Challenging Our Assumptions: A Cultural Competencies Reader

Ohio University Writing Program
Editors: Rachael Ryerson and Courtney A. Mauck

VAN-GRINER
LEARNING

Challenging Our Assumptions:
A Cultural Competencies Reader
Ohio University Writing Program
Editors: Rachael Ryerson and Courtney A. Mauck
Fifth Edition

Printed in the United States of America
10 9 8 7 6 5 4 3 2 1
ISBN: 978-1-61740-862-5

Van-Griner Publishing
Cincinnati, Ohio
www.van-griner.com

President: Dreis Van Landuyt
Project Manager: Maria Walterbusch
Customer Care Lead: Lauren Houseworth

Holt 862-5 Su20
316122

VAN-GRINER
LEARNING

Table of Contents

How to Tame a Wild Tongue

GLORIA ANZALDÚA

"We're going to have to control your tongue," the dentist says, pulling out all the metal from my mouth. Silver bits plop and tinkle into the basin. My mouth is a motherlode.

The dentist is cleaning out my roots. I get a whiff of the stench when I gasp. "I can't cap that tooth yet, you're still draining," he says.

"We're going to have to do something about your tongue," I hear the anger rising in his voice. My tongue keeps pushing out the wads of cotton, pushing back the drills, the long thin needles. "I've never seen anything as strong or as stubborn," he says. And I think, how do you tame a wild tongue, train it to be quiet, how do you bridle and saddle it? How do you make it lie down?

> "Who is to say that robbing a people of
> its language is less violent than war?"
>
> —Ray Gwyn Smith[1]

I remember being caught speaking Spanish at recess—that was good for three licks on the knuckles with a sharp ruler. I remember being sent to the corner of the classroom for "talking back" to the Anglo teacher when all I was trying to do was tell her how to pronounce my name. "If you want to be American, speak 'American.' If you don't like it, go back to Mexico where you belong."

5 "I want you to speak English. *Pa' hallar buen trabajo tienes que saber hablar el inglés bien. Qué vale toda tu educación sí todavía hablas inglés con un* 'accent,'" my mother would say, mortified that I spoke English like a Mexican. At Pan American University, I and all Chicano students were required to take two speech classes. Their purpose: to get rid of our accents.

Attacks on one's form of expression with the intent to censor are a violation of the First Amendment. *El Anglo con cara de inocentene nos arrancó la lengua.* Wild tongues can't be tamed, they can only be cut out.

Overcoming the Tradition of Silence

> *Ahogadas, escupimos el oscuro.*
> *Peleando con nuestra propia sombra*
> *el silencio nos sepulta.*

En boca cerrada no entran moscas. "Flies don't enter a closed mouth" is a saying I kept hearing when I was a child. *Ser habladora* was to be a gossip and a liar, to talk too much. *Muchachitas bien criadas,* well-bred girls don't answer back. *Es una falta de respeto* to talk back to one's mother or father. I remember one of the sins I'd recite to the priest in the confession box the few times I went to confession: talking back to my mother, *hablar pa' 'tras, repelar. Hocicona, repelona, chismosa,* having a big mouth, questioning, carrying tales are all signs of being *mal criada*. In my culture they are all words that are derogatory if applied to women—I've never heard them applied to men.

The first time I heard two women, a Puerto Rican and a Cuban, say the word *"nosotras,"* I was shocked. I had not known the word existed. Chicanas use *nosotros* whether we're male or female. We are robbed of our female being by the masculine plural. Language is a male discourse.

> And our tongues have become
> dry the wilderness has
> dried out our tongues
> and we have forgotten speech.
>
> —Irena Klepfisz[2]

Even our own people, other Spanish speakers *nos quieren poner candados en la boca*. They would hold us back with their bag of *reglas de academia*.

Oyé coma ladra: el lenguaje de la frontera.

> *Quien tiene boca se equivoca.*
>
> —Mexican Saying

10 *"Pacho,* cultural traitor, you're speaking the oppressor's language by speaking English, you're ruining the Spanish language," I have been accused by various Latinos and Latinas. Chicano Spanish is considered by the purist and by most Latinos deficient, a mutilation of Spanish.

But Chicano Spanish is a border tongue which developed naturally. Change, *evolución, enriquecimiento de palabras nuevas por invención o adopción* have created variants of Chicano Spanish, *un nuevo lenguaje. Un lenguaje que corresponde a un modo de vivir.* Chicano Spanish is not incorrect, it is a living language.

For a people who are neither Spanish nor live in a country in which Spanish is the first language; for a people who live in a country in which English is the reigning tongue but who are not Anglo; for a people who cannot entirely identify with either standard (formal, Castillian) Spanish nor standard English, what recourse is left to them but to create their own language? A language which they can connect their identity to, one capable of communicating the realities and values true to themselves—a language with terms that are neither *español ni inglés,* but both. We speak a patois, a forked tongue, a variation of two languages.

Chicano Spanish sprang out of the Chicanos' need to identify ourselves as a distinct people. We needed a language with which we could communicate with ourselves, a secret language. For some of us, language is a homeland closer than the Southwest—for many Chicanos today live in the Midwest and the East. And because we are a complex, heterogeneous people, we speak many languages. Some of the languages we speak are:

1. Standard English
2. Working class and slang English
3. Standard Spanish
4. Standard Mexican Spanish
5. North Mexican Spanish dialect.
6. Chicano Spanish (Texas, New Mexico, Arizona, and California have regional variations)
7. Tex-Mex
8. *Pachuco* (called *caló*)

My "home" tongues are the languages I speak with my sister and brothers, with my friends. They are the last five listed, with 6 and 7 being closest to my heart. From school, the media, and job situations, I've picked up standard and working class English. From Mamagrande Locha and from reading Spanish and Mexican literature, I've picked up Standard Spanish and Standard Mexican Spanish. From *los recién llegados,* Mexican immigrants, and *braceros,* I learned the North Mexican dialect. With Mexicans I'll try to speak either Standard Mexican Spanish or the North Mexican dialect. From my parents and Chicanos living in the Valley, I picked up Chicano Texas Spanish, and I speak it with my mom, younger brother (who married a Mexican and who rarely mixes Spanish with English), aunts, and older relatives.

15 With Chicanas from *Nuevo México* or *Arizona* I will speak Chicano Spanish a little, but often they don't understand what I'm saying. With most California Chicanas I speak entirely in English (unless I forget). When I first moved to San Francisco, I'd rattle off something in Spanish, unintentionally embarrassing them. Often it is only with another Chicana *tejana* that I can talk freely.

Words distorted by English are known as anglicisms or *pochismos*. The *pocho* is an anglicized Mexican or American of Mexican origin who speaks Spanish with an accent characteristic of North Americans and who distorts and reconstructs the language according to the influence of English.[3] Tex-Mex, or Spanglish, comes most naturally to me. I may switch back and forth from English to Spanish in the same sentence or in the same word. With my sister and my brother Nune and with Chicano *tejano* contemporaries I speak in Tex-Mex.

From kids and people my own age I picked up *Pachuco. Pachuco* (the language of the zoot suiters) is a language of rebellion, both against Standard Spanish and Standard English. It is a secret language. Adults of the culture and outsiders cannot understand it. It is made up of slang words from both English and Spanish. *Ruca* means girl or woman, *vato* means guy or dude, *chale* means no, *simón* means yes, *churro* is sure, talk is *periquiar, pigionear* means petting, *que gacho* means how nerdy, *ponte águila* means watch out, death is called *la pelona*. Through lack of practice and not having others who can speak it, I've lost most of the *Pachuco* tongue.

Chicano Spanish

Chicanos, after 250 years of Spanish/Anglo colonization, have developed significant differences in the Spanish we speak. We collapse two adjacent vowels into a single syllable and sometimes shift the stress in certain words such as *maíz/maiz, cohete/cuete*. We leave out certain consonants when they appear between vowels: *lado/lao, mojado/mojao*. Chicanos from South Texas pronounce *f* as *j* as in *jue* (*fue*). Chicanos use "archaisms," words that are no longer in the Spanish language, words that have been evolved out. We say *semos, truje, haiga, ansina, and naiden*. We retain the "archaic" *j*, as in *jalar*, that derives from an earlier *h*, (the French *halar* or the Germanic *halon* which was lost to standard Spanish in the 16th century), but which is still found in several regional dialects such as the one spoken in South Texas. (Due to geography, Chicanos from the Valley of South Texas were cut off linguistically from other Spanish speakers. We tend to use words that the Spaniards brought over from Medieval Spain. The majority of the Spanish colonizers in Mexico and the Southwest came from Extremadura—Hernán Cortés was one of them—and Andalucía. Andalucians pronounce *ll* like a *y*, and their *d's* tend to be absorbed by adjacent vowels: *tirado* becomes *tirao*. They brought *el lenguaje popular, dialectos y regionalismos*.[4])

Chicanos and other Spanish speakers also shift *ll* to *y* and *z* to *s*.[5] We leave out initial syllables, saying *tar* for *estar; toy* for *estoy, hora* for *ahora* (*cubanos* and *puertorriqueños* also leave out initial letters of some words). We also leave out the final syllable such as *pa* for *para*. The intervocalic *y*, the *ll* as in *tortilla, ella, botella*, gets replaced by *tortia* or *tortiya, ea, botea*. We add an additional syllable at the beginning of certain words: *atocar* for *tocar, agastar* for *gastar*. Sometimes we'll say *lavaste las vacijas*, other times *lavates* (substituting the *ates* verb endings for the *aste*).

20 We use anglicisms, words borrowed from English: *bola* from ball, *carpeta* from carpet, *máchina de lavar* (instead of *lavadora*) from washing machine. Tex-Mex argot, created by adding a Spanish sound at the beginning or end of an English word such as *cookiar* for cook, *watchar* for watch, *parkiar* for park, and *rapiar* for rape, is the result of the pressures on Spanish speakers to adapt to English.

We don't use the word *vosotros/as* or its accompanying verb form. We don't say *claro* (to mean yes), *imagínate,* or *me emociona,* unless we picked up Spanish from Latinas, out of a book, or in a classroom. Other Spanish-speaking groups are going through the same, or similar development in their Spanish.

Linguistic Terrorism

> *Deslenguadas. Somos los del español deficiente.* We are your linguistic nightmare, your linguistic aberration, your linguistic *mestisaje,* the subject of your *burla.* Because we speak with tongues of fire we are culturally crucified. Racially, culturally, and linguistically *somos huérfanos*—we speak an orphan tongue.

Chicanas who grew up speaking Chicano Spanish have internalized the belief that we speak poor Spanish. It is illegitimate, a bastard language. And because we internalize how our language has been used against us by the dominant culture, we use our language differences against each other.

Chicana feminists often skirt around each other with suspicion and hesitation. For the longest time I couldn't figure it out. Then it dawned on me. To be close to another Chicana is like looking into the mirror. We are afraid of what we'll see there. *Pena.* Shame. Low estimation of self. In childhood we are told that our language is wrong. Repeated attacks on our native tongue diminish our sense of self. The attacks continue throughout our lives.

Chicanas feel uncomfortable talking in Spanish to Latinas, afraid of their censure. Their language was not outlawed in their countries. They had a whole lifetime of being immersed in their native tongue; generations, centuries in which Spanish was a first language, taught in school, heard on radio and TV, and read in the newspaper.

25 If a person, Chicana or Latina, has a low estimation of my native tongue, she also has a low estimation of me. Often with *mexicanas y latinas* we'll speak English as a neutral language. Even among Chicanas we tend to speak English at parties or conferences. Yet, at the same time, we're afraid the other will think we're *agringadas* because we don't speak Chicano Spanish. We oppress each other trying to out-Chicano each other, vying to be the "real" Chicanas, to speak like Chicanos. There is no one Chicano language just as there is no one Chicano

experience. A monolingual Chicana whose first language is English or Spanish is just as much a Chicana as one who speaks several variants of Spanish. A Chicana from Michigan or Chicago or Detroit is just as much a Chicana as one from the Southwest. Chicano Spanish is as diverse linguistically as it is regionally.

By the end of this century, Spanish speakers will comprise the biggest minority group in the U.S., a country where students in high schools and colleges are encouraged to take French classes because French is considered more "cultured." But for a language to remain alive it must be used.[6] By the end of this century English, and not Spanish, will be the mother tongue of most Chicanos and Latinos.

So, if you want to really hurt me, talk badly about my language. Ethnic identity is twin skin to linguistic identity—I am my language. Until I can take pride in my language, I cannot take pride in myself. Until I can accept as legitimate Chicano Texas Spanish, Tex-Mex, and all the other languages I speak, I cannot accept the legitimacy of myself. Until I am free to write bilingually and to switch codes without having always to translate, while I still have to speak English or Spanish when I would rather speak Spanglish, and as long as I have to accommodate the English speakers rather than having them accommodate me, my tongue will be illegitimate.

I will no longer be made to feel ashamed of existing. I will have my voice: Indian, Spanish, white, I will have my serpent's tongue—my woman's voice, my sexual voice, my poet's voice. I will overcome the tradition of silence.

> My fingers
> move sly against your palm
> Like women everywhere, we speak in code. …
>
> —Malanie Kaye/Kantrowitz[7]

"Vistas," corridos, y conzida: My Native Tongue

In the 1960s, I read my first Chicano novel. It was *City of Night* by John Rechy, a gay Texan, son of a Scottish father and a Mexican mother. For days I walked around in stunned amazement that a Chicano could write and could get published. When I read *I Am Joaquín*[8] I was surprised to see a bilingual book by a Chicano in print. When I saw poetry written in Tex-Mex for the first time, a feeling of pure joy flashed through me. I felt like we really existed as a people. In 1971, when I started teaching High School English to Chicano students, I tried to supplement the required texts with works by Chicanos, only to be reprimanded and forbidden to do so by the principal. He claimed that I was supposed to teach "American" and English literature. At the risk of being fired,

I swore my students to secrecy and slipped in Chicano short stories, poems, a play. In graduate school, while working toward a Ph.D., I had to "argue" with one advisor after the other; semester after semester, before I was allowed to make Chicano literature an area of focus.

30 Even before I read books by Chicanos or Mexicans, it was the Mexican movies I saw at the drive-in—the Thursday night special of $1.00 a carload—that gave me a sense of belonging. *"Vámonos a las vistas,"* my mother would call out and we'd all—grandmother, brothers, sister, and cousins—squeeze into the car. We'd wolf down cheese and bologna white bread sandwiches while watching Pedro Infante in melodramatic tearjerkers like *Nosotros los pobres.* the first "real" Mexican movie (that was not an imitation of European movies). I remember seeing *Cuando los hijos se van* and surmising that all Mexican movies played up the love a mother has for her children and what ungrateful sons and daughters suffer when they are not devoted to their mothers. I remember the singing-type "westerns" of Jorge Negrete and Miquel Aceves Mejía. When watching Mexican movies, I felt a sense of homecoming as well as alienation. People who were to amount to something didn't go to Mexican movies, or *bailes,* or tune their radios to *bolero, rancherita,* and *corrido* music.

The whole time I was growing up, there was *norteño* music sometimes called North Mexican border music, or Tex-Mex music, or Chicano music, or *cantina* (bar) music. I grew up listening to *conjuntos,* three- or four-piece bands made up of folk musicians playing guitair, *bajo sexto,* drums, and button accordion, which Chicanos had borrowed from the German immigrants who had come to Central Texas and Mexico to farm and build breweries. In the Rio Grande Valley, Steve Jordan and Little Joe Hernández were popular, and Flaco Jiménez was the accordion king. The rhythms of Tex-Mex music are those of the polka, also adapted from the Germans, who in turn had borrowed the polka from the Czechs and Bohemians.

I remember the hot, sultry evenings when *corridos*—songs of love and death on the Texas-Mexican borderlands—reverberated out of cheap amplifiers from the local *cantinas* and wafted in through my bedroom window.

Corridos first became widely used along the South Texas/Mexican border uring the early conflict between Chicanos and Anglos. The *corridos* are usually about Mexican heroes who do valiant deeds against the Anglo oppressors. Pancho Villa's song, *"La cucaracha,"* is the most famous one. *Corridos* of John F. Kennedy and his death are still very popular in the Valley. Older Chicanos remember Lydia Mendoza, one of the great border *corrido* singers who was called *la Gloria de Tejas.* Her *"El tango negro,"* sung during the

Great Depression, made her a singer of the people. The everpresent *corridos* narrated one hundred years of border history, bringing news of events as well as entertaining. These folk musicians and folk songs are our chief cultural mythmakers, and they made our hard lives seem bearable.

I grew up feeling ambivalent about our music. Country-western and rock-and-roll had more status. In the 50s and 60s, for the slightly educated and *agringado* Chicanos, there existed a sense of shame at being caught listening to our music. Yet I couldn't stop my feet from thumping to the music, could not stop humming the words, nor hide from myself the exhilaration I felt when I heard it.

35 There are more subtle ways that we internalize identification, especially in the forms of images and emotions. For me food and certain smells are tied to my identity, to my homeland. Woodsmoke curling up to an immense blue sky; woodsmoke perfuming my grandmother's clothes, her skin. The stench of cow manure and the yellow patches on the ground; the crack of a .22 rifle and the reek of cordite. Homemade white cheese sizzling in a pan, melting inside a folded *tortilla*. My sister Hilda's hot, spicy *menudo, chile colorado* making it deep red, pieces of *panza* and hominy floating on top. My brother Carito barbequing *fajitas* in the backyard. Even now and 3,000 miles away, I can see my mother spicing the ground beef, pork, and venison with *chile*. My mouth salivates at the thought of the hot steaming *tamales* I would be eating if I were home.

Si le preguntas a mi mamá, "¿Qué eres?"

> "Identity is the essential core of who
> We are as individuals, the conscious
> expelience of the self inside."
>
> —Gershen Kaufman[9]

Nosotros los Chicanos straddle the borderlands. On one side of us, we are constantly exposed to the Spanish of the Mexicans, on the other side we hear the Anglos' incessant clamoring so that we forget our language. Among ourselves we don't say *nosotros los americanos, o nosotros los españoles, o nosotros los hispanos*. We say *nosotros los mexicanos* (by *mexicanos* we do not mean citizens of Mexico; we do not mean a national identity, but a racial one). We distinguish between *mexicanos del otro lado* and *mexicanos de este lado*. Deep in our hearts we believe that being Mexican has nothing to do with which country one lives in. Being Mexican is a state of soul—not one of mind, not one of citizenship. Neither eagle nor serpent, but both. And like the ocean, neither animal respects borders.

> *Dime con quien andas y te diré quien eres.*
> (Tell me who your friends are and I'll tell you who you are.)
>
> —Mexican Saying

Si le preguntas a mi mamá, "¿Qué eres?" te dirá, "Soy mexicana." My brothers and sister say the same. I sometimes will answer *"soy mexicana"* and at others will say *"soy Chicana" o "soy tejana."* But I identified as *"Raza"* before I ever identified as *"mexicana"* or "Chicana."

As a culture, we call ourselves Spanish when referring to ourselves as a linguistic group and when copping out. It is then that we forget our predominant Indian genes. We are 70–80 percent Indian.[10] We call ourselves Hispanic[11] or Spanish-American or Latin American or Latin when linking ourselves to other Spanish speaking peoples of the Western hemisphere and when copping out. We call ourselves Mexican-American[12] to signify we are neither Mexican nor American, but more the noun "American" than the adjective "Mexican" (and when copping out).

Chicanos and other people of color suffer economically for not acculturating. This voluntary (yet forced) alienation makes for psychological conflict, a kind of dual identity—we don't identify with the Anglo-American cultural values and we don't totally identify with the Mexican cultural values. We are a synergy of two cultures with various degrees of Mexicanness or Angloness. I have so internalized the borderland conflict that sometimes I feel like one cancels out the other and we are zero, nothing, no one. *A veces no soy nada ni nadie. Pero hasta cuando no lo soy, lo soy.*

40 When not copping out, when we know we are more than nothing, we call ourselves Mexican, referring to race and ancestry; *mestizo* when affirming both our Indian and Spanish (but we hardly ever own our Black ancestory); Chicano when referring to a politically aware people born and/or raised in the U.S.; *Raza* when referring to Chicanos; *tejanos* when we are Chicanos from Texas.

Chicanos did not know we were a people until 1965 when Ceasar Chavez and the farmworkers united and *I Am Joaquín* was published and *la Raza Unida* party was formed in Texas. With that recognition, we became a distinct people. Something momentous happened to the Chicano soul—we became aware of our reality and acquired a name and a language (Chicano Spanish) that reflected that reality. Now that we had a name, some of the fragmented pieces began to fall together—who we were, what we were, how we had evolved. We began to gel glimpses of what we might eventually become.

Yet the struggle of identities continues, the struggle of borders is our reality still. One day the inner struggle will cease and a true integration take place. In the meantime, *tenémos que hacer la lucha. ¿Quien está protegiendo los ranchos de mi gente? ¿Quién está tratando de cerrar la fisura entre la india y el blanco en nuestra sangre? El Chicano, si, el Chicano que anda como un ladrón en su propia casa.*

Los Chicanos, how patient we seem, how very patient. There is the quiet of the Indian about us.[13] We know how to survive. When other races have given up their tongue, we've kept ours. We know what it is to live under the hammer blow of the dominant *norte-americano* culture. But more than we count the blows, we count the days the weeks the years the centuries the eons until the white laws and commerce and customs will rot in the deserts they've created, lie bleached. *Humildes* yet proud, *quietos* yet wild, *nosotros losmexicanos-Chicanos* will walk by the crumbling ashes as we go about our business. Stubborn, persevering, impenetrable as stone, yet possessing a malleability that renders us unbreakable, we, the *mestizas* and *mestizos* will remain.

Credit

Anzaldúa, Gloria. *Borderlands/La Frontera: The New Mestiza.* San Francisco: Aunt Lute Books, 1987.

Fun Home Excerpt

ALISON BECHDEL

THEN THERE WAS A BOY MY SENIOR YEAR OF COLLEGE.
WHEN I WAS LITTLE, I REALLY WANTED TO BE A GIRL.
I'D DRESS UP IN GIRLS' CLOTHES.
I WANTED TO BE A BOY! I DRESSED IN BOYS' CLOTHES!
REMEMBER?
IT WAS NOT THE SOBBING, JOYOUS RE-UNION OF ODYSSEUS AND TELEMACHUS.
IT WAS MORE LIKE FATHERLESS STEPHEN AND SONLESS BLOOM...
...HAVING THEIR EQUIVO-CAL LATE-NIGHT COCOA AT 7 ECCLES STREET.
BUT WHICH OF US WAS THE FATHER?
I HAD FELT DISTINCTLY PARENTAL LISTENING TO HIS SHAMEFACED RECITATION.
AND ALL TOO SOON WE WERE AT THE THEATER.

THE MOVIE WAS GOOD. IT WAS ABOUT HOW LORETTA LYNN MAKES IT OUT OF APPALACHIA TO BECOME A BIG COUNTRY-WESTERN STAR.
I AIN'T NEVER GONNA SEE YOU AGAIN.
YES YOU WILL, DADDY.
EXIT
INDEED, DADDY CROAKED OF BLACK LUNG DISEASE A FEW SCENES LATER, BEFORE SHE GOT BACK TO VISIT.
COLOR BY TECHNICOLOR
No. 25842
MOTION PICTURE ASSOCIATION
COPYRIGHT MCMLXXX · UNIVERSAL PICTURES
ALL RIGHTS RESERVED
I WOULD SEE MY FATHER ONE MORE TIME AFTER THIS. BUT WE WOULD NEVER DISCUSS OUR SHARED PREDILECTION AGAIN.
NOW SHOWING
Coal Miner's Daughter
Did Bloom discover common factors of similarity between
their respective like and unlike reactions to experience?
Both were sensitive to artistic impressions musical in prefer-
preferred a continental to an
tic to a transatlantic place of
rly domestic training and an
resistance professed their dis-
us, national, social and ethical
doctrines. Both admitted the alternately stimulating and obtunding influence of heterosexual magnetism.
obtunding?
WE HAD HAD OUR ITHACA MOMENT.

IN OUR CASE, OF COURSE, SUBSTITUTE THE ALTERNATELY STIMULATING AND OBTUNDING INFLUENCE OF HOMOSEXUAL MAGNETISM.
MY-O-MY BAR
AFTER THE MOVIE, DAD TOOK ME TO A NOTORIOUS LOCAL NIGHTSPOT. THE FRONT WAS A TOPLESS CLUB. THE BACK WAS A GAY BAR.
I.D.?
PSU
THIS MIGHT HAVE BEEN OUR CIRCE CHAPTER, LIKE WHEN STEPHEN AND BLOOM DRINK AT THE BROTHEL IN NIGHTTOWN.
I'M HER FATHER.
TWENTY-ONE, BUD.
OR AT LEAST, IT COULD HAVE BEEN A FUNNY STORY ONE DAY.
AS IT WAS, WE DROVE HOME IN MORTIFIED SILENCE.

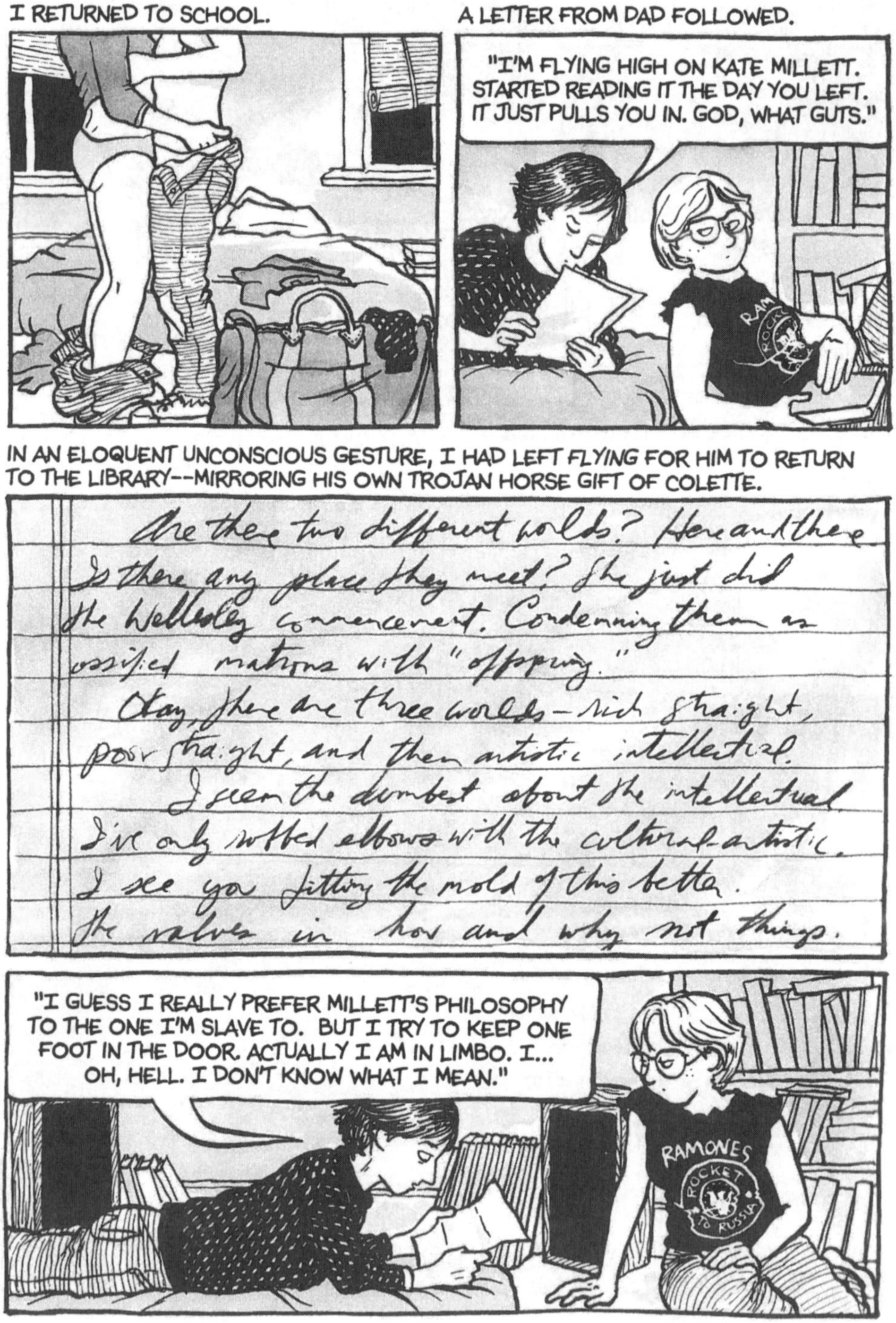
I RETURNED TO SCHOOL.
A LETTER FROM DAD FOLLOWED.
"I'M FLYING HIGH ON KATE MILLETT. STARTED READING IT THE DAY YOU LEFT. IT JUST PULLS YOU IN. GOD, WHAT GUTS."
IN AN ELOQUENT UNCONSCIOUS GESTURE, I HAD LEFT *FLYING* FOR HIM TO RETURN TO THE LIBRARY--MIRRORING HIS OWN TROJAN HORSE GIFT OF COLETTE.
Are there two different worlds? Here and there.
Is there any place they meet? She just did
the Wellesley commencement. Condemning them as
ossified matrons with "offspring."
Okay, there are three worlds—rich straight,
poor straight, and then artistic intellectual.
I seem the dumbest about the intellectual.
I've only rubbed elbows with the cultural-artistic.
I see you fitting the mold of this better.
The values in how and why not things.
"I GUESS I REALLY PREFER MILLETT'S PHILOSOPHY TO THE ONE I'M SLAVE TO. BUT I TRY TO KEEP ONE FOOT IN THE DOOR. ACTUALLY I AM IN LIMBO. I... OH, HELL. I DON'T KNOW WHAT I MEAN."
RAMONES
ROCKET TO RUSSIA

AT THE END OF THE SEMESTER JOAN CAME HOME WITH ME FOR A VISIT. I DID NOT INTRODUCE HER AS MY GIRLFRIEND.

THIS WAS THE LAST TIME I'D SEE DAD.

ON OUR FINAL EVENING, A FAMILY FRIEND REMARKED ADMIRINGLY TO JOAN ON THE CLOSE RELATIONSHIP BETWEEN MY FATHER AND ME.

IT WAS UNUSUAL, AND WE WERE CLOSE. BUT NOT CLOSE ENOUGH.

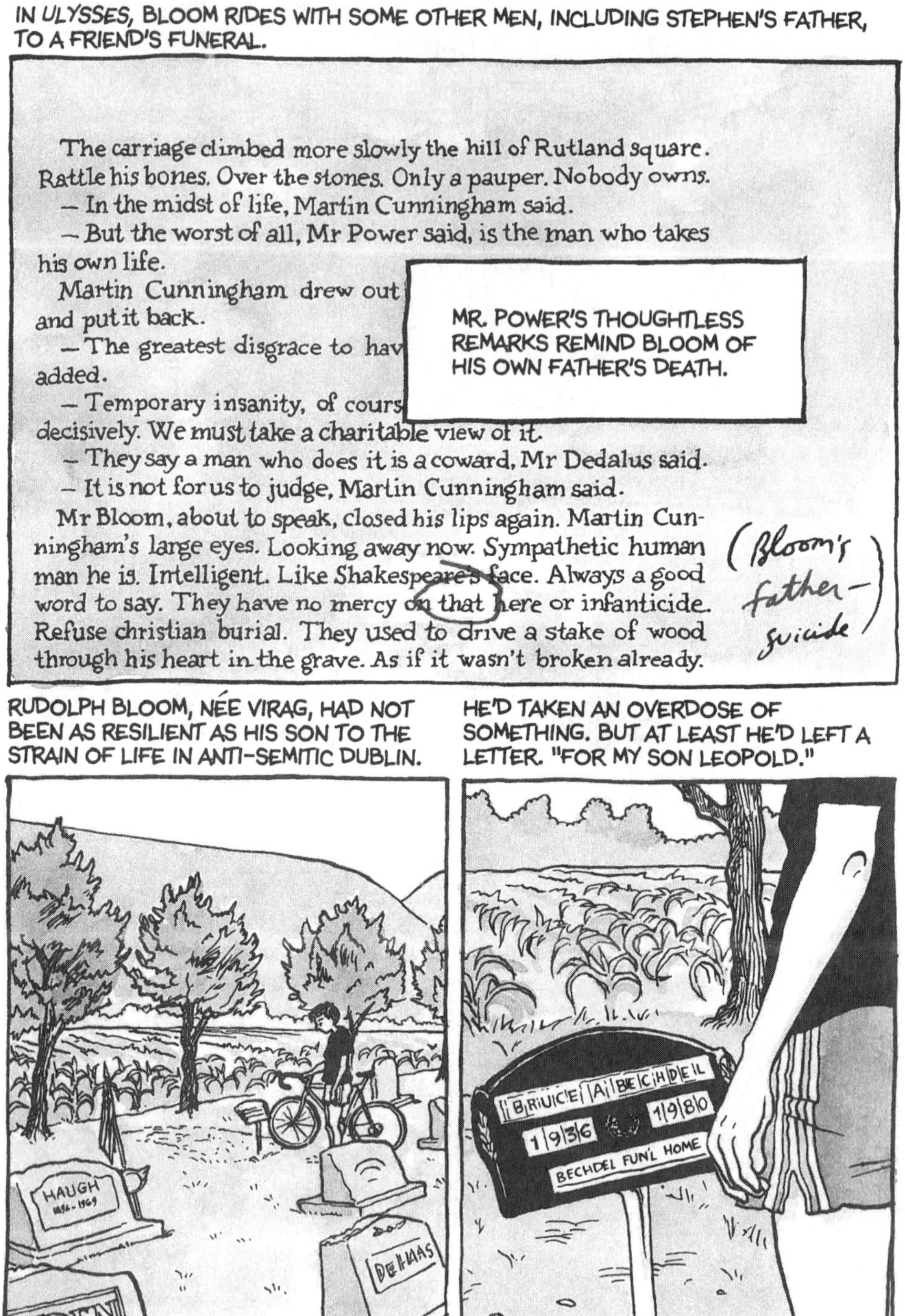
IN ULYSSES, BLOOM RIDES WITH SOME OTHER MEN, INCLUDING STEPHEN'S FATHER, TO A FRIEND'S FUNERAL.
The carriage climbed more slowly the hill of Rutland square. Rattle his bones. Over the stones. Only a pauper. Nobody owns.
— In the midst of life, Martin Cunningham said.
— But the worst of all, Mr Power said, is the man who takes his own life.
Martin Cunningham drew out
and put it back.
— The greatest disgrace to hav
added.
— Temporary insanity, of cours
decisively. We must take a charitable view of it.
— They say a man who does it is a coward, Mr Dedalus said.
— It is not for us to judge, Martin Cunningham said.
Mr Bloom, about to speak, closed his lips again. Martin Cunningham's large eyes. Looking away now. Sympathetic human man he is. Intelligent. Like Shakespeare's face. Always a good word to say. They have no mercy on that here or infanticide. Refuse christian burial. They used to drive a stake of wood through his heart in the grave. As if it wasn't broken already.
MR. POWER'S THOUGHTLESS REMARKS REMIND BLOOM OF HIS OWN FATHER'S DEATH.
(Bloom's father — suicide)
RUDOLPH BLOOM, NÉE VIRAG, HAD NOT BEEN AS RESILIENT AS HIS SON TO THE STRAIN OF LIFE IN ANTI-SEMITIC DUBLIN.
HAUGH
1886-1969
DE HAAS
HE'D TAKEN AN OVERDOSE OF SOMETHING. BUT AT LEAST HE'D LEFT A LETTER. "FOR MY SON LEOPOLD."
BRUCE A BECHDEL
1936
1980
BECHDEL FUN'L HOME

DAD LEFT NO NOTE. AFTER THE FUNERAL, LIFE PRETTY MUCH RESUMED ITS COURSE. THEY SAY GRIEF TAKES MANY FORMS, INCLUDING THE ABSENCE OF GRIEF.

IN ONE OF DAD'S COURTSHIP LETTERS TO MOM, HE PRAISES SOMETHING SHE'D WRITTEN IN HER LAST POST BY COMPARING IT TO JAMES JOYCE.

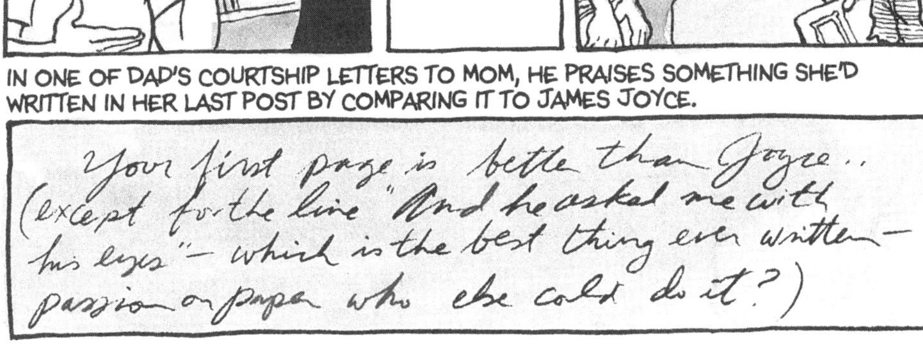

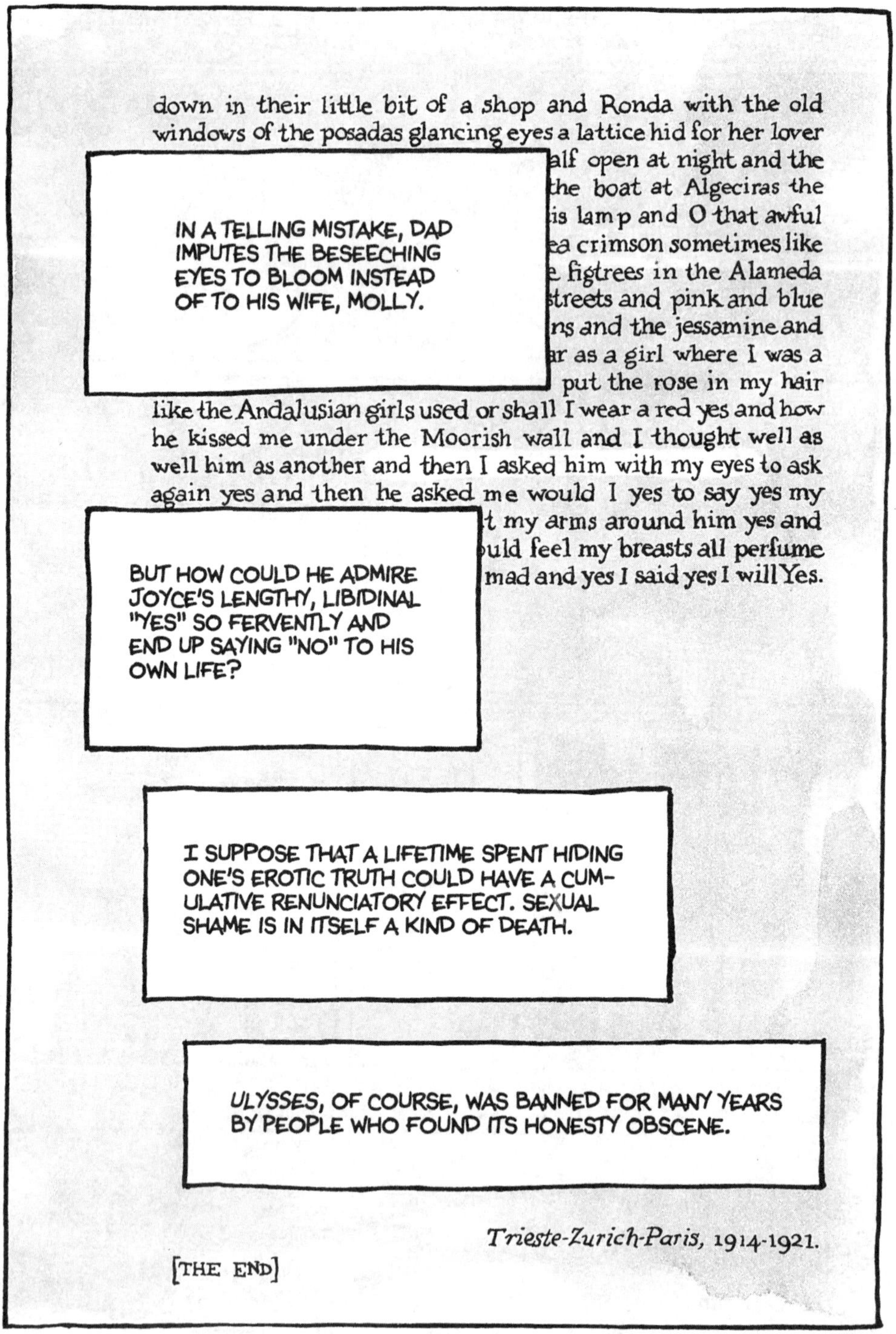
down in their little bit of a shop and Ronda with the old
windows of the posadas glancing eyes a lattice hid for her lover
alf open at night and the
the boat at Algeciras the
is lamp and O that awful
ea crimson sometimes like
e figtrees in the Alameda
treets and pink and blue
ns and the jessamine and
ar as a girl where I was a
put the rose in my hair
like the Andalusian girls used or shall I wear a red yes and how
he kissed me under the Moorish wall and I thought well as
well him as another and then I asked him with my eyes to ask
again yes and then he asked me would I yes to say yes my
t my arms around him yes and
uld feel my breasts all perfume
mad and yes I said yes I will Yes.
IN A TELLING MISTAKE, DAD IMPUTES THE BESEECHING EYES TO BLOOM INSTEAD OF TO HIS WIFE, MOLLY.
BUT HOW COULD HE ADMIRE JOYCE'S LENGTHY, LIBIDINAL "YES" SO FERVENTLY AND END UP SAYING "NO" TO HIS OWN LIFE?
I SUPPOSE THAT A LIFETIME SPENT HIDING ONE'S EROTIC TRUTH COULD HAVE A CUMULATIVE RENUNCIATORY EFFECT. SEXUAL SHAME IS IN ITSELF A KIND OF DEATH.
ULYSSES, OF COURSE, WAS BANNED FOR MANY YEARS BY PEOPLE WHO FOUND ITS HONESTY OBSCENE.
Trieste-Zurich-Paris, 1914-1921.
[THE END]

THE FRONT MATTER OF MY MODERN LIBRARY EDITION INCLUDES THE DECISION BY THE JUDGE WHO LIFTED THE BAN IN 1933.
ALONG WITH A LETTER FROM JOYCE TO RANDOM HOUSE, DETAILING *ULYSSES'* PUBLICATION HISTORY TO DATE.
HE MENTIONS THAT MARGARET ANDERSON AND JANE HEAP WERE PROSECUTED FOR RUNNING EPISODES IN THEIR MAGAZINE, THE *LITTLE REVIEW*.
HE ACKNOWLEDGES THE RISK SYLVIA BEACH TOOK IN PUBLISHING A MANU-SCRIPT NO ONE ELSE WOULD TOUCH.
akespeare and Compa
PERHAPS IT'S JUST A COINCIDENCE THAT THESE WOMEN--ALONG WITH SYLVIA'S LOVER ADRIENNE MONNIER, WHO PUBLISHED THE FRENCH EDITION OF *ULYSSES*--WERE ALL LESBIANS.
YOU SHOULD LEARN ABOUT PARIS IN THE TWENTIES, THAT WHOLE SCENE.
COLETTE'S AUTO-BIOGRAPHY
EARTHLY PARADISE
BUT I LIKE TO THINK THEY WENT TO THE MAT FOR THIS BOOK *BECAUSE* THEY WERE LESBIANS, BECAUSE THEY KNEW A THING OR TWO ABOUT EROTIC TRUTH.
EARTHLY PARADISE
Colette

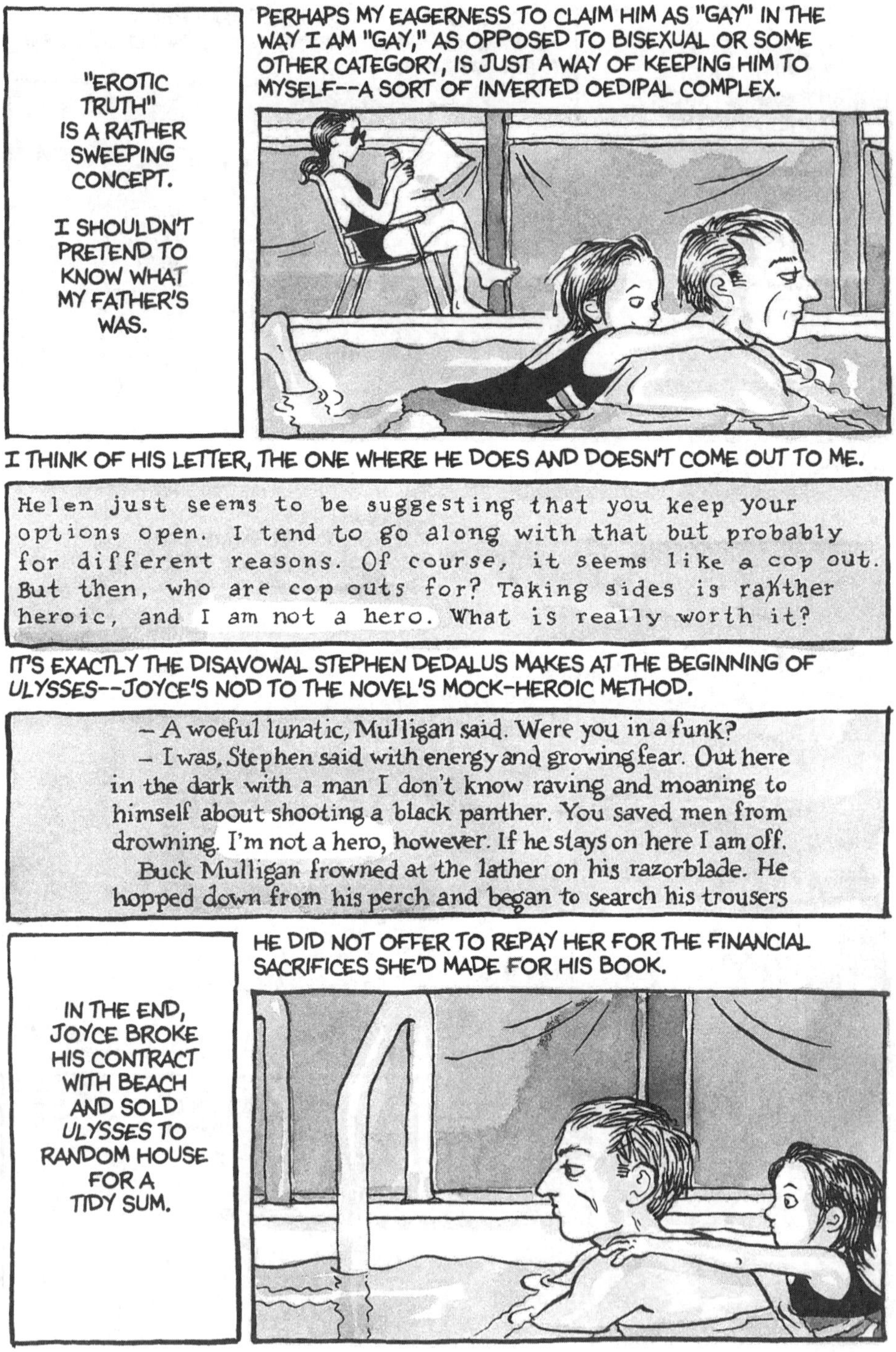
"EROTIC TRUTH" IS A RATHER SWEEPING CONCEPT.
I SHOULDN'T PRETEND TO KNOW WHAT MY FATHER'S WAS.
PERHAPS MY EAGERNESS TO CLAIM HIM AS "GAY" IN THE WAY I AM "GAY," AS OPPOSED TO BISEXUAL OR SOME OTHER CATEGORY, IS JUST A WAY OF KEEPING HIM TO MYSELF--A SORT OF INVERTED OEDIPAL COMPLEX.
I THINK OF HIS LETTER, THE ONE WHERE HE DOES AND DOESN'T COME OUT TO ME.
Helen just seems to be suggesting that you keep your options open. I tend to go along with that but probably for different reasons. Of course, it seems like a cop out. But then, who are cop outs for? Taking sides is rakther heroic, and I am not a hero. What is really worth it?
IT'S EXACTLY THE DISAVOWAL STEPHEN DEDALUS MAKES AT THE BEGINNING OF ULYSSES--JOYCE'S NOD TO THE NOVEL'S MOCK-HEROIC METHOD.
– A woeful lunatic, Mulligan said. Were you in a funk?
– I was, Stephen said with energy and growing fear. Out here in the dark with a man I don't know raving and moaning to himself about shooting a black panther. You saved men from drowning. I'm not a hero, however. If he stays on here I am off.
Buck Mulligan frowned at the lather on his razorblade. He hopped down from his perch and began to search his trousers
IN THE END, JOYCE BROKE HIS CONTRACT WITH BEACH AND SOLD ULYSSES TO RANDOM HOUSE FOR A TIDY SUM.
HE DID NOT OFFER TO REPAY HER FOR THE FINANCIAL SACRIFICES SHE'D MADE FOR HIS BOOK.

BEACH PUT A GOOD FACE ON IT, WRITING "A BABY BELONGS TO ITS MOTHER, NOT TO THE MIDWIFE, DOESN'T IT?"
AND AS LONG AS WE'RE LIKENING ULYSSES TO A CHILD, IT FARED MUCH BETTER THAN JOYCE'S ACTUAL CHILDREN.
WENT MAD
BECAME AN ALCOHOLIC
BUT I SUPPOSE THIS IS CONSISTENT WITH THE BOOK'S THEME THAT SPIRITUAL, NOT CONSUBSTANTIAL, PATERNITY IS THE IMPORTANT THING.
IS IT SO UNUSUAL FOR THE TWO THINGS TO COINCIDE?
WHAT IF ICARUS HADN'T HURTLED INTO THE SEA? WHAT IF HE'D INHERITED HIS FATHER'S INVENTIVE BENT? WHAT MIGHT HE HAVE WROUGHT?

HE DID HURTLE INTO THE SEA, OF COURSE.
BUT IN THE TRICKY REVERSE NARRATION THAT IMPELS OUR ENTWINED STORIES, HE WAS THERE TO CATCH ME WHEN I LEAPT.

Credit

Black Lives Matter

PATRISSE KHAN-CULLORS AND ASHA BANDELE

This was a teenager just trying to get home.

Sybrina Fulton

1 It is July 13, 2013, and I have stepped away from monitoring events at the trial of the man who killed Trayvon Martin, 17, a year and a half before.

I had learned about Trayvon one day while I was at the Strategy Center in 2012 and going through Facebook. I came across a small article from a local paper. Was it Sanford's? I read that a white man—that's how the killer was identified and self-identified until we raised the issue of race—had killed a Black boy and was not going to be charged.

I start cursing. I am outraged. In what fucking world does this make sense? I put a call out: Have people heard about 17-year-old Trayvon Martin? I have loved so many young men who look just like this boy. I feel immediate grief, and as my friends begin to respond, they, too, are grief stricken. We meet at my home. We circle up. A multiracial group of roughly 15 people dedicated to ending white supremacy and creating a world in which all of our children can thrive. We process. We talk about what we've seen and experienced in our lives. We cry.

At some point Al Sharpton hears about what happened to Trayvon and a huge rally is held in New York. An arrest is demanded. And at first it seems ignored. But the demand is elevated in Florida by a group of brilliant and brave young organizers, the Dream Defenders, led by Umi Agnew. They occupy the governor's office, bringing direct action back into the fore for our generation. They use social media to amplify their voices, and they inspire a nation of organizers, including me, as I am working into LA to build our Dignity and Power Now. After weeks of protest, the killer is arrested and the world begins to know the extent to which he is a sick and deranged man, a man whose violence was known, a man who had had police called on him. A man who was not called a terrorist or put on a national database despite, before he murdered Trayvon, having committed actual violence.

5 Before the killer's trial begins, there are several things that we know:

In July 2005, he was arrested for "resisting an officer with violence." According to Jonathan Capehart, reporting for *The Washington Post,* the man who was allowed to carry a gun and become a neighborhood watch volunteer "got into a scuffle with cops who were questioning a friend for alleged underage drinking." The *Post* continued: "The charges were reduced and then waived after he entered an alcohol education program."

In August 2005, the killer's fiancée sought and received a restraining order against him because of his alleged violence against her.

Over an eight-year period, the killer made more than 45 unsubstantiated calls to the Sanford, Florida, police department about people he termed as "suspicious black males."

The killer's cousin had accused him of molesting her *before* the case made national news—meaning before any attention-seeking could have been her motive—and reported to the police, "I know George. And I know that he does not like black people." She pleaded for anonymity, and she continued: "He would start something. He's a very confrontational person. It's in his blood. Let's just say that. I don't want this poor kid and his family to just be overlooked." She begged police to ask around, to find out what kind of man this was.

10 All of this was in the record before Reverend Sharpton's rally.

Before the demand that he be arrested. Before the Dream Defenders occupied the governor's office.

Before Black Lives Matter.

But on July 13, 2013, I am traveling to Susanville, California, to visit an 18-year-old young man named Richie whom I have known and cherished since he was 14 years old. Richie has been sentenced to a decade in prison for a robbery in which no one was physically harmed. What kind of time will Trayvon's killer get?

We have driven fully half a day to be here, to be with Richie, whom I met when Mark Anthony, Jason and I worked as youth counselors at Cleveland. We initiated various forms of restorative justice programming in the school, and Richie stood out, even among a cohort of young people who were all standouts. He was part of a group of Black boys at the high school who couldn't stay out of trouble—we were told. But we believed punishment was the wrong interrupter for them.

15 Suspensions, for example, did little to move young people to wholeness or better performance. And they were used for even the most minor of offenses—being "disrespectful" was a common cause. Black children were far more at risk, suspended at nearly four times the rate of white students despite similar

behavior patterns. Black children taught by white teachers were particularly at risk for suspension, the data showed again and again. (Although the reverse was not true. Black teachers did not move to suspend white children at higher rates.)

Nearly seven million kids in the nation, some as young as four, were suspended in 2011 and 2012, when we were at Cleveland. Still, suspensions, for as widely as they were used, were a failure. All they did, as the data indicated, was alienate young people from school, teachers and often their peers. And they, like other punitive measures, did not address the external life and social factors that impacted children, including food and housing insecurity and police harassment or having lost a parent or close family member to mass incarceration.

But our job, in any case, was to interrupt that trouble and we were determined to do it in a way that elevated the humanity of the students. For a year our small team sat in circle with the young men. We talked about racism and homophobia. We talked about classism and sexism. We pulled apart concepts of addiction, and not so much addiction as in drugs but as in all of the behaviors that can compel a person to behave in ways that are detrimental. Our vision was to interrupt the process that had led the young men to see themselves outside of their own dreams.

Richie was the intellectual and the artist in the crew. He was the first one to publicly declare that he was a feminist, to say he wanted to be a Black man unlike his father, whose definition of manhood was prescribed by a limited Judeo-Christian ethos: making money, marry, have a child, rule your home, die. Richie eventually became the editor of the school newspaper and for the Valentine's Day edition one year, he supported a young woman writer who, like many of the students, had been reading Eve Ensler and wanted to proclaim V-Day as a day to celebrate and honor vaginas.

She wrote about how sacred they were, about how they must no longer be the site of male assault. Richie commissioned art to accompany the story and when the paper came out, he made it front-page news, along with a huge picture of a vulva. The school administration went wild, confiscating all the copies of the paper, threatening Richie with suspension. He stood his ground.

He said it was their responsibility to talk about sexual assault, their duty to force people to think about women's sexual organs differently. He said women were powerful and ought to be honored as such.

20 His position would garner global attention. Richie was called for interviews from as far away as India. Eventually the school backed down from their censure of and threats against him. The experience changed him and by the time he was 18, he had moved out of his parents' home, wanting desperately to break away from the silence of his mother and the harsh boundaries of his father. And after staying with me and Mark Anthony for a time, and then with other friends, he found a small apartment in Reseda, not far from Cleveland, and got a job with the LA Unified School District, working with students not so different than the student he had once been. Life was going well.

Until one day it wasn't.

Without warning, the district cut his hours. And that was that. They didn't fire him, but they didn't give him a steady schedule or allow him to earn a living wage. And because his schedule was erratic, it was hard for him to find anything else. Richie, a six-foot-five, young Black man who was living on his own and who had tattoos, and who was good enough to be hired but not good enough to really include and provide a career path for—and yet not bad enough to fire, was left in limbo and desperate. And his rent was due.

Later, after he was arrested, he said to me that when he felt desperate, when he didn't have the money to pay his rent, the voice he heard in his head was the one he was raised with: Men don't ask for help. Men make it happen.

You had already done so much for me, he said to me in the LA County Jail visitor's room. I didn't want to appear weak, he said. I know that's stupid, he said, but it's how I felt.

25 I told him he could always ask me for help. He said, I don't know what I was thinking. I guess I figured if I didn't hurt anyone, if I just got the money, it would get me through and no one would have to know, he said. I know that sounds crazy. I didn't want to hurt anyone. I just needed to pay the rent.

And in fact no one was physically hurt, although I'm sure they were terrified. But Richie was still handed down a sentence of ten years. Like Monte, who also never hurt anyone, was handed a sentence of eight years. When I think about them as I write these words, I don't only think about all the killer cops, the cops who lied, the cops who never got charged or when they were got acquitted. I also think about men like Brock Turner, the Stanford star swimmer, who raped a woman and got six months. Six months because the judge said Turner couldn't make it in prison, that prison wasn't for him.

But it was made for Richie? For Monte? For my father? My God. Is that not reason enough to shut it down?

But on this hot July day in 2013, Richie is thick in the first year of that sentence and we, his wife, Taina, his best friend Haewon and I, are sitting in a prison visiting room in Susanville that is like most California prison visiting rooms, sterile and windowless, with tables that have the legs cut down to three inches off the ground, so no playing footsies. There are the requisite vending machines against a wall where we can buy overpriced food that ensures lucrative contracts for white-owned companies and salty, sugary, processed food items that are loaded guns for we who have no real choice but to eat them.

And on this day in Susanville we are talking about a million things, although eventually everything will come back to what is unfolding in Central Florida and Trayvon Martin's killer: Will he walk?

30 For as much as we are there in California for and with Richie, together, loving each other and laughing as much as is possible, we are also in Florida and our hearts are full with the Fulton and Martin family and we are afraid. We do not speak of our fear about the decision that looms, knowing that our children so rarely receive justice in this nation. We speak about hope because after all, what else? At some point I recall thinking, My God. The world knows that, against a 911 operator's orders, this man chased down and killed 17-year-old Trayvon Martin.

And Trayvon Martin, a Black boy who was just walking home. Walking with a can of Arizona Iced Tea and a pack of Skittles he'd bought for his little brother. Walking and speaking on his cell to his friend Rachel, a girl who was bullied and a girl he protected. Walking and wearing a hoodie like teenagers everywhere wear hoodies. Walking and at once set upon by a large, white-presenting man who decided that because the boy was Black and because he wore a hoodie like most teens, he was a threat.

We learn that the man was ordered by a police dispatcher to stop.

We learn that the man chased the boy, who was running errands for his little brother, who was talking to his friend, his friend who was bullied.

We learn that the man pulled the trigger on this unarmed child who weighed what, 50, 75 pounds less than the man with the gun?

35 We learn that the man believed he had a right to do what he did. A right to stand ground that wasn't being challenged by a boy carrying iced tea and Skittles. He believed that his assumed rights superseded this child's right to walk home to his own house to bring his little brother a treat.

And we are scared that a jury of this man's peers would agree.

We are scared because of the work and time it took even to get the man arrested.

We are scared because Trayvon's beautiful life and terrible death is meant to be erased; the reporting of it made no front-page news, no *Dateline,* no Anderson Cooper. The story on my Facebook feed was a tiny blog post, a post not connected with mainstream media. A white man is questioned and then released after he shoots and kills an unarmed Black boy who was walking home. And in that instant I was filled with rage and confusion. Was this 2012 or 1955?

We could be talking about Emmett Till. This is who I think about throughout the course of the trial and the weeks and months leading up to it. I think of Emmett Till and his family and also my nephew, Chase, Monte's son, who is 14 the year Trayvon is killed. Will he be shot down and killed for walking while Black, and will his murder matter so little it doesn't even make the news and no one will be held accountable?

40 I grew up in a neighborhood that was impoverished and in pain and bore all the modern-day outcomes of communities left without resources and yet supplied with tools of violence. But when someone in my neighborhood committed a crime, let alone murder, all of us were held accountable, my God. Metal detectors, searchlights and constant police presence, full-scale sweeps of kids just walking home from school—all justified by politicians and others who said they represented our needs. Where were these representatives when white guys shot us down?

Were it not for the brave and determined young people who formed the Dream Defenders joining forces with the brave and heartbroken parents of Trayvon, Sybrina Fulton and Tracey Martin, and had there not been sit-ins, protests, occupations, and Al Sharpton, this boy's name would be on no one's tongue, save for his family and the friends who loved him.

Because of all this, we know and we are afraid, but still, in that prison in Susanville on July 13, 2013, in the state that would give a desperate Black boy who physically harmed no one ten years but a rapist six months, we hold on to hope.

Because what else?

Seven hours after it begins, the visit with Richie ends, and we head back to the motel we are staying at in the small town. Of the just under 20,000 residents, nearly half, 46 percent, live in one of the town's two prisons.

45 Susanville, incorporated in 1860, was named for the child of the man who laid claim to founding it at a time when founding something was a euphemism for manifest destiny and homesteading and all the blood and death both of these wrought. "Founding," a term like the phrase "collateral damage," the use of which was ratcheted up in the 90s so they didn't have to say dead Iraqi children.

But the point is that we are an 11-hour drive from Los Angeles because Susanville is deep in Northern California, farther up than the Bay Area and at the border of Nevada, near Reno. And it's entirely unlike the vibrancy and wealth generally associated with our state and its outsize imagery of glittery Beverly Hills and shiny Silicon Valley. If you saw a picture of it, West Virginia would likely come to mind before California would.

But Susanville is actually more reflective of the average California town than anything that is marketed to tourists. And it looks like American towns across the rest of the country: small and working class, except here the demographics report an extraordinary diversity—if, that is, diversity is distorted, like a horror-house mirror or a story from *The Twilight Zone.* In Susanville, there is almost no one who is Black and free at the same time, although a cursory reading of census reports could have you believing it's a racial Kumbaya.

Once a place where loggers and miners worked, today Susanville's singular growth industry is prisons; roughly half of all the adults who live here work at one of the two facilities. Of course those numbers intensify wildly if you count the work done, the labor extracted, from the prisoners who are shipped here predominantly from LA County, from the Bay.

Being here, looking at the storefronts, the people, it feels like we are trapped in a black-and-white photograph from the deep South in the 1950s, and the images of hard rural living come stuttering back as if to taunt us that freedom has never arrived and won't. All you can feel are the walls and the bars, the gun towers and barbed wire, which is only offset by all the military. The random appearance of soldiers who are based near Susanville. The sense of impending war. The American flags in every size you can imagine. What must it be like to live hoping for and invested in war and crime because without them the people of Susanville must believe that the world would collapse?

50 On the way back to the motel we stop at a small store to buy microwavables. There are no restaurants we want to eat in, plus this is cheaper. We buy pre-made chicken sandwiches or something like that. We are trying to be healthy. The motel has a microwave. We eat and we get on my laptop. Eating and waiting for the verdict to come in. I go on my Facebook page because that's where everyone is updating what's happening. I am nervous but Facebook keeps me connected.

And then it happens.

I start seeing the timelines update. The killer is acquitted of the first charge. And then he is acquitted of all of them. Every. Single. One. Of. Them. I go into shock. I lose my breath. My heart drops to my stomach. I am stunned and for a moment cannot move. When I begin to move I go into denial.

No! This is impossible. Wait a minute. Hold on. This doesn't make sense.

But as soon as I deny it I know that it is true, and I am overcome with embarrassment and shame. How could this have happened? Why couldn't we make this not happen? And then I start crying. And I feel wrong about crying. My tears make me want to hide. I feel like I have to be the particular kind of strong Black people are always asked to be. The impossible strong. The strong where there's no space to think about your own vulnerability. The space to cry.

55 I look around the room, this small motel room, and I look at the two women I have traveled here with. In my role as a counselor at Cleveland, I played such a particular role for them. Haewon, a junior when Richie entered their high school as a ninth grader, embraced him as her little brother. I held them both close to me, mentored them both, trained them to be organizers for justice in our communities, organizers against the prison industrial complex, organizers for human rights.

And Taina, Taina, who fell in love with Richie months before he was arrested, committed to him, which made me commit to her. When they decided to marry after learning of his sentence, I was the one to marry them. I had become ordained in 2004, primarily because I was determined to marry Queer people despite what was then marriage inequity in California and the nation. As time moved forward and marriage equity took hold, my ordination and desire to marry people expanded to include all those who for different reasons were prevented from legally being families. Including prisoners and their wives. I officiated Taina and Richie's service, their exchange of vows inside of jail, and there has not been a weekend in all the years that they've been together when she has missed seeing him.

So even though I am not so much older than they are, whether Richie or Taina or Haewon or even Trayvon, I am old enough to feel responsible. I have become my big brother Paul. I feel the weight of being with two Black women who are younger than me in this prison town, and I wonder, if it came down to it, would I be able to protect them, protect us? Do I have any power to ensure that they will live long—that their Black lives will be full and healthy?

I cannot stop myself from crying. As much as I want to. I weep hard. We all do. And then I get angry. Once again my world is defined by cognitive dissonance: to be in this town where this little boy, literally this 18-year-old boy, who had hurt no one, would be locked up for ten years and this white-presenting man could kill us and go home.

And then my friend Alicia writes a Facebook post. Alicia, who I'd known for seven years at this point, who I'd met at a political gathering in Rhode Island where at the end of the day our goal was to dance until we couldn't dance anymore. She and I danced with one another all night long and began a friendship that holds us together to this very day. But she writes these words in the wake of the acquittal:

> btw stop saying that we are not surprised. that's a damn shame in itself. I continue to be surprised at how little Black lives matter. And I will continue that. stop giving up on black life. black people, I will NEVER give up on us. NEVER.
>
> And then I respond. I wrote back with a hashtag:
>
> #BlackLivesMatter

Alicia and I brainstorm over the course of the next few days. We know we want to develop something. We know we want whatever we create to have global reach. Alicia reaches out to her friend Opal Tometi, a dedicated organizer who is running Black Alliance for Just Immigration, based in Brooklyn, New York. Opal is a master communicator and develops all the initial digital components we need to even get people to feel comfortable saying the words Black Lives Matter, for even among those closest to us, there are many who feel the words will be viewed as separatist, that they will isolate us. Opal pulls together the architecture for our first website and Twitter accounts, our Facebook and Tumblr. We are determined to take public this basic concept: That our lives mean something. That Black Lives Matter.

After a few days I return to Facebook and I begin to post.

I write that we are going to begin organizing.

I write: *I hope it impacts more than we can ever imagine.*

Credit

Is He Boyfriend Material? Representation of Males in Teenage Girls' Magazines

KIRSTEN B. FIRMINGER

Abstract

Teenage girls' magazines play an important role in shaping the norms of the millions of girls who read them. In this article, I examine, through the discursive analysis of two issues each of five different popular teenage girls' magazines (ten issues total), how males and male behavior are represented. Guided by the magazines, girls are "empowered" to be informed consumers of boys, who are written about as shallow, highly sexual, emotionally inexpressive, and insecure, but also as potential boyfriends, providing romance, intimacy, and love. Framed by fashion and beauty products in both the advertisement and magazine content, success in attracting the "right" boy and finding love is presented as a result of girls' self-regulation, personal responsibility, and good choices, with only their own lack of self-esteem and effort holding them back.

Keywords

Adolescents, gender norms, consumption, magazines, content analysis

> It seems like guys lock up their feelings tighter than Fort Knox, right? Well, here's the key to opening that emotional vault! ... CG! Epiphany: When a guy finally opens up to you, you'll know he has set you apart from other girls.
>
> —*CosmoGirl,* All About Guys Section, "Guy Magnet Cheat Sheet"

On the pages of popular teenage girls' magazines, boys are presented (in)congruently as the providers of potential love, romance, and excitement and as highly sexual, attracted to the superficial, and emotionally inexpressive. The magazines guide female readers toward avoiding the "bad" male and male behavior (locking up their feelings tighter than Fort Knox) and obtaining the "good" male and male behavior (setting you apart from other girls). Within girls' magazines, success in life and (heterosexual) love is girls' responsibility, tied to their ability to self-regulate, make good choices, and present themselves in the "right"way. The only barriers are girls' own lack of self-esteem or limited effort (Harris 2004). While the "girl power" language of the feminist movement is used, its politics and questioning of patriarchal gender norms are not discussed. Instead, the magazines advocate relentless surveillance of self, boys, and peers. Embarrassing and confessional tales, quizzes, and opportunities to rate and judge boys and girls on the basis of their photos and profiles encourage young women to "fashion" identities through clothes, cosmetics, beauty items, and consumerism.

Popular teenage girls' magazines. In the United States, teenage girls' magazines are read by more than 75 percent of teenage girls (Market profile: Teenagers 2000). The magazines play an important role in shaping the norms and expectations during a crucial stage of identity and relationship development. Currie (1999) found that some readers consider the magazines' content to be more compelling than their own personal experiences and knowledge. Magazines are in the business of both selling themselves to their audience and selling their audience to advertisers (Kilborne 1999). Teenage girls are advertised as more loyal to their favorite magazines than to their favorite television programs, with magazines touted as "a sister and a friend rolled into one" (Market profile: Teenagers 2000). Magazines attract and keep advertisers by providing the right audience for their products and services, suppressing information that might offend the advertiser, and including editorial content saturated in advertiser-friendly advice (Kilborne 1999).

In this textual environment, consumerist and individualist attitudes and values are promoted to the exclusion of alternative perspectives. Across magazines, one relentless message is clear: "the road to happiness is attracting males for successful heterosexual life by way of physical beautification" (Evan et al. 1991; see also Carpenter 1998, Currie 1999, Signorelli 1997). Given the clarity of this message, little work has been done focusing on the portrayal of males that the girls are supposed to attract. I began my research examining this question: how are males and male behavior portrayed in popular teenage girls' magazines?

Method

To explore these questions, I designed a discursive analysis of a cross-section of adolescent girls' magazines, sampling a variety of magazines and analyzing across them for common portrayals of males. *Seventeen* and *YM* are long-running adolescent girls' magazines. *Seventeen* has a base circulation of 2.4 million while *YM* has a circulation of 2.2 million (*Advertising Age* 74: 21). As a result of the potential of the market, the magazines that are directed at adolescent girls have expanded to include the new *CosmoGirl* (launched in 1999) and *ELLEgirl* (in 2001). Very successful, *CosmoGirl* has a base circulation of 1 million. *ELLEgirl* reports a smaller circulation of 450,000 (*Advertising Age* 74: 21). Chosen as an alternative to the other adolescent girls' magazines, *Girls' Life* is directed at a younger female audience and is the winner of the 2000, 1999, and 1996 Parents' Choice Awards Medal and of the 2000 and 1998 Parents' Guide to Children's Media Association Award of Excellence. The magazine reports it is the number one magazine for girls ages 10 to 15, with a circulation of 3 million (http://www.girlslife.com/infopage.php, retrieved May 23, 2004).

5 I coded two issues each of *Seventeen, YM, CosmoGirl, ELLEgirl,* and *Girls' Life,* for a total of ten issues. Magazines build loyalty with their readers by presenting the same kinds of material, in a similar form, month after month (Duke 2002). To take into account seasonal differences in content, I purchased the magazines six months apart, once during December 2002 and once during July 2003. While the magazines range in their dates of publication (for instance, Holiday issue, December issue, January issue, etc.), all the magazines were together at the same newsstand at the singular time of purchase.

Results

Within the pages of the magazines, articles and photo layouts focus primarily on beauty, fashion, celebrities and entertainment, boys and love, health and sex, and self-development. The magazines specialize, with emphasis more or less on one of these topics over the other: *ElleGirl* presents itself as more fashion focused, while self-development is the emphasis for *Girls' Life*'s younger audience. Within the self-development sections, one can find articles focusing on topics such as activities, school, career aspirations, volunteering, sports, and politics. However, even in these articles, focus is on the social, interpersonal aspects of relationships and on consumption instead of the actual doing and mastery of activities.

Advertising permeates the magazines, accounting for 20.8 percent to 44.8 percent of the pages. Additionally, many of the editorial articles, presumably noncommercial, are written in ways that endorse specific products and services (see Currie 1999, for more information on "advertorials"). For instance, one advice column responded to a reader's inquiry about a first kiss by recommending " ... [having] the following supplies [handy] for when the magical moment finally arrives: Sugarless mints, yummy flavored lip gloss (I dig Bonne Bell Lip Smackers) ..."

Male-focused content. On average, 19.7 percent of the pages focused on males[1], ranging from a minimum of 13.6 percent in *ELLEGirl* to a maximum percent in *Seventeen*. Articles on boys delve into boys' culture, points of view, opinions, interests, and hobbies, while articles on girls' activities focus more pointedly on the pursuit of boys. Girls learn "Where the boys are," since the "next boyfriend could be right under your nose." They are told,

> Where to go: Minor-league ballparks. Why: Cute guys! ... Who'll be there: The players are just for gazing at; your targets are the cuties in the stands. And don't forget the muscular types lugging soda trays up and down the aisles. What to say: Ask him what he thinks about designated hitters (they're paid just to bat). He'll be totally impressed that you even brought up the subject.

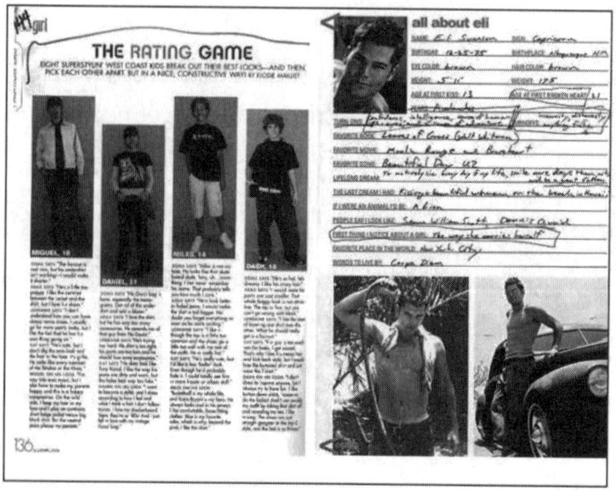

Figure 1: "The Rating Game" and "All About Eli"
SOURCE: Image 1 (left): ElleGirl May/June 2003, p. 136, "Fashion Lab," published by Hachette Filipacchi Media, New York, NY.

10 Males are offered up to readers in several different formats. First we read profiles, then we meet "examples," we are allowed question and answer, we are quizzed, and then we are asked to judge the males. Celebrity features contain in-depth interviews with male celebrities, while personal short profiles of celebrities or "regular" guys include a photo, biographical information, hobbies, interests, and inquiries such as his "three big requirements for a girl-friend" and "his perfect date." *CosmoGirl*'s fold-out photo centerfold (see Figure 1) informs readers that the first thing 27-year-old Eli notices about a girl is "the way she carries herself," his turn-ons are "Confidence, intelligence, sense of humor, lips, eyes, and a sense of adventure," and his turn-offs are "insecurity, dishonesty, and anything fake." In question-and-answer articles, regular columnists answer selected questions that the readers have submitted.[2] Some columns consistently focus on boys, such as "GL Guys by Bill and Dave" and *YM*'s "Love Q and A," while others focus on a variety of questions, for instance *ELLEgirl*'s "Ask Jennifur" profiles of noncelebrity males are presented and judged in rating articles. The magazines publish their criteria for rating boys, via rhetorical devices such as "the magazine staffs' opinions" or the opinion polls of other teenage girls (see Figure 1).

C#2

Ratings include categories such as "his style," "dateable?," and "style factor." For example, in *CosmoGirl*'s Boy-O-Meter article, "Dateable?: I usually go for dark hair, olive skin, and thick eyebrows. But his eyes make me feel like I could confide in him," or *ELLEgirl*'s The Rating Game, "He's cute, but I don't dig the emo look and the hair in the face. It's girlie." Readers can then assess their opinions in relation to those of other girls' and the magazine staff.

E#2

R#2

Romantic stories and quotes enable readers to witness "real" romance and love and compare their "personal experiences" to those presented in the magazines. For instance, "Then one day I found a note tucked in my locker that said, 'You are different than everyone else. But that is why you are beautiful.' At the bottom of the note it said, 'From Matt—I'm in your science class. 'We started dating the next day." These can also be rated, as the magazine staff then responded, "Grade: A. He sounds like a very smart boy."

Finally, the readers can then test their knowledge and experiences through the quizzes in the magazines, such as *Seventeen*'s quiz, "Can your summer love last?" with questions and multiple-choice answers:

> As he's leaving for a weeklong road trip with the guys, he: A) tells you at least 10 times how much he's going to miss you. B) promises to call you when he gets a chance. C) can't stop talking about how much fun it will be to "get away" with just his buddies for seven whole days.

15 Over the pages, boys as a "product" begin to merge with the [other] products and services being sold to girls in "training" as informed consumers, learning to feel "empowered" and make good "choices." While a good boy is a commodity of value, the young women readers learn that relationships with boys should be considered disposable and interchangeable like the other products being sold, "Remember, BFs come and go, but best friends are for- ever! Is he worth it? Didn't think so."

Embarrassing and confessional stories. Short embarrassing or confessional stories submitted by the readers for publication provide another textual window through which young women can view gender politics; one issue of *YM* included a special pull-out book focused exclusively on confessionals.[3] Kaplan and Cole (2003) found in their four focus groups that the girls enjoy the embarrassing and confessional stories because they reveal "what it is like to be a teenage girl."

On average, two-thirds of the confessional/embarrassing stories were male focused; in 42–100 percent of the stories males were the viewing audience for, or participant in, a girl's embarrassing/confessional moment. Often these stories involve a "cute boy," "my boyfriend," or "my crush." For example:

> My friends and I noticed these cute guys at the ice cream parlor. As we were leaving with our cones, the guys offered to walk with us. I was wearing my chunky-heeled shoes and feeling pretty awesome … until I tripped. My double scoop flew in the air and hit one of the guys. Oops.

Teenage girls within these stories are embarrassed about things that have happened, often accidentally, with males typically as the audience. While this may allow the female readers to see that they are not the only ones who have experienced embarrassing moments, it also reinforces the notion of self-surveillance as well as socializes girls to think of boys as the audience and judges of their behavior (Currie 1999).

20 *Representations of males.* To assess how males are represented, I coded content across male-focused feature articles and "question and answer" columns.[4] These articles contained the most general statements about boys and their behaviors, motivations, and characteristics (for example, "Guys are a few steps behind girls when it comes to maturity level"[5]).

A dominant tension in the representations of boys involves males' splitting of intimacy from sexuality (see Whitney Missildine's article in this issue). The magazine advises girls as they negotiate these different behaviors and situations, trying to choose the "right" guy (who will develop an intimate relationship with a girl), reject the "bad" guy (who is focused only on sex), or if possible, change the "bad" guy into the "good" guy (through a girl's decisions and interactions with the male).

> My boyfriend and I were together for 10 months when he said he wanted to take a break—he wasn't sure he was ready for such a commitment. The thought of him seeing other people tore me apart. So every day while we were broken up, I gave him something as a sign of my feelings for him: love sayings cut out from magazines, or cute comics from the paper. Eventually he confessed that he had just been confused and that he loved me more than ever.

As girls are represented as responsible for good shopping, they are represented also as responsible for selecting/changing/shaping male behavior. If girls learn to make the right choices, they can have the right relationship with the right guy, or convert a "bad"/confused boy into a good catch.

The tension is most evident in stories about males' high sex drive, attraction to superficial appearances, emotional inexpressiveness, and fear of rejection and contrasted with those males who are "keepers": who keep their sex drive in check, value more than just girls' appearances, and are able to open up. The articles and advice columns blend the traditional and the feminist; encompassing both new and old meanings and definitions of what it means to be female and male within today's culture (Harris 2004).

25 *The males' sex drive*. The "naturally" high sex drive of males rises as the most predominant theme across the magazines. Viewed as normal and unavoidable in teenage boys, girls write to ask for an explanation and advice, and they are told:

> You invited a guy you kind of like up to your room (just to talk!) and he got the wrong idea. This was not your fault. Guys—especially unchaperoned guys on school trips—will interpret any move by a girl as an invitation to get heavy. And I mean any move. You could have sat down next to him at a lab table and he would have taken that as a sign from God that you wanted his body.

When it comes to the topic of sexuality, traditional notions surround "appropriate behavior" for young women and men. Girls learn that males respect and date girls who are able to keep males' sex drive in check and who take time building a relationship. Girls were rarely shown as being highly sexual or interested only in a sexual relationship with a boy. Girls are supposed to avoid potentially dangerous situations (such as being alone with a boy) and draw the line (since the males frequently are unable to do so). If they don't, they can be labeled sluts.

> Don't even make out with someone until you're sure things are exclusive. When you hook up with him too early, you're giving him the message that you are something less than a goddess (because, as you know, a goddess is guarded in a temple, and it's not easy to get to her). Take it from me when I tell you that guys want to be with girls they consider goddesses. So treat your body as a temple—don't let just any one in.

> Most guys would probably assume that a girl who ditches guys after intimacy is slutty. I know, I know—there's a double standard. It seems like the "players" among us can date and dump as frequently as they please, but it's only a social no-no when you girls do it.

30

> A guy in heat tried to take advantage of you and you wouldn't give in. That's all that matters. You may have kissed him, but, ultimately, the decision to draw the line was yours and you did it. That's nothing to feel slutty about.

Valuing superficial appearances. Driven by sex, males were shown as judging and valuing girls based on their appearance.

> That's bad, but it's scarier when combined with another sad male truth: They're a lot more into looks than we are.

> Okay, I'm the first to admit that guys can be shallow and insipid and *Baywatch* brainwashed to the point where the sight of two balloons on a string will turn them on.

Since males are thought to be interested in the superficial, girls sought advice on how to be most superficially appealing, asking what do guys prefer, including the size of a girl's breasts, hair color, eye color, height, and weight. Girls are portrayed as wanting to know how to present themselves to attract boys, demonstrating an interaction between girls' ideas and understanding of what males want and girls' own choices and behaviors.

35 *Boys are emotionally inexpressive*. Across features, readers learn about boys' inability or unwillingness to open up and share their feelings. However, the articles suggest also that if a girl is able to negotiate the relationship correctly, she could get a guy to trust her.

> Let's say you go to the pet store and see a really cute puppy you'd like to pet, but every time you try, he pulls away because he was treated badly in the past. People aren't much different. Move very slowly, and build up trust bit by bit. Show this guy you're into him for real, and he'll warm up to you. Puppy love is worth the wait.

Girls are responsible for doing the emotional work and maintenance and for being change agents in relationships, not allowing room for or even expecting males to take on any of these tasks (see also Chang 2000).

Boys' insecurity and fear of rejection. Boys are displayed as afraid of rejection. Reflecting the neoliberal ideology of "girl power," girls were urged by the magazines to take the initiative in seeking out and approaching boys. This way they are in control of and responsible for their fate, with only lack of confidence, self-esteem, and effort holding them back from finding romance and love.

> So in the next week (why waste more time?), write him a note, pull him aside at a party, or call him up with your best friend by your side for support. Hey, he could be psyched that you took the initiative.

40

> So I think you may have to do the work. If there's a certain guy you're feelin' and you think he's intimidated by you, make the first move. Say something to relax him, like, "What's up? My name is Chelsea." After that, he'll probably start completing sentences.

Males' potential—the "keepers." "Consider every guy to be on a level playing field—they all have potential." Boys were shown to have "potential" and girls were advised to search out the "right" guys.

> He does indeed sound dreamy. He also sounds like a total gentleman, considering he hasn't attempted to jump your bones yet, so the consensus is: He's a keeper.

> Most guys are actually smarter than you think and are attracted to all sorts of things about the female species. Yes, big boobs definitely have their dedicated fan base, but so do musical taste, brains, a cute laugh, style and the ability to throw a spiral football (to name just a few). What's a turn-on or deal breaker for one guy is a nonevent for another.

> The streets are filled with guys who are nice, hot, smart, fun, and half-naked (joking … sort of!). And they all want to spend some time with an unattached pumpkin like you.

45 These boys become the center of the romantic stories and quotes about love and relationships. Resulting from and sustained by girls' self-regulation, personal responsibility, effort, and good choices (as guided by the tools and advice provided by the magazines), these boys are for keeps.

Discussion

Within the magazines, girls are invited to explore boys as shallow, highly sexual, emotionally inexpressive, and insecure and boys who are potential boyfriends, providing romance, intimacy, and love. Males' high sex drive and interest in superficial appearances are naturalized and left unquestioned in the content of the magazines; within a "girl power" version of compulsory heterosexuality, girls should too learn the right way to approach a boy in order to get what they want—"the road to happiness is attracting males for successful heterosexual life by way of physical beautification" (Evans et al. 1991). Girls walk the fine line of taking advantage of males' interest in sex and appearance, without crossing over into being labeled a slut. Socialized to be purchasers of beauty and fashion products that promise to make them attractive to boys, girls are "in charge" of themselves and the boys they "choose." It's a competitive market so they better have the right understanding of boys, as well as the right body and outfit to go with it.

The magazines' portrayals, values, and opinions are shaped by their need to create an advertiser-friendly environment while attracting and appealing to the magazines' audience of teenage girls. Skewing the portrayal of males and females to their target audience, magazine editors, writers, and, though I have not highlighted it here—advertisers, take advantage of gender-specific fantasies, myths, and fears (Craig 1993). Boys become another product, status symbol, and identity choice. If girls' happiness requires finding romance and love, girls should learn to be informed consumers of boys. By purchasing the magazines, they have a guide to this process, guaranteed to help them understand "What his mixed signals really mean." In addition, if boys are concerned with superficial appearances, it is to the benefit of girls to buy the advertised products and learn "The best swimsuit for [their] bod[ies]."

As girls survey and judge themselves and others, possessions and consumption become the metric for assessing status (Rohlinger 2002; Salamon 2003), the cultural capital for teenagers in place of work, community, and other activities (Harris 2004). The feminist "girl empowerment" becomes personal, appropriated to sell products. The choice and purchase of products and services sold in the magazines promise recreation and transformation, of not only one's outward appearance but also of one's inner self, leading to happiness, satisfaction, and success (Kilborne 1999). Money is the underlying driving force in magazine content. However, while the magazines focus on doing good business, girls are being socialized by the magazines' norms and expectations.

"Bottom line: look at dating as a way to sample the menu before picking your entrée. In the end, you'll be much happier with the choice you make! Yum!"

Works Cited

Carpenter, L. M. 1998. From girls into women: Scripts for sexuality and romance in Seventeen Magazine, 1974–1994. *The Journal of Sex Research* 35: 158–168.

Chang, J. 2000. Agony-resolution pathways: How women perceive American men in Cosmopolitan's agony (advice) column. *The Journal of Men's Studies* 8: 285–308.

Currie, D. H. 1999. Girl talk: Adolescent magazines and their readers. Toronto: University of Toronto Press.

Craig, S. 1993. Selling masculinities, selling femininities: Multiple genders and the economics of television. *The Mid-Atlantic Almanack* 2: 15–27.

Duke, L. 2002. Get real!: Cultural relevance and resistance to the mediated feminine ideal. *Psychology and Marketing* 19: 211–233.

Evans, E., J. Rutberg, and C. Sather. 1991. Content analysis of contemporary teen magazines for adolescent females. *Youth and Society* 23: 99–120.

Girls' Life magazine: About us. Retrieved May 23, 2004 from http://www.girlslife.com/infopage.php.

Kaplan, E. B. and L. Cole. 2003. I want to read stuff on boys": White, Latina, and Black girls reading Seventeen magazine and encountering adolescence. *Adolescence* 38: 141–159.

Market profile: Teenagers. 2000. Magazine Publishers of America.

McRobbie, A. 1991. Feminism and Youth Culture. London: Macmillan.

Rohlinger, D. 2002. Eroticizing men: Cultural influences on advertising and male objectification. *Sex Roles: A Journal of Research* 46: 61–74.

Salamon, S. 2003. From hometown to nontown: Rural community effects of suburbanization. *Rural Sociology* 68: 1–24.

Signorelli, N. 1997. A content analysis: Reflections of girls in the media, a study of television shows and commercials, movies, music videos, and teen magazine articles and ads. Children Now and Kaiser Family Foundation Publication.

Tolman, D. L., R. Spencer, T. Harmon, M. Rosen-Reynoso, and M. Stripe. 2004. Getting close, staying cool: Early adolescent boys' experiences with romantic relationships, In *Adolescent boys: Exploring diverse cultures of boyhood,* edited by N.Way and J. Chu. New York: NYU Press.

Tolman, D. L., R. Spencer, M. Rosen-Reynoso, and M. Porche. 2002. Sowing the seeds of violence in heterosexual relationships: Early adolescents narrate compulsory heterosexuality. *Journal of Social Issues* 59: 159–178.

Van Roosmalen, E. 2000. Forces of patriarchy: Adolescent experiences of sexuality and conceptions of relationships. *Youth and Society* 32: 202–227.

Where the girls are. 2003. *Advertising Age* 74: 21.

Peculiar Benefits

ROXANE GAY

When I was young, my parents took our family to Haiti during the summers. For them, it was a homecoming. For my brothers and me it was an adventure, sometimes a chore, and always a necessary education on privilege and the grace of an American passport. Until visiting Haiti, I had no idea what poverty really was or the difference between relative and absolute poverty. To see poverty so plainly and pervasively left a profound mark on me.

To this day, I remember my first visit, and how at every intersection, men and women, shiny with sweat, would mob our car, their skinny arms stretched out, hoping for a few gourdes or American dollars. I saw the sprawling slums, the shanties housing entire families, the trash piled in the streets, and also the gorgeous beach and the young men in uniforms who brought us Coca-Cola in glass bottles and made us hats and boats out of palm fronds. It was hard for a child to begin to grasp the contrast of such inescapable poverty alongside almost repulsive luxury, and then the United States, a mere eight hundred miles away, with its gleaming cities rising out of the landscape and the well-maintained interstates stretching across the country, the running water and the electricity. It wasn't until many, many years later that I realized my education on privilege began long before I could appreciate it in any meaningful way.

Privilege is a right or immunity granted as a peculiar benefit, advantage, or favor. There is racial privilege, gender (and identity) privilege, heterosexual privilege, economic privilege, able-bodied privilege, educational privilege, religious privilege, and the list goes on and on. At some point, you have to surrender to the kinds of privilege you hold. Nearly everyone, particularly in the developed world, has something someone else doesn't, something someone else yearns for.

The problem is, cultural critics talk about privilege with such alarming frequency and in such empty ways, we have diluted the word's meaning. When people wield the word "privilege," it tends to fall on deaf ears because we hear that word so damn much it has become white noise.

5 One of the hardest things I've ever had to do is accept and acknowledge my privilege. It's an ongoing project. I'm a woman, a person of color, and the child of immigrants, but I also grew up middle class and then upper middle class. My parents raised my siblings and me in a strict but loving environment. They were and are happily married, so I didn't have to deal with divorce or crappy intramarital dynamics. I attended elite schools. My master's and doctoral degrees were funded. I got a tenure-track position my first time out. My bills are paid. I have the time and resources for frivolity. I am reasonably well published. I have an agent and books to my name. My life has been far from perfect, but it's somewhat embarrassing for me to accept just how much privilege I have.

It's also really difficult for me to consider the ways in which I lack privilege or the ways in which my privilege hasn't magically rescued me from a world of hurt. On my more difficult days, I'm not sure what's more of a pain in my ass—being black or being a woman. I'm happy to be both of these things, but the world keeps intervening. There are all kinds of infuriating reminders of my place in the world—random people questioning me in the parking lot at work as if it is unfathomable that I'm a faculty member, the persistence of lawmakers trying to legislate the female body, street harassment, strangers wanting to touch my hair.

We tend to believe that accusations of privilege imply we have it easy, which we resent because life is hard for nearly everyone. Of course we resent these accusations. Look at white men when they are accused of having privilege. They tend to be immediately defensive (and, at times, understandably so). They say, "It's not my fault I am a white man," or "I'm [insert other condition that discounts their privilege]," instead of simply accepting that, in this regard, yes, they benefit from certain privileges others do not. To have privilege in one or more areas does not mean you are wholly privileged. Surrendering to the acceptance of privilege is difficult, but it is really all that is expected. What I remind myself, regularly, is this: the acknowledgment of my privilege is not a denial of the ways I have been and am marginalized, the ways I have suffered.

You don't necessarily *have* to do anything once you acknowledge your privilege. You don't have to apologize for it. You need to understand the extent of your privilege, the consequences of your privilege, and remain aware that people who are different from you move through and experience the world in ways you might never know anything about. They might endure situations you can never know anything about. You could, however, use that privilege for the greater good—to try to level the playing field for everyone, to work for social justice, to bring attention to how those without certain privileges are disenfranchised. We've seen what the hoarding of privilege has done, and the results are shameful.

When we talk about privilege, some people start to play a very pointless and dangerous game where they try to mix and match various demographic characteristics to determine who wins at the Game of Privilege. Who would win in a privilege battle between a wealthy black woman and a wealthy white man? Who would win a privilege battle between a queer white man and a queer Asian woman? Who would win in a privilege battle between a working-class white man and a wealthy, differently abled Mexican woman? We could play this game all day and never find a winner. Playing the Game of Privilege is mental masturbation—it only feels good to those playing the game.

10 Too many people have become self-appointed privilege police, patrolling the halls of discourse, ready to remind people of their privilege whether those people have denied that privilege or not. In online discourse, in particular, the specter of privilege is always looming darkly. When someone writes from experience, there is often someone else, at the ready, pointing a trembling finger, accusing that writer of having various kinds of privilege. How dare someone speak to a personal experience without accounting for every possible configuration of privilege or the lack thereof? We would live in a world of silence if the only people who were allowed to write or speak from experience or about difference were those absolutely without privilege.

When people wield accusations of privilege, more often than not, they want to be heard and seen. Their need is acute, if not desperate, and that need rises out of the many historical and ongoing attempts to silence and render invisible marginalized groups. Must we satisfy our need to be heard and seen by preventing anyone else from being heard and seen? Does privilege automatically negate any merits of what a privilege holder has to say? Do we ignore everything, for example, that white men have to say?

We need to get to a place where we discuss privilege by way of observation and acknowledgment rather than accusation. We need to be able to argue beyond the threat of privilege. We need to stop playing Privilege or Oppression Olympics because we'll never get anywhere until we find more effective ways of talking through difference. We should be able to say, "This is my truth," and have that truth stand without a hundred clamoring voices shouting, giving the impression that multiple truths cannot coexist. Because at some point, doesn't privilege become beside the point?

Privilege is relative and contextual. Few people in the developed world, and particularly in the United States, have no privilege at all. Among those of us who participate in intellectual communities, privilege runs rampant. We have disposable time and the ability to access the Internet regularly. We have the freedom to express our opinions without the threat of retaliation. We have smartphones and iProducts and desktops and laptops. If you are reading this essay, you have some kind of privilege. It may be hard to hear that, I know, but if you cannot recognize your privilege, you have a lot of work to do; get started.

Argument as Conversation
The Role of Inquiry in Writing a Researched Argument

STUART GREENE

Argument is very much a part of what we do every day: We confront a public issue, something that is open to dispute, and we take a stand and support what we think and feel with what we believe are good reasons. Seen in this way, argument is very much like a conversation. By this, I mean that making an argument entails providing good reasons to support your viewpoint, as well as counterarguments, and recognizing how and why readers might object to your ideas. The metaphor of conversation emphasizes the social nature of writing. Thus inquiry, research, and writing arguments are intimately related. If, for example, you are to understand the different ways others have approached your subject, then you will need to do your "homework." This is what Doug Brent (1996) means when he says that research consists of "the looking-up of facts in the context of other worldviews, other ways of seeing" (78).

In learning to argue within an academic setting, such as the one you probably find yourself in now, it is useful to think about writing as a form of inquiry in which you convey your understanding of the claims people make, the questions they raise, and the conflicts they address. As a form of inquiry, then, writing begins with problems, conflicts, and questions that you identify as important. The questions that your teacher raises and that you raise should be questions that are open to dispute and for which there are not prepackaged answers. Readers within an academic setting expect that you will advance a scholarly conversation and not reproduce others' ideas. Therefore, it is important to find out who else has confronted these problems, conflicts, and questions in order to take a stand within some ongoing scholarly conversation. You will want to read with an eye toward the claims writers make, claims that they are making with respect to you, in the sense that writers want you to think and feel in a certain way. You will want to read others' work critically, seeing if the reasons writers use to support their arguments are what you would consider good reasons. And finally, you will want to consider the possible counterarguments to the claims writers make and the views that call your own ideas into question.

Like the verbal conversations you have with others, effective arguments never take place in a vacuum; they take into account previous conversations that have taken place about the subject under discussion. Seeing research as a means for advancing a conversation makes the research process more *real*, especially if you recognize that you will need to support your claims with evidence in order to persuade readers to agree with you. The concept and practice of research arises out of the specific social context of your readers' questions and skepticism.

Reading necessarily plays a prominent role in the many forms of writing that you do, but not simply as a process of gathering information. This is true whether you write personal essays, editorials, or original research based on library research. Instead, as James Crosswhite suggests in his book *The Rhetoric of Reason,* reading "means making judgments about which of the many voices one encounters can be brought together into productive conversation" (131).

5 When we sit down to write an argument intended to persuade someone to do or to believe something, we are never really the first to broach the topic about which we are writing. Thus, learning how to write a researched argument is a process of learning how to enter conversations that are already going on in written form. This idea of writing as dialogue—not only between author and reader but between the text and everything that has been said or written beforehand—is important. Writing is a process of balancing our goals with the history of similar kinds of communication, particularly others' arguments that have been made on the same subject. The conversations that have already been going on about a topic are the topic's historical context.

Perhaps the most eloquent statement of writing as conversation comes from Kenneth Burke (1941) in an oft-quoted passage:

> Imagine that you enter a parlor. You come late. When you arrive, others have long preceded you, and they are engaged in a heated discussion, a discussion too heated for them to pause and tell you exactly what it is about. In fact the discussion had already begun long before any of them got there, so that no one present is qualified to retrace for you all the steps that had gone before. You listen for a while, until you decide that you have caught the tenor of the argument; then you put in your oar. Someone answers; you answer him; another comes to your defense; another aligns himself against you, to either the embarrassment or gratification of your opponent, depending on the quality of your ally's assistance. However, the discussion is interminable. The hour grows late, you must depart, with the discussion still vigorously in progress. (110–111)

As this passage describes, every argument you make is connected to other arguments. Every time you write an argument, the way you position yourself will depend on three things: which previously stated arguments you share, which previously stated arguments you want to refute, and what new opinions and supporting information you are going to bring to the conversation. You may, for example, affirm others for raising important issues, but assert that they have not given those issues the thought or emphasis that they deserve. Or you may raise a related issue that has been ignored entirely.

Entering the Conversation

To develop an argument that is akin to a conversation, it is helpful to think of writing as a process of understanding conflicts, the claims others make, and the important questions to ask, not simply as the ability to tell a story that influences readers' ways of looking at the world or to find good reasons to support our own beliefs. The real work of writing a researched argument occurs when you try to figure out the answers to the following:

- What topics have people been talking about?
- What is a relevant problem?
- What kinds of evidence might persuade readers?
- What objections might readers have?
- What is at stake in this argument? (What if things change? What if things stay the same?)

10 In answering these questions, you will want to read with an eye toward identifying an *issue,* the *situation* that calls for some response in writing, and framing a *question.*

Identify an Issue

An issue is a fundamental tension that exists between two or more conflicting points of view. For example, imagine that I believe that the best approach to educational reform is to change the curriculum in schools. Another person might suggest that we need to address reform by considering social and economic concerns. One way to argue the point is for each writer to consider the goals of education that they share, how to best reach those goals, and the reasons why their approach might be the best one to follow. One part of the issue is (*a*) that some people believe that educational reform should occur through changes in the curriculum; the second part is (*b*) that some people believe that reform should occur at the socioeconomic level. Notice that in defining different parts of an issue, the conflicting claims may not necessarily invalidate each other. In fact, one could argue that reform at the levels of curriculum and socioeconomic change may both be effective measures.

Keep in mind that issues are dynamic and arguments are always evolving. One of my students felt that a book he was reading placed too much emphasis on school-based learning and not enough on real-world experience. He framed the issue in this way: "We are not just educated by concepts and facts that we learn in school. We are educated by the people around us and the environments that we live in every day." In writing his essay, he read a great deal in order to support his claims and did so in light of a position he was writing against: "that education in school is the most important type of education."

Identify the Situation

It is important to frame an issue in the context of some specific situation. Whether curricular changes make sense depends on how people view the problem. One kind of problem that E. D. Hirsch identified in his book *Cultural Literacy* is that students do not have sufficient knowledge of history and literature to communicate well. If that is true in a particular school, perhaps the curriculum might be changed. But there might be other factors involved that call for a different emphasis. Moreover, there are often many different ways to define an issue or frame a question. For example, we might observe that at a local high school, scores on standardized tests have steadily decreased during the past five years. This trend contrasts with scores during the ten years prior to any noticeable decline. Growing out of this situation is the broad question, "What factors have influenced the decline in standardized scores at this school?" Or one could ask this in a different way: "To what extent have scores declined as a result of the curriculum?"

The same principle applies to Anna Quindlen's argument about the homeless in her commentary "No Place Like Home," which illustrates the kinds of connections an author tries to make with readers. Writing her piece as an editorial in the *New York Times,* Quindlen addresses an issue that appears to plague New Yorkers. And yet many people have come to live with the presence of homelessness in New York and other cities. This is the situation that motivates Quindlen to write her editorial: People study the problem of homelessness, yet nothing gets done. Homelessness has become a way of life, a situation that seems to say to observers that officials have declared defeat when it comes to this problem.

Frame a Good Question

15 A good question can help you think through what you might be interested in writing; it is specific enough to guide inquiry and meets the following criteria:

- It can be answered with the tools you have.
- It conveys a clear idea of who you are answering the question for.
- It is organized around an issue.
- It explores "how," "why," or "whether," and the "extent to which."

A good question, then, is one that can be answered given the access we have to certain kinds of information. The tools we have at hand can be people or other texts. A good question also grows out of an issue, some fundamental tension that you identify within a conversation. Through identifying what is at issue, you should begin to understand for whom it is an issue—who you are answering the question for.

Framing as a Critical Strategy for Writing, Reading, and Doing Research

Thus far, I have presented a conversational model of argument, describing writing as a form of dialogue, with writers responding to the ways others have defined problems and anticipating possible counterarguments. In this section, I want to add another element that some people call framing. This is a strategy that can help you orchestrate different and conflicting voices in advancing your argument.

Framing is a metaphor for describing the lens, or perspective, from which writers present their arguments. Writers want us to see the world in one way as opposed to another, not unlike the way a photographer manipulates a camera lens to frame a picture. For example, if you were taking a picture of friends in front of the football stadium on campus, you would focus on what you would most like to remember, blurring the images of people in the background. How you set up the picture, or frame it, might entail using light and shade to make some images stand out more than others. Writers do the same with language (see also Chapter 4).

For instance, in writing about education in the United States, E. D. Hirsch uses the term *cultural literacy* as a way to understand a problem, in this case the decline of literacy. To say that there is a decline, Hirsch has to establish the criteria against which to measure whether some people are literate and some are not. Hirsch uses *cultural literacy* as a lens through which to discriminate between those who fulfill his criteria for literacy and those who do not. He defines *cultural literacy* as possessing certain kinds of information. Not all educators agree. Some oppose equating literacy and information, describing literacy as an *event* or as a *practice* to argue that literacy is not confined to acquiring bits of information; instead, the notion of literacy as an *event* or *practice* says something about how people use what they know to accomplish the work of a community. As you can see, any perspective or lens can limit readers' range of vision: readers will see some things and not others.

20 In my work as a writer, I have identified four reasons to use framing as a strategy for developing an argument. First, framing encourages you to name your position, distinguishing the way you think about the world from the ways others do. Naming also makes what you say memorable through key terms and theories. Readers may not remember every detail of Hirsch's argument, but they recall the principle—cultural literacy—around which he organizes his details. Second, framing forces you to offer both a definition and description of the principle around which your argument develops. For example, Hirsch defines *cultural literacy* as "the possession of basic information needed to thrive in the modern world." By defining your argument, you give readers something substantive to respond to. Third, framing specifies your argument, enabling others to respond to your argument and to generate counterarguments that you will want to engage in the spirit of conversation. Fourth, framing helps you organize your thoughts, and readers', in the same way that a title for an essay, a song, or a painting does.

To extend this argument, I would like you to think about framing as a strategy of critical inquiry when you read. By critical inquiry, I mean that reading entails understanding the framing strategies that writers use and using framing concepts in order to shed light on our own ideas or the ideas of others. Here I distinguish *reading as inquiry* from *reading as a search for information.* For example, you might consider your experiences as readers and writers through the lens of Hirsch's conception of cultural literacy. You might recognize that schooling for you was really about accumulating information and that such an approach to education served you well. It is also possible that it has not. Whatever you decide, you may begin to reflect upon your experiences in new ways in developing an argument about what the purpose of education might be.

Alternatively, you might think about your educational experiences through a very different conceptual frame in reading the following excerpt from Richard Rodriguez's memoir, *Hunger of Memory.* In this book, Rodriguez explains the conflicts he experienced as a nonnative speaker of English who desperately sought to enter mainstream culture, even if this meant sacrificing his identity as the son of Mexican immigrants. Notice how Rodriguez recalls his experience as a student through the framing concept of "scholarship boy" that he reads in Richard Hoggart's 1957 book, *The Uses of Literacy.* Using this notion of "scholarship boy" enables him to revisit his experience from a new perspective.

As you read this passage, consider what the notion of "scholarship boy" helps Rodriguez to understand about his life as a student. In turn, what does such a concept help you understand about your own experience as a student?

> For weeks I read, speed-read, books by modern educational theorists, only to find infrequent and slight mention of students like me .... Then one day, leafing through Richard Hoggart's *The Uses of Literacy,* I found, in his description of the scholarship boy, myself. For the first time I realized that there were other students like me, and so I was able to frame the meaning of my academic success, its consequent price—the loss.

Motivated to reflect upon his life as a student, Rodriguez comes across Richard Hoggart's book and a description of "the scholarship boy."

His initial response is to identify with Hoggart's description. Notice that Rodriguez says he used what he read to "frame the meaning of my academic success."

> 25 Hoggart's description is distinguished, at least initially, by deep understanding. What he grasps very well is that the scholarship boy must move between environments, his home and the classroom, which are at cultural extremes, opposed. With his family, the boy has the intense pleasure of intimacy, the family's consolation in feeling public alienation. Lavish emotions texture home life. *Then,* at school, the instruction bids him to trust lonely reason primarily. Immediate needs set the pace of his parents' lives. From his mother and father the boy learns to trust spontaneity and nonrational ways of knowing. *Then,* at school, there is mental calm. Teachers emphasize the value of a reflectiveness that opens a space between thinking and immediate action.

The scholarship boy moves between school and home, between moments of spontaneity and reflectiveness.

> Years of schooling must pass before the boy will be able to sketch the cultural differences in his day as abstractly as this. But he senses those differences early. Perhaps as early as the night he brings home an assignment from school and finds the house too noisy for study.
>
>> He has to be more and more alone, if he is going to 'get on.' He will have, probably unconsciously, to oppose the ethos of the hearth, the intense gregariousness of the working-class family group .... The boy has to cut himself off mentally, so as to do his homework, as well as he can. (47)

Rodriguez uses Hoggart's words and idea to advance his own understanding of the problem he identifies in his life: that he was unable to find solace at home and within his working-class roots.

In this excerpt, the idea of framing highlights the fact that other people's texts can serve as tools for helping you say more about your own ideas. If you were writing an essay using Hoggart's term *scholarship boy* as a lens through which to say something about education, you might ask how Hoggart's term illuminates new aspects of another writer's examples or your own—as opposed to asking, "How well does Hoggart's term *scholarship boy* apply to my experience?" (to which you could answer, "Not very well"). Further, you might ask, "To what extent does Hirsch's concept throw a more positive light on what Rodriguez and Haggart describe?" or "Do my experiences challenge, extend, or complicate such a term as *scholarship boy*?"

Now that you have a sense of how framing works, let's look at an excerpt from a researched argument a first-year composition student wrote, titled "Learning 'American' in Spanish." The full text of this essay can be found at the end of this essay. The assignment to which she responded asked her to do the following:

> 30 Draw on your life experiences in developing an argument about education and what it has meant to you in your life. In writing your essay, use two of the four authors (Freire, Hirsch, Ladson-Billings, Pratt) included in this unit to frame your argument or any of the reading you may have done on your own. What key terms, phrases, or ideas from these texts help you teach your readers what you want them to learn from your experiences? How do your experiences extend or complicate your critical frames?
>
> In the past, in responding to this assignment, some people have offered an overview of almost their entire lives, some have focused on a pivotal experience, and others have used descriptions of people who have influenced them. The important thing is that you use those experiences to argue a position: for example, that even the most well-meaning attempts to support students can actually hinder learning. This means going beyond narrating a simple list of experiences, or simply asserting an opinion. Instead you must use—and analyze your experiences, determining which will most effectively convince your audience that your argument has a solid basis.

As you read the excerpt from this student's essay, ask yourself how the writer uses two framing concepts—"transculturation" and "contact zone"—from Mary Louise Pratt's article "Arts of the Contact Zone." What do these ideas help the writer bring into focus? What experience do these frames help her to name, define, and describe?

Exactly one week after graduating from high school, with thirteen years of American education behind me, I boarded a plane and headed for a Caribbean island. I had fifteen days to spend on an island surrounded with crystal blue waters, white sandy shores, and luxurious ocean resorts. With beaches to play on by day and casinos to play in during the night, I was told that this country was an exciting new tourist destination. My days in the Dominican Republic, however, were not filled with snorkeling lessons and my nights were not spent at the blackjack table. Instead of visiting the ritzy East Coast, I traveled inland to a mountain community with no running water and no electricity. The bus ride to this town, called Guayabal, was long, hot, and uncomfortable. The mountain roads were not paved and the bus had no air-conditioning. Surprisingly, the four-hour ride flew by. I had plenty to think about as my mind raced with thoughts of the next two weeks. I wondered if my host family would be welcoming, if the teenagers would be friendly, and if my work would be hard. I mentally prepared myself for life without the everyday luxuries of a flushing toilet, a hot shower, and a comfortable bed. Because Guayabal was without such basic commodities, I did not expect to see many reminders of home. I thought I was going to leave behind my American ways and immerse myself into another culture. These thoughts filled my head as the bus climbed the rocky hill toward Guayabal. When I finally got off the bus and stepped into the town square, I realized that I had thought wrong: There was no escaping the influence of the American culture.

The writer has not yet named her framing concept; but notice that the concrete details she gathers here set readers up to expect that she will juxtapose the culture of Guayabal and the Dominican Republic with that of the United States.

In a way, Guayabal was an example of what author Mary Louise Pratt refers to as a contact zone. Pratt defines a contact zone as "a place where cultures meet, clash, and grapple with each other, often in contexts of highly asymmetrical relations of power" (76). In Guayabal, American culture and American consumerism were clashing with the Hispanic and Caribbean culture of the Dominican Republic. The clash came from the Dominicans' desire to be American in every sense, and especially to be consumers of American products. This is nearly impossible for Dominicans to achieve due

The writer names her experience as an example of Pratt's conception of a "contact zone." Further, the writer expands on Pratt's quote by relating it to her own observations. And finally, she uses this frame as a way to organize the narrative (as opposed to ordering her narrative chronologically).

to their extreme poverty. Their poverty provided the "asymmetrical relation of power" found in contact zones, because it impeded not only the Dominican's ability to be consumers, but also their ability to learn, to work, and to live healthily. The effects of their poverty could be seen in the eyes of the seven-year-old boy who couldn't concentrate in school because all he had to eat the day before was an underripe mango. It could be seen in the brown, leathered hands of the tired old man who was still picking coffee beans at age seventy.

35 The moment I got off the bus I noticed the clash between the American culture, the Dominican culture, and the community's poverty. It was apparent in the Dominicans' fragmented representation of American pop culture. Everywhere I looked in Guayabal I saw little glimpses of America. I saw Coca-Cola ads painted on raggedy fences. I saw knockoff Tommy Hilfiger shirts. I heard little boys say, "I wanna be like Mike" in their best English, while playing basketball. I listened to merengue house, the American version of the traditional Dominican merengue music. In each instance the Dominicans had adopted an aspect of American culture, but with an added Dominican twist. Pratt calls this transculturation. This term is used to "describe processes whereby members of subordinated or marginal groups select and invent from materials transmitted by a dominant or metropolitan culture" (80). She claims that transculturation is an identifying feature of contact zones. In the contact zone of Guayabal, the marginal group, made up of impoverished Dominicans, selected aspects of the dominant American culture, and invented a unique expression of a culture combining both Dominican and American styles. My most vivid memory of this transculturalization was on a hot afternoon when I heard some children yelling, "Helado! Helado!" or "Ice cream! Ice cream!" I looked outside just in time to see a man ride by on a bicycle, ringing a hand bell and balancing a cooler full of ice cream in the front bicycle basket. The Dominican children eagerly chased after him, just as American children chase after the ice-cream truck.

The writer provides concrete evidence to support her point.

The writer offers an illustration of what she experienced, clarifying how this experience is similar to what Pratt describes. Note that Pratt's verb clash, *used in the definition of* contact zone, *reappears here as part of the author's observation.*

The author adds another layer to her description, introducing Pratt's framing concept of "transculturation." Here again she quotes Pratt in order to bring into focus her own context here. The writer offers another example of transculturation.

Although you will notice that the writer does not challenge the framing terms she uses in this paper, it is clear that rather than simply reproducing Pratt's ideas and using her as the Voice of Authority, she incorporates Pratt's understandings to enable her to say more about her own experiences and ideas. Moreover, she uses this frame to advance an argument in order to affect her readers' views of culture. In turn, when she mentions others' ideas, she does so in the service of what she wants to say.

Conclusion: Writing Researched Arguments

I want to conclude this chapter by making a distinction between two different views of research. On the one hand, research is often taught as a process of collecting information for its own sake. On the other hand, research can also be conceived as the discovery and purposeful use of information. The emphasis here is upon *use* and the ways you can shape information in ways that enable you to enter conversations. To do so, you need to demonstrate to readers that you understand the conversation: what others have said in the past, what the context is, and what you anticipate is the direction this conversation might take. Keep in mind, however, that contexts are neither found nor located. Rather, context, derived from the Latin *contexere,* denotes a process of weaving together. Thus your attempt to understand context is an active process of making connections among the different and conflicting views people present within a conversation. Your version of the context will vary from others' interpretations.

Your attempts to understand a given conversation may prompt you to do research, as will your attempts to define what is at issue. Your reading and inquiry can help you construct a question that is rooted in some issue that is open to dispute. In turn, you need to ask yourself what is at stake for you and your reader other than the fact that you might be interested in educational reform, homelessness, affirmative action, or any other subject. Finally, your research can provide a means for framing an argument in order to move a conversation along and to say something new.

If you see inquiry as a means of entering conversations, then you will understand research as a social process. It need not be the tedious task of collecting information for its own sake. Rather, research has the potential to change readers' worldviews and your own.

Acknowledgment

I wish to thank Robert Kachur and April Lidinsky for helping me think through the notions of argument as conversation and framing.

Works Cited

Bartholomae, David, and Anthony Petrosky. 1996. *Ways of Reading: An Anthology for Writers.* New York: Bedford Books.

Brent, Doug. 1996. "Rogerian Rhetoric: Ethical Growth Through Alternative Forms of Argumentation." In *Argument Revisited; Argument Redefined: Negotiating Meaning in a Composition Classroom,* 73–96. Edited by Barbara Emmel, Paula Resch, and Deborah Tenney. Thousand Oaks, CA: Sage Publications.

Burke, Kenneth. 1941. *The Philosophy of Literary Form.* Berkeley: University of California Press.

Crosswhite, James. 1996. *The Rhetoric of Reason: Writing and the Attractions of Argument.* Madison, WI: University of Wisconsin Press.

Freire, Paulo. 1970. *Pedagogy of the Oppressed.* New York: Continuum.

Hirsch, E. D. 1987. *Cultural Literacy.* New York: Vintage Books.

Ladson-Billings, Gloria. 1994. *The Dreamkeepers: Successful Teachers of African American Children.* New York: Teachers College Press.

Quindlen, Anna. 1993. "No Place Like Home." In *Thinking Out Loud: On the Personal, the Public, and the Private,* 42–44. New York: Random House.

Rodriguez, Richard. 1983. Hunger of Memory: *The Education of Richard Rodriguez.* New York: Bantam Books.

Credit

Trans Representation*

JACK HALBERSTAM

Transgender is a shape.

—Jeanne Vacarro, "Feelings and Fractals" (2015)

A few years ago I attended a queer, transnational performance studies conference where a play was staged about a queer historical figure. This figure greatly resembled the gender-ambiguous Juana Aguilar, researched by María Elena Martínez, whom I discussed earlier. And indeed, the play, staged by Mexican performance artist Jesusa Rodríguez, was based on Martínez's research. Rather than receiving the play as an interesting piece of period theater, audience members became irate and angered by the depiction, especially since some parts of the life of the hermaphroditic character were played for comedic effect. The conference turned, overnight, from a wildly imaginative series of performances, talks, and theatre productions into a somber event filled with roundtables, short tables, long tables, and turned tables on what had gone wrong with this representation of a "transgender" figure. The dramaturg was accused of transphobia, historical reference points were thrown to the wind, and many tears were shed. I later wrote a blog in response to what I had seen, and I linked the event and the hard feelings it produced to calls for trigger warnings and protests that targeted queer cultural producers rather than homophobes and transphobes. My essay was received enthusiastically at first, but it quickly became obvious that my piece was the journalistic equivalent of waving a red flag at a rampaging bull. People accused me of all manner of perfidy, and one wit dubbed me the "sports dad of queer theory" for my grumpy attitude toward "the kids today."

Since then there have been other, similar, transgender protests of queer representation. I end this chapter with one such example, in an attempt to see what we can make of these battles over the project of representing trans* bodies. My goal is not at all to chastise young people or tut-tut about how young people have lost the plot on political engagement. After all, I am not a particularly skilled or dynamic activist myself. Rather, my goal has long been to try to understand the visual protocols for representing the trans* body, trans* experience, and trans* identity, be it in texts that are positive or negative, abstract or realistic. It is generally a good idea not to approach the visual materials documenting trans* life with a moral framework that leads only to adjudication; instead, we are better served by considering the formal methods by which trans* experience can be represented and the benefits and liabilities therein.

In my 2005 book *In a Queer Time and Place: Transgender Bodies, Subcultural Lives* I argued that the regular temporal frameworks that organize life expectations in Euro-American contexts were themselves part and parcel of a normalizing system that orients diverse communities with heterogeneous desires toward a remarkably narrow swath of life narratives. Those orderly and predictable life narratives become the stuff of all kinds of governmental logics of rule and make possible everything from inheritance claims to insurance algorithms. If we situate queerness as a contrary temporal logic, we begin to see how and where and why certain bodies are perceived as threatening, destabilizing, and aberrant. Reading queerness as an altered relation to time and place also takes us out of the ambit of stable social identities and provides a non-identitarian language for social, sexual and political eccentricity. In this chapter I ask about the visual language that captures queerness, transitivity and trans* identities across variables understandings of time and space.

Since I wrote *In a Queer Time and Place,* many other books have emerged on queer temporality. Elizabeth Freeman's widely read *Time Binds: Queer Temporalities, Queer Histories,* for example, theorizes a queer history that can be found in "nonsequential time," an erotic temporality that inheres to discontinuity, a "body's microtemporalities," and the libidinal pull of the anachronistic.[1] Similarly, Lee Edelman has used the notion of queer time to make visible the mostly hidden logics of political structures that draw us into hackneyed and normative formulations of self and politics by situating the future itself as a function of reproductive normativity.[2] In a critique of Edelman's rallying cry of "no future," the late José Esteban Muñoz, in *Cruising Utopia,* conjured the (im)possibility of "Brown futures," offering instead a queer phenomenological vision of utopian horizons that allow for the possibility that "we are not yet queer" and that queerness is very much still to come.[3] More recently, this conjuring of a queer future has preoccupied Black queer scholars such as Kara Keeling and Tavia Nyong'o, who have reminded us of the difference that race makes to the ways in which we imagine futurity, the archaic, the child, spoiled pasts, intransigent presents, and so on.[4]

5 As part of the first wave of books on queer temporality, mine laid out the implications of a model of queerness that is not simply about what kinds of bodies have sex with what kinds of bodies, but about different life narratives, alternative ways of being in relation to others, and new practices of occupying space. For example, I proposed that we might privilege friendship networks over extended families when assessing the structures of intimacy that sustain queer

lives, and we might also think about transgenderism in particular as not simply a contrapuntal relationship between bodily form and content but as an altered relation to seeing and being seen. Transgenderism, in other words, has never been simply a new identity among many others competing for space under the rainbow umbrella. Rather, it constitutes radically new knowledge about the experience of being in a body and can be the basis for very different ways of seeing the world.

This is, at least in part, one of the arguments Kara Keeling makes in her work on race and transgender visuality. In an essay titled "Looking for M—: Queer Temporality, Black Political Possibility, and Poetry from the Future," Keeling fuses a theory of anticolonial temporality gleaned from Fanon with an understanding of the experience of cinematic affect taken from Deleuze to situate Black trans* futurity as something that exceeds the knowledge of conventional documentary film. Keeling develops this argument in "Looking for M—" to propose the appearance in Black film of an "impossible possibility," or worlds and modes of being that escape "recognition, meaning, and valuation." In Daniel Peddle's film *The Aggressives* (2005), a Black trans* character named M disappears and the filmmaker is unable to track hir down. For Keeling, *The Aggressives* provided a template for the dis-appearance of gender-queer Black bodies. M's disappearance within the arc of the film is not simply unfortunate or even tragic, it is rather a "political act" that resists the narrative closure which the film tries to impose on unruly lives and, just as importantly, refuses the classifications of LGBT by turning to the subcultural designation of "*aggressives*," a term that does not neatly match up with L, G, B, or T. Keeling's theoretically innovative reading disrupts the easy narratives of gender-variant lives that would place very different life narratives alongside each other under the headings of queer or trans and across time and space.

If, as Keeling's work has shown, bodies often exceed the apparatuses (medical, cinematic, narrative, or social) available to represent them, what methods *should* we use to track the disorderly histories of trans*? We also need to remember Sandy Stone's important intervention in her "Posttranssexual Manifesto" from over twenty years ago. Stone argued against the standard narratives of transsexual identity that had been advanced by doctors, psychiatrists, feminists, and anthropologists, insisting instead on the importance of transsexuals self-representing and refusing to be the object of knowledge. Commenting on some popular accounts of transsexual life written by nontranssexuals—notably Gary Kates's work on Chevalier d'Éon and Anne Bolin's early ethnographies of "traversing gender"—Stone writes: "Both Kates' and Bolin's studies are in most respects excellent work, and were published in the same collection as an earlier version of this essay; but still there are no subjects in these discourses, only homogenized, totalized objects—fractally replicating earlier histories of minority discourses in the large. So when I speak the forgotten word, it will perhaps wake memories of other debates. The word is *some.*"[5] The fragmentation, segmentation, multiplicity of the category trans* can only emerge within an optic that recognizes trans* as a capacious and fluid category rather than a diagnosis.

Seeing trans* bodies differently, then—not simply as trans bodies that provide an image of the nonnormative against which normative bodies can be discerned, but as bodies that are fragmentary and internally contradictory, bodies that remap gender and its relations to race, place, class, and sexuality, bodies that are in pain or that represent a play of surfaces, bodies that sound different than they look, bodies that represent palimpsestic relations to identity—means finding different visual, aural, and haptic codes through which to figure the experience of being in a body. After all, the trans* body is not so easy to represent, and the visual frame that captures such bodies either has to reveal sites of contradiction on the gender-variant body (through nakedness perhaps, which risks sensationalizing such bodies) or through other kinds of exposure, violent, intrusive, or otherwise.

Jeanne Vacarro has offered the experience of touch as an alternative method for reading trans* bodies; she describes, under the heading "Handmade," a logic of knowing that departs totally from the diagnostic forms of classification that have mediated trans* people's ability to say who they are. Vacarro writes: "If we are to dislodge transgender from the event of its medicalization and meditate, alternatively, on the handmade dimensionality of experience, what might transgender come to mean? … The handmade is a haptic, affective theorization of the transgender body, a mode of animating material experience and accumulative felt matter. As bodily feeling and sensation transform flesh parallel to diagnostic and administrative forces, a handmade orientation foregrounds the work of crafting identity."[6] This is a gorgeous understanding of embodiment through the worldmaking activities of craft and crafting, and it opens out onto visual methodologies deployed by various artists for representing without fetishizing bodies that might either seamlessly pass or seem lodged between the systems of representation that promise to deliver orderly arrangements of binary gender to viewing audiences whose sense of visual pleasure depends on such tidy systems. The haptic offers one path around the conundrum of a binary visual plane (what is not male appears to be female, what is not female appears to be male).

10 Indeed, the haptic offers a great aesthetic frame for trans* representation in general. As explained by theorist Laura Marks in her book *Touch,* the haptic is a sensory mode of perception that engages a model of knowing and perception that is not oriented toward mastery, not deployed simply at the level of the visual. The haptic both names the way the mind grasps for meanings that elude it while still holding on to the partial knowledge available. It violates the opposition between subject and object and demands that the viewer/namer/authority feel implicated in the act of looking, naming, and judging. For Marks, the haptic is "a visual erotics that offers its object to the viewer but only on condition that its unknowability remain intact, and that the viewer, in coming closer, give up his or her own mastery."[7] As this quote indicates, hapticality organizes meaning, knowing, and seeing in ways that exceed rational, sense-making enterprises and instead force the viewer to examine their own relations to truth and authenticity. This is a perfect frame for the trans* body, which, in the end, does not seek to be seen and known but rather wishes to throw the organization of all bodies into doubt.

A great example of haptic work on trans* bodies that points to new forms of embodiment without seeking to know or master them can be found in the outlandish sculptures, goofy drawings, and loopy films by trans* artist Harry Dodge.[8] His work partakes wholeheartedly and joyfully in the haptic while performing a practice given over to humor, hybridity, and exploration of the unnameable. He identifies the unnamable in an interview as "anti-authoritarian leakage, overflow, and profusion."[9] His sculptures, made from discarded materials, trash, and found objects and materials, capture beautifully this other language for embodiment—a play of surfaces, a humorous engagement with being, a flirtation with becoming, a reckoning with the "dynamic indeterminacy" that trans* bodies point to and inhabit, narrate, and even historicize. In some of Dodge's work, cheery objects point and wave to one another, and in drawings Dodge creates cartoonlike scenes within which hybrid but allegorical bodies speak in poetic ways to each other. In the pencil drawing "Lobster Boy (regarding articulation)," for example, a boyish figure holds up his gigantic claw of a hand and thinks: "The spirit of if I had each of my separate fingers lives in my heart." Meanwhile, another figure, perhaps a rock, counters: "There's not a name for everything." This drawing is fantastical, imaginative, and hilarious. It opposes the desire to grasp meaning with the impossibility of naming, situating unknowability in many forms of able and disabled embodiment, not just the gender variable. The haptic, which describes a mode of sensing through touch, lives in the massive claw hands, in their pointing mechanisms, and in the rock's pronouncement about unnameability. In visual artist Micha Cárdenas's performances, too, the haptic frames the trans* body, in the form of wearable electronics, immersive virtual environments, and various forms of hacktivism and new media productive of what she calls "transrealities."[10]

Scholars like Jeanne Vacarro have offered the language of the haptic as an alternative to the medical, the legal, and the mediatized will to know and as a remapping of the gendered body, not around having or lacking the phallus but around manipulating and knowing via the hand, the finger, the arm, the body in bits and pieces. The haptic body and the haptic self are not known in advance but improvised over and over on behalf of a willful and freeing sense of bewilderment.

Taking the haptic as well as the sense of queer temporality and the unnameable and unknowable experience of embodiment as our foundation, let's examine how trans* bodies have been represented over the past two decades—what kinds of contestations have emerged about these representations—and then think through some indefinite, nonspecific, and open-ended approaches to trans* representation.

In the late 1990s and early 2000s, some films were in circulation that took the transgender body as their topic or that deployed the transgender body as a metaphor for other unstable forms of identity. But most films featuring trans* identities still cast transgenderism as a kind of aberration, as something in need of explanation, or as a symbol for illegible social identities. That said, in the 1990s mainstream cinema parted ways with the tendency to represent transgender people as mad, bad, and dangerous. Films like Brian De Palma's *Dressed to Kill* from 1980, not to mention Alfred Hitchcock's *Psycho* from 1960, had made the connection between gender variance and serial murder seem obvious and inevitable. But that changed when three different films shifted the protocols for conventional cinematic representations of transgender lives.

15 *The Crying Game,* directed by Neil Jordan (1992). In some films, but most notably in Neil Jordan's *The Crying Game,* the transgender body came to serve as a metaphor for other sites of instability and for the fraught and contradictory sets of political commitments that accumulate around and through race, nation, and class. In this film, the trans* character Dil Oaye Davidson) provides an occasion for an extended discourse on appearance and reality, the Irish Republican Army (IRA) versus English nationalism, and racist and transphobic

fetishism. For all its fetishistic looking at the Black trans* body, however, the film did manage to situate transgenderism within a larger political and social context and as part of an ongoing revolutionary project. The story involves a Black English soldier, Jody (Forest Whitaker), kidnapped by IRA members Fergus (Stephen Rea) and Jude (Miranda Richardson), who dies while trying to escape, but not before he forms a bond with Fergus and asks him to visit his girlfriend, Dil, in London. Fergus follows through on his promise, and the subsequent encounter leads to romance and the revelation of her transgenderism.

Despite Fergus's revulsion when he confronts Dil's "incomplete" transition—namely, her penis—the film allows a learning curve for the main characters. Fergus and Dil learn what Jody had already known, namely that all forms of nationalism require fictions of the natural, the communal, and the unified, when in fact the only thing holding people together is fear and violence. In this configuration, each character finds themself both inside and outside of national belonging, and Dil's mismatched body becomes a symbol for the patchwork of social contradictions that nationalisms attempt to smooth over. The film also highlighted erotic tensions between the transgender woman and the cis-gender man, and while Fergus's first reaction to Dil's embodiment was revulsion, the film tracks an unorthodox trajectory for his desire, within which neither Dil's gender nor Fergus's sexual orientation is definitively fixed.

Boys Don't Cry, directed By Kim Peirce (1999). *Boys Don't Cry* by Kim Peirce is the breakthrough film for thinking about the trans* body as simultaneously viable and vulnerable, sexy and powerful. This film about the real-life murder of a trans*masculine youth, Brandon Teena, was sensitive to the ambiguity of Brandon Teena's embodiment and expansive on his desires and gender practices.

In my earlier readings of the film, I accounted for a "transgender gaze" within which time, space, desire, and embodied identification all splinter, representing a collapse of the matrices of gender and sexuality.[11] While certain shots through a car's windshield give viewers a sense of the beauty and desolation of the Nebraska landscape, jump cuts collapse time and space, fantasy and reality, reminding us that the trans* body not only asks that we slow down the lightning-fast calculations by which we assign genders to bodies, but also stalls systems of signification that attach masculinity to maleness, femininity to femaleness, leaving nothing in between. In *Boys Don't Cry,* the murder of Brandon Teena, whose gender has been recognized by the young woman he loves but not by her family and friends, represents the shattered and uneven nature of the reception of trans* visuality. The film eloquently conjures the shared vision of the trans* person and their lover, even as it confronts the violence that seeks to destroy that vision.

In my original reading of the film, I noted how we move with this film from looking or staring at the transgender body to seeing the world through hir eyes. This is captured most effectively in a brutal sequence where Brandon is exposed by local men and where he momentarily leaves his body, allowing him to see himself being displayed. I then explored the cinematic techniques that allow viewers to participate in a "transgender gaze" or "glance." Experimental interludes in this film give us access, as viewers, not only to the experience of transgenderism—as a split, a contradiction (pleasurable or otherwise), a friction—but also to the experience of those who desire transgender people. The film made Brandon Teena into a cultural hero, a martyr, and a victim. Later I will recount what happened when a group of activists at a U.S. college, fifteen years after its release, understood *Boys Don't Cry* as a transphobic film organized around the dismantling of a young transsexual man's body.

20 *By Hook Or By Crook,* directed by Harry Dodge and Silas Howard (2001). Finally, there is Dodge/Howard's brilliant independent film *By Hook or by Crook,* which focuses on trans* friendship, shared masculinities, the quest narrative, and road movie as a metaphor for transition and the nature of love in trans* contexts. This film was pioneering in terms of its ability to create a truly alternative vision while making no concessions to a straight viewer. *By Hook or by Crook* is the story of a friendship between two trans* masculine subjects. The transgender figures are just "he," with no explanation for their eccentric gendering given. Instead, the film highlights intimate bonds, sex, and love as the real themes of the film, showing the buddies on a quest that has no stable outcome; it is a road movie without an obvious destination. The quest functions instead as a metaphor for "continuous transition"—one of the features of trans* identity that makes it different from transsexualism. Here, the trans* character of Valentine in particular (played by Dodge) becomes a quixotic figure tilting not only at conventional gender norms but also at normative notions of family, sex, love, and belonging.

Looking at these films, one must remember and try to recreate the context in which they originally appeared. In the late 1990s and early 2000s transgenderism, and particularly transsexualism, was very much a focus of talk shows and media fascination. The media dealt with transsexuality as an exotic phenomenon for which the public was not ready. The mainstream media represented transgender people as "dysphoric," dishonest, disoriented, or worse, and this sense of disorientation, rather than being folded into a general postmodern condition, was cast as uninhabitable and pathologically unstable. Transgender bodies, indeed, represented a condition of radical instability against which other gendered identities appeared legible, knowable, and natural.

So far, I have argued that the representation of transgenderism depends on a repudiation of the veracity of the visual (passing), an embrace of the haptic (unknowing), and a narrative framework of continual transition (becoming). In earlier texts filmmakers and artists have used a number of techniques to visualize the trans* body without reducing it to the binary template of male or female, and so we have witnessed the representation of the self as split (*Boys Don't Cry*), the representation of the body as inherently unstable and contradictory (*The Crying Game*), and the representation of the body as an absurd site that eludes linguistic and visual codes (*By Hook or by Crook* as well as Dodge's artwork). As a result of these pioneering efforts, contemporary filmmakers and television producers are neither trying to garner recognition of the trans* body nor claiming it as exceptional. Influenced by the work of Jin Haritawarn, Riley Snorton, and Jasbir Puar on transnormalization, by Mel Chen on the materiality of grammar, and by Nikki Sullivan and others on the meaning of somatechnics, contemporary visual artists astutely rethink the intersections between technology, embodiment, identity, and biopolitical mechanisms of control.[12] In this way, in contemporary art and culture we can begin to rethink gender histories, the role of technology in reimagining the body and the interactions between bodies and landscapes/spaces, and dynamics of race, class, and ability.

In the contemporary landscape of representation, television has become more dominant than cinema; with its episodic structure and evolving plot lines, TV series allow for much more information and contradiction to enter into the representation of complex lives. An excellent example for our purposes is *Transparent* (2014–present), created and directed by Jill Soloway. In its first season, *Rolling Stone* credited it with "making the world safer for trans people"; *Out* dubbed it the first show to handle properly not only transgenderism but also bisexuality; and the *Advocate* called *Transparent,* simply, "great television."[13] Telling the story of a dysfunctional Jewish family in Los Angeles that falls apart and regroups around the patriarch's revelation of her transition from male to female, *Transparent* covers new ground for television. The refusal to trade only in positive images of trans people, never mind Jews, lesbians, female rabbis, and butch security guards, makes it unique in the media history of queer representation. Though less avant-garde than Dodge/Howard's work,

Transparent nonetheless builds upon the carefully crafted trans* regimes of representation that came before it. (Indeed, Silas Howard is a regular director of episodes of *Transparent.*) The series showcases some new techniques of representation in relation to the transgender body. And as in Sara Davidmann's text *Ken. To Be Destroyed* (examined in chapter 4), the narrative of the trans* body appears both in relation to contemporary Jewish life and under the sign of potential destruction.

The challenge for *Transparent* lies in its ability to represent a specific trans experience ("someness," in Sandy Stone's terms) without making it representative of *all* trans experience. The show manages to convey, with some subtlety, the relief of coming out, the stress of feeling exposed, the sadness of being late to the table. With a writing team that includes queer writer Ali Liebegott and consultants who include artists Zachary Drucker and Rhys Ernst, *Transparent* made the wise decision to work with trans people's *own* narratives rather than to cleave faithfully to Jill Soloway's autobiographical story. Soloway's experience with her father's transition still forms the spine of the piece, but it is rounded out with a clutch of other stories about aging, sexual experimentation, addiction, sibling tension, and so on. Aspects of this episodic TV series stand out from previous trans representations: it is not committed to repairing the negative facets of representations of transgenderism, for example, but it also refuses to situate the trans* body as a lonely and singular entity. Rather, the trans* characters (some of whom appear in the present, some in a Jewish past in prewar Berlin) all appear in relation to and firmly within real-world events. The appearance of trans* characters throughout the series also offers critiques of the family and of all idealized notions of community.

25 *Transparent* continuously flirts with the archive of negative representations of trans* life and identities. Thus, part of the framing of Maura, the trans*parent, is as a wealthy person who has been cloistered in privilege and whose trans* identity means something very different from those of the trans* women she meets out in the "community." In season three, for example, Maura staffs an LGBT crisis hotline, and after taking a call from a troubled queer trans" person of color, Elizah, she goes off on a wild goose chase to find and potentia!ly "save" this woman. The script pillories this rescue mission, however, and it is Maura who ends up in the hospital, not the object of her ministrations.

Transparent beautifully shows how the bourgeois family expands to embrace its own, even when its "own" is an aging patriarch turned transwoman, and it gives audiences a warts-and-all view into trans* life. Indeed, perhaps because *Transparent* is a TV series, it has to produce and invest not only in characters who are basically good people, trying hard and forging new ground, but also in those who screw up, hurt each other, and take two steps back for every one step forward. The range of characters is far-ranging and complex, as in real life.

Some transgender audiences of *Transparent* have complained that neither Jill Soloway nor the actor playing Maura, Jeffrey Tambor, is transgender. Tambor himself, in accepting his second Emmy Award for the role, urged producers and directors to "give transgender talent a chance." Not only that, but "give them auditions. Give them their story. Do that. And also, one more thing, I would not be unhappy were I the last cisgender male playing a female transgender on television. We have work to do."[14]

We have work to do. In this extraordinarily self-aware speech, Tambor made excellent use of his position as perhaps one of the most beloved transgender characters in the history of visual representation. But transgender activists, never mind transgender actors, remain irritated, to say the least, by the long history of casting nontransgender actors in transgender roles. *Transamerica* starred Felicity Huffman as a preoperative transsexual woman; *The Dallas Buyers Club* starred Jared Leto as a trans woman with AIDS; and of course, *Boys Don't Cry* starred Hilary Swank as Brandon Teena, the young trans* masculine youth who was killed for passing as male.

In recent years, transgender audiences have become more and more incensed by the casting of nontransgender actors, and a number of skirmishes have broken out over this practice. These skirmishes are symptomatic of a deeply felt sense of the injustice of having ones life depicted by people who have benefited from the binary of normative and nonnormative genders. But these protests also misrecognize the longer arc of trans* representation, a trajectory I have tried to sketch here, and there is a tendency to try to adjudicate the injustice in relation not to new films and TV shows but to films like *Boys Don't Cry,* retroactively critiquing and calling for a reckoning with the way that visual culture has framed transgender life. While I am sympathetic to such attempts to address a history of unfair and often toxic representations, I also want to consider the many ways we can refuse, resist and recast these visual mechanisms in the present. I therefore close this chapter with an account of an event that unites both some of the tensions expressed in chapter 4 about trans* generational conflict and new tensions over the representation of trans* lives in an age of social media.

30 The film *Boys Don't Cry* was made in 1999. It took years to research, fund, cast, and shoot; was released to superb reviews; and went on to garner awards and praise for the lead actor, Hilary Swank, and the young director, Kim Peirce, not to mention the film's production team led by Christine Vachon. The film was hard hitting, visually innovative, and marked a massive breakthrough in the representation of gender-variant bodies. While there were certainly debates about decisions that Peirce made within the film's narrative arc (the omission of the murder of an African American friend, Philip DeVine, at the same time that Brandon was killed), *Boys Don't Cry* was received at the time as a magnificent film honoring the life of a gender-queer youth and conveying cinematically a sense of the jeopardy of gendervariant experiences. It was also seen as a sensitive depiction of life in small-town U.S.A. Kim Peirce went on to speak widely about the film in public venues, explaining her relationship to the subject matter of gender variance, working-class life, and gender-based violence.

In a screening of the film in 2016, with Peirce as a speaker, younger audiences took offense at the film and accused the filmmaker of making money off the representation of violence against trans people. This happened when Peirce showed up to speak at a special screening of the film at Reed College in Oregon, just days after the presidential election in November 2016. Unbeknownst to the organizers of the screening, student protesters had removed posters from around campus that advertised the film and lecture, and they arrived early to the cinema on the night of the screening to hang new posters. These posters voiced a range of reactions to the film, including "You don't fucking get it!" and "Fuck Your Transphobia!" as well as "Trans Lives Do Not Equal $$." To cap it all off, the sign hung on the podium read: "Fuck this cis white bitch"!! The protesters waited until after the film had screened (at Peirce's request), then entered the auditorium shouting, "Fuck your respectability politics," and yelling over her commentary. Peirce finally left the room. After establishing some ground rules for a discussion, Peirce returned, but the conversation again got out of hand, and finally a student yelled at Peirce: "Fuck you, scared bitch." At which point the protesters filed out and Peirce left campus.

This is an astonishing set of events to reckon with for those of us who remember the events surrounding Brandon Teena's murder, the debates in the months that followed over Brandon Teena's identity, and, later, the reception of the film itself. The murder of Brandon Teena spurred early transgender activists into action, and many showed up at the trial of his killers. Despite much discussion at the time about whether Brandon was "butch" or "transgender," queer and transgender audiences were mostly satisfied with the depiction of Brandon Teena in *Boys Don't Cry.* The film appealed to many audiences, queer and straight, and it continues to play around the world.

The accounts of this protest give evidence of enormous vitriol, much of it blatantly misogynist (the repeated use of the word "bitch," for example), directed at a queer, butch filmmaker, and they leave us with an enormous number of questions about representational dynamics, clashes between different historical paradigms of queer and transgender life, and the expression of queer anger that, instead of being directed at murderous enemies in the mainstream of American political life, has been turned onto independent filmmakers within the queer and LGBT communities. After this incident at Reed, I heard from other students that they, too, felt "uncomfortable" with the representations of transgender life and death in *Boys Don't Cry.*

How might we respond to these objections in ways that do not dismiss the feelings of the students but that ask for different relations to protest, to the reading of complex texts, and to how anger about transphobic and homophobic texts might be directed? Here are a few thoughts.

35 *We need to situate this film properly within the history of the representation of transgender characters.* At the time that Peirce made *Boys Don't Cry,* most films featured transgender people only as monsters, killers, sociopaths, or isolated misfits (e.g., *Psycho* [Hitchcock, 1960]; *Dressed To Kill* [de Palma, 1980]; *The Silence of The Lambs* [Demme, 1991]). Few treated transgender people with even a modicum of comprehension, and even fewer dealt with the transphobic environments that were part of heteronormative family life. Very few films prior to *Boys* focused on transgender masculinity at all, and when transgender male characters did appear in film, they were often depicted as women who passed as men for pragmatic reasons (e.g., *The Ballad of Little Jo,* 1993) or as androgynous figures of whimsy (e.g., *Orlando,* 1992). *Boys Don't Cry* is the first film in history to build a credible story line around the credible masculinity of a credible trans-masculine figure. Period.

We cannot always demand a perfect match between directors, actors, and the material in any given narrative. As a masculine person from a working-class background who had experienced sexual abuse, Peirce identified strongly with the life and struggles of Brandon Teena. Peirce, though not a transgender man, is gender variant. The film she produced was sensitive to Brandon Teena's social environment, his gender identity, his hard upbringing, and his struggle to understand himself and to be understood by others. If Peirce told a story in which the transgender body was punished, she did so not in order to participate in that punishment but because it would have been dishonest to tell the story any other way. The violence he suffered stood, at the time, as emblematic of the many forms of violence that transgender people suffered, and it called on the audiences of the film to rebuke the world in which such violence was commonplace.

Transgender actors should play transgender roles, but that is not always possible and certainly was a long shot at the time Peirce made her film. Peirce conducted a national search for a trans-masculine actor for *Boys Don't Cry*. She did screen tests with many trans-identified people, and she ultimately gave the role to the best actor available who was credible as a young female-bodied person passing for male. That actor was Hilary Swank, best known at the time for her role in *The Next Karate Kid* and occasional appearances on *Buffy the Vampire Slayer*. It was vital to have a strong performer in the role of Brandon Teena, and Swank was cast accordingly. Also, why should a transgender actor only play transgender roles—shouldn't we be asking cis-gendered directors to cast transgender men and women as romantic leads, dramatic protagonists, superheroes, and so forth?

We should not be asking for films to make detours around scenes of sexual violence; instead, we should be asking what we actually mean by violence in any given context. In *Boys Don't Cry*, the rape scene was brutal, hard to shoot, hard to act in, and overall a difficult, emotionally draining piece of filmmaking. But it is also a crucial part of the film, a way of representing faithfully the brutal violence that at the time was meted out regularly to gender-nonconforming bodies, and it was true to the specific fate of Brandon Teena. The brutality of the rape also cuts in and out of scenes in the police station as Brandon Teena reports the rape. The police treat Brandon as a "girl" who must have been "pleased" by the attention of the young men, whom they consider normal, sexual subjects. Thus, the rape scene damns the police, highlights the role of violence in the enforcement of normativity, and draws the audience's sympathies to Brandon in a way that makes transphobia morally reprehensible.

When we target scenes of rape and sexual violence in independent films about historical characters and call them unwatchable, we are making it difficult to grapple with all kinds of historical material that involves systemic violence and oppression. But we are also limiting the meaning of "violence" to physical assault. As so many theorists have shown, violence can also appear in the form of civility, empathy, absence, indifference, and non-appearance.[15] Violence is the glue of contemporary representation: we regularly watch films in which cars are blown up (every film with a chase scene); planes are shot down (many films featuring Tom Cruise or James Bond); superheroes sweep the streets of evil, taking out hundreds of people at a time (*Iron Man* but also *Ghostbusters*);

tidal waves destroy entire cities (*Deep Impact*); complete colonies of fish are swallowed up by marauding sharks (*Finding Nemo*); aliens land and eliminate buildings (*The War of the Worlds*); zombie mobs chase humans and slowly eat them (*The Walking Dead*)—and so forth and so on. To focus solely on sexual violence and ignore the more general context of cinematic violence, never mind taking complaints only to queer directors who are struggling to represent queer life rather than to straight directors ignoring queer and trans* life, betrays a limited vision of representational systems and ideologies and ultimately leaves those systems and their biases completely intact.

40 The incident at Reed College offers an example of how hard it can be to share activist goals across different generations of people who experience their marginalized identities very differently and who may or may not be able to access and identify with the experiences of those who came before or after them. I offer the account of this screening and what followed not to mark it as outrageous or extraordinary but to highlight how central film and video were to struggles around visibility and viability in the 1990s and how more recently visual representation in the cinema has given way to the multi-platforms of social media. The material that, in the late years of the twentieth century, gave queer and trans* people hope for easier days ahead today fuels anger and revulsion on the part of younger trans* people and leads them to protest the very filmmakers who helped to create the privileges they currently enjoy. We can expect more such skirmishes in the future, given the rifts between generations of activists, but maybe the hinge of the * as it attaches to trans can be used to open up dialogue, difficult though it may be, rather than slam the door on further conversation.

Understanding Patriarchy

BELL HOOKS

Patriarchy is the single most life-threatening social disease assaulting the male body and spirit in our nation. Yet most men do not use the word "patriarchy" in everyday life. Most men never think about patriarchy—what it means, how it is created and sustained. Many men in our nation would not be able to spell the word or pronounce it correctly. The word "patriarchy" just is not a part of their normal everyday thought or speech. Men who have heard and know the word usually associate it with women's liberation, with feminism, and therefore dismiss it as irrelevant to their own experiences. I have been standing at podiums talking about patriarchy for more than thirty years. It is a word I use daily, and men who hear me use it often ask me what I mean by it.

Nothing discounts the old antifeminist projection of men as all-powerful more than their basic ignorance of a major facet of the political system that shapes and informs male identity and sense of self from birth until death. I often use the phrase "imperialist white-supremacist capitalist patriarchy" to describe the interlocking political systems that are the foundation of our nation's politics. Of these systems the one that we all learn the most about growing up is the system of patriarchy, even if we never know the word, because patriarchal gender roles are assigned to us as children and we are given continual guidance about the ways we can best fulfill these roles.

Patriarchy is a political-social system that insists that males are inherently dominating, superior to everything and everyone deemed weak, especially females, and endowed with the right to dominate and rule over the weak and to maintain that dominance through various forms of psychological terrorism and violence. When my older brother and I were born with a year separating us in age, patriarchy determined how we would each be regarded by our parents. Both our parents believed in patriarchy; they had been taught patriarchal thinking through religion.

At church they had learned that God created man to rule the world and everything in it and that it was the work of women to help men perform these tasks, to obey, and to always assume a subordinate role in relation to a powerful man. They were taught that God was male. These teachings were reinforced in every institution they encountered—schools, courthouses, clubs, sports arenas, as well as churches. Embracing patriarchal thinking, like everyone else around them, they taught it to their children because it seemed like a "natural" way to organize life.

5 As their daughter I was taught that it was my role to serve, to be weak, to be free from the burden of thinking, to caretake and nurture others. My brother was taught that it was his role to be served; to provide; to be strong; to think, strategize, and plan; and to refuse to caretake or nurture others. I was taught that it was not proper for a female to be violent, that it was "unnatural." My brother was taught that his value would be determined by his will to do violence (albeit in appropriate settings). He was taught that for a boy, enjoying violence was a good thing (albeit in appropriate settings). He was taught that a boy should not express feelings. I was taught that girls could and should express feelings, or at least some of them. When I responded with rage at being denied a toy, I was taught as a girl in a patriarchal household that rage was not an appropriate feminine feeling, that it should not only not be expressed, but it should be eradicated. When my brother responded with rage at being denied a toy, he was taught as a boy in a patriarchal household that his ability to express rage was good but that he had to learn the best setting to unleash his hostility. It was not good for him to use his rage to oppose the wishes of his parents, but later, when he grew up, he was taught that rage was permitted and that allowing rage to provoke him to violence would help him protect home and nation.

We lived in farm country, isolated from other people. Our sense of gender roles was learned from our parents, from the ways we saw them behave. My brother and I remember our confusion about gender. In reality I was stronger and more violent than my brother, which we learned quickly was bad. And he was a gentle, peaceful boy, which we learned was really bad. Although we were often confused, we knew one fact for certain: we could not be and act the way we wanted to, doing what we felt like. It was clear to us that our behavior had to follow a predetermined, gendered script. We both learned the word "patriarchy" in our adult life, when we learned that the script that had determined what we should be, the identities we should make, was based on patriarchal values and beliefs about gender.

I was always more interested in challenging patriarchy than my brother was because it was the system that was always leaving me out of things that I wanted to be part of. In our family life of the fifties, marbles were a boy's game. My brother had inherited his marbles from men in the family; he had a tin box to keep them in. All sizes and shapes, marvelously colored, they were to my eye the most beautiful objects. We played together with them, often with me aggressively clinging to the marble I liked best, refusing to share. When Dad was at work, our stay-at-home mom was quite content to see us playing marbles together. Yet Dad, looking at our play from a patriarchal perspective, was disturbed by what he saw. His daughter, aggressive and competitive, was a better player than his son. His son was passive; the boy did not really seem to care who won and was willing to give over marbles on demand. Dad decided that this play had to end, that both my brother and I needed to learn a lesson about appropriate gender roles.

One evening my brother was given permission by Dad to bring out the tin of marbles. I announced my desire to play and was told by my brother that "girls did not play with marbles," that it was a boy's game. This made no sense to my four- or five-year-old mind, and I insisted on my right to play by picking up marbles and shooting them. Dad intervened to tell me to stop. I did not listen. His voice grew louder and louder. Then suddenly he snatched me up, broke a board from our screen door, and began to beat me with it, telling me, "You're just a little girl. When I tell you to do something, I mean for you to do it." He beat me and he beat me, wanting me to acknowledge that I understood what I had done. His rage, his violence captured everyone's attention. Our family sat spellbound, rapt before the pornography of patriarchal violence. After this beating I was banished—forced to stay alone in the dark. Mama came into the bedroom to soothe the pain, telling me in her soft southern voice, "I tried to warn you. You need to accept that you are just a little girl and girls can't do what boys do." In service to patriarchy her task was to reinforce that Dad had done the right thing by, putting me in my place, by restoring the natural social order.

I remember this traumatic event so well because it was a story told again and again within our family. No one cared that the constant retelling might trigger post-traumatic stress; the retelling was necessary to reinforce both the message and the remembered state of absolute powerlessness. The recollection of this brutal whipping of a little-girl daughter by a big strong man, served as more than just a reminder to me of my gendered place; it was a reminder to everyone watching/remembering, to all my siblings, male and female, and to our grownwoman mother that our patriarchal father was the ruler in our household. We were to remember that if we did not obey his rules, we would be punished, punished even unto death. This is the way we were experientially schooled in the art of patriarchy.

10 There is nothing unique or even exceptional about this experience. Listen to the voices of wounded grown children raised in patriarchal homes and you will hear different versions with the same underlying theme, the use of violence to reinforce our indoctrination and acceptance of patriarchy. In *How Can I Get Through to You?* family therapist Terrence Real tells how his sons were

initiated into patriarchal thinking even as their parents worked to create a loving home in which antipatriarchal values prevailed. He tells of how his young son Alexander enjoyed dressing as Barbie until boys playing with his older brother witnessed his Barbie persona and let him know by their gaze and their shocked, disapproving silence that his behavior was unacceptable:

> Without a shred of malevolence, the stare my son received transmitted a message. You are not to do this. And the medium that message was broadcast in was a potent emotion: shame. At three, Alexander was learning the rules. A ten second wordless transaction was powerful enough to dissuade my son from that instant forward from what had been a favorite activity. I call such moments of induction the "normal traumatization" of boys.

To indoctrinate boys into the rules of patriarchy, we force them to feel pain and to deny their feelings.

My stories took place in the fifties; the stories Real tells are recent. They all underscore the tyranny of patriarchal thinking, the power of patriarchal culture to hold us captive. Real is one of the most enlightened thinkers on the subject of patriarchal masculinity in our nation, and yet he lets readers know that he is not able to keep his boys out of patriarchy's reach. They suffer its assaults, as do all boys and girls, to a greater or lesser degree. No doubt by creating a loving home that is not patriarchal, Real at least offers his boys a choice: they can choose to be themselves or they can choose conformity with patriarchal roles. Real uses the phrase "psychological patriarchy" to describe the patriarchal thinking common to females and males. Despite the contemporary visionary feminist thinking that makes clear that a patriarchal thinker need not be a male, most folks continue to see men as the problem of patriarchy. This is simply not the case. Women can be as wedded to patriarchal thinking and action as men.

Psychotherapist John Bradshaw's clear-sighted definition of patriarchy in *Creating Love* is a useful one: "The dictionary defines 'patriarchy' as a 'social organization marked by the supremacy of the father in the clan or family in both domestic and religious functions'. "Patriarchy is characterized by male domination and power. He states further that "patriarchal rules still govern most of the world's religious, school systems, and family systems." Describing the most damaging of these rules, Bradshaw lists "blind obedience—the foundation upon which patriarchy stands; the repression of all emotions except fear; the destruction of individual willpower; and the repression of thinking whenever it departs from the authority figure's way of thinking." Patriarchal thinking shapes the values of our culture. We are socialized into this system, females as well as males. Most of us learned patriarchal attitudes in our family of origin, and they were usually taught to us by our mothers. These attitudes were reinforced in schools and religious institutions.

15 The contemporary presence of female-headed house holds has led many people to assume that children in these households are not learning patriarchal values because no male is present. They assume that men are the sole teachers of patriarchal thinking. Yet many female-headed households endorse and promote patriarchal thinking with far greater passion than two-parent households. Because they do not have an experiential reality to challenge false fantasies of gender roles, women in such households are far more likely to idealize the patriarchal male role and patriarchal men than are women who live with patriarchal men every day. We need to highlight the role women play in perpetuating and sustaining patriarchal culture so that we will recognize patriarchy as a system women and men support equally, even if men receive more rewards from that system. Dismantling and changing patriarchal culture is work that men and women must do together.

Clearly we cannot dismantle a system as long as we engage in collective denial about its impact on our lives. Patriarchy requires male dominance by any means necessary, hence it supports, promotes, and condones sexist violence. We hear the most about sexist violence in public discourses about rape and abuse by domestic partners. But the most common forms of patriarchal violence are those that take place in the home between patriarchal parents and children. The point of such violence is usually to reinforce a dominator model, in which the authority figure is deemed ruler over those without power and given the right to maintain that rule through practices of subjugation, subordination, and submission.

Keeping males and females from telling the truth about what happens to them in families is one way patriarchal culture is maintained. A great majority of individuals enforce an unspoken rule in the culture as a whole that demands we keep the secrets of patriarchy, thereby protecting the rule of the father. This rule of silence is upheld when the culture refuses everyone easy access even to the word "patriarchy." Most children do not learn what to call this system of institutionalized gender roles, so rarely do we name it in everyday speech. This silence promotes denial. And how can we organize to challenge and change a system that cannot be named?

It is no accident that feminists began to use the word "patriarchy" to replace the more commonly used "male chauvanism" and "sexism." These courageous voices wanted men and women to become more aware of the way patriarchy affects us all. In popular culture the word itself was hardly used during the heyday of contemporary feminism. Antimale activists were no more eager than their sexist male counterparts to emphasize the system of patriarchy and the way it works. For to do so would have automatically exposed the notion that men were all-powerful and women powerless, that all men were oppressive and women always and only victims. By placing the blame for the perpetuation of sexism solely on men, these women could maintain their own allegiance to patriarchy, their own lust for power. They masked their longing to be dominators by taking on the mantle of victimhood.

Like many visionary radical feminists I challenged the misguided notion, put forward by women who were simply fed up with male exploitation and oppression, that men were "the enemy." As early as 1984 I included a chapter with the title "Men: Comrades in Struggle" in my book *Feminist Theory: From Margin to Center* urging advocates of feminist politics to challenge any rhetoric which placed the sole blame for perpetuating patriarchy and male domination onto men:

20 > Separatist ideology encourages women to ignore the negative impact of sexism on male personhood. It stresses polarization between the sexes. According to Joy Justice, separatists believe that there are "two basic perspectives" on the issue of naming the victims of sexism: "There is the perspective that men oppress women. And there is the perspective that people are people, and we are all hurt by rigid sex roles." ... Both perspectives accurately describe our predicament. Men do oppress women. People are hurt by rigid sexist role patterns, These two realities coexist. Male oppression of women cannot be excused by the recognition that there are ways men are hurt by rigid sexist roles. Feminist activists should acknowledge that hurt, and work to change it—it exists. It does not erase or lessen male responsibility for supporting and perpetuating their power under patriarchy to exploit and oppress women in a manner far more grievous than the serious psychological stress and emotional pain caused by male conformity to rigid sexist role patterns.

Throughout this essay I stressed that feminist advocates collude in the pain of men wounded by patriarchy when they falsely represent men as always and only powerful, as always and only gaining privileges from their blind obedience to patriarchy. I emphasized that patriarchal ideology brainwashes men to believe that their domination of women is beneficial when it is not:

> Often feminist activists affirm this logic when we should be constantly naming these acts as expressions of perverted power relations, general lack of control of one's actions, emotional powerlessness, extreme irrationality, and in many cases, outright insanity. Passive male absorption of sexist ideology enables men to falsely interpret this disturbed behavior positively. As long as men are brainwashed to equate violent domination and abuse of women with privilege, they will have no understanding of the damage done to themselves or to others, and no motivation to change.

Patriarchy demands of men that they become and remain emotional cripples. Since it is a system that denies men full access to their freedom of will, it is difficult for any man of any class to rebel against patriarchy, to be disloyal to the patriarchal parent, be that parent female or male.

The man who has been my primary bond for more than twelve years was traumatized by the patriarchal dynamics in his family of origin. When I met him he was in his twenties. While his formative years had been spent in the company of a violent, alcoholic dad, his circumstances changed when he was twelve and he began to live alone with his mother. In the early years of our relationship he talked openly about his hostility and rage toward his abusing dad. He was not interested in forgiving him or understanding the circumstances that had shaped and influenced his dad's life, either in his childhood or in his working life as a military man.

In the early years of our relationship he was extremely critical of male domination of women and children. Although he did not use the word "patriarchy," he understood its meaning and he opposed it. His gentle, quiet manner often led folks to ignore him, counting him among the weak and the powerless. By the age of thirty he began to assume a more macho persona, embracing the dominator model that he had once critiqued. Donning the mantle of patriarch, he gained greater respect and visibility. More women were drawn to him. He was noticed more in public spheres. His criticism of male domination ceased. And indeed he begin to mouth patriarchal rhetoric, saying the kind of sexist stuff that would have appalled him in the past.

These changes in his thinking and behavior were triggered by his desire to be accepted and affirmed in a patriarchal workplace and rationalized by his desire to get ahead. His story is not unusual. Boys brutalized and victimized by patriarchy more often than not become patriarchal, embodying the abusive patriarchal masculinity that they once clearly recognized as evil. Few men brutally abused as boys in the name of patriarchal maleness courageously resist the brainwashing and remain true to themselves. Most males conform to patriarchy in one way or another.

Indeed, radical feminist critique of patriarchy has practically been silenced in our culture. It has become a subcultural discourse available only to well-educated elites. Even in those circles, using the word "patriarchy" is regarded as passé. Often in my lectures when I use the phrase "imperialist white-supremacist capitalist patriarchy" to describe our nation's political system, audiences laugh. No one has ever explained why accurately naming this system is funny. The laughter is itself a weapon of patriarchal terrorism. It functions as a disclaimer, discounting the significance of what is being named. It suggests that the words themselves are problematic and not the system they describe. I interpret this laughter as the audience's way of showing discomfort with being asked to ally themselves with an antipatriarchal disobedient critique. This laughter reminds me that if I dare to challenge patriarchy openly, I risk not being taken seriously.

Citizens in this nation fear challenging patriarchy even as they lack overt awareness that they are fearful, so deeply embedded in our collective unconscious are the rules of patriarchy. I often tell audiences that if we were to go door-to-door asking if we should end male violence against women, most people would give their unequivocal support. Then if you told them we can only stop male violence against women by ending male domination, by eradicating patriarchy, they would begin to hesitate, to change their position. Despite the many gains of contemporary feminist movement—greater equality for women in the workforce, more tolerance for the relinquishing of rigid gender roles—patriarchy as a system remains intact, and many people continue to believe that it is needed if humans are to survive as a species. This belief seems ironic, given that patriarchal methods of organizing nations, especially the insistence on violence as a means of social control, has actually led to the slaughter of millions of people on the planet.

Until we can collectively acknowledge the damage patriarchy causes and the suffering it creates, we cannot address male pain. We cannot demand for men the right to be whole, to be givers and sustainers of life. Obviously some patriarchal men are reliable and even benevolent caretakers and providers, but still they are imprisoned by a system that undermines their mental health.

30 Patriarchy promotes insanity. It is at the root of the psychological ills troubling men in our nation. Nevertheless there is no mass concern for the plight of men. In *Stiffed: The Betrayal of the American Man,* Susan Faludi includes very little discussion of patriarchy:

> Ask feminists to diagnose men's problems and you will often get a very clear explanation: men are in crisis because women are properly challenging male dominance. Women are asking men to share the public reins and men can't bear it. Ask antifeminists and you will get a diagnosis that is, in one respect, similar. Men are troubled, many conservative pundits say, because women have gone far beyond their demands for equal treatment and are now trying to take power and control away from men ... The underlying message: men cannot be men, only eunuchs, if they are not in control. Both the feminist and antifeminist views are rooted in a peculiarly modern American perception that to be a man means to be at the controls and at all times to feel yourself in control.

Faludi never interrogates the notion of control. She never considers that the notion that men were somehow in control, in power, and satisfied with their lives before contemporary feminist movement is false.

Patriarchy as a system has denied males access to full emotional well-being, which is not the same as feeling rewarded, successful, or powerful because of one's capacity to assert control over others. To truly address male pain and male crisis we must as a nation be willing to expose the harsh reality that patriarchy has damaged men in the past and continues to damage them in the present. If patriarchy were truly rewarding to men, the violence and addiction in family life that is so all-pervasive would not exist. This violence was not created by feminism. If patriarchy were rewarding, the overwhelming dissatisfaction most men feel in their work lives—a dissatisfaction extensively documented in the work of Studs Terkel and echoed in Faludi's treatise—would not exist.

In many ways *Stiffed* was yet another betrayal of American men because Faludi spends so much time trying not to challenge patriarchy that she fails to highlight the necessity of ending patriarchy if we are to liberate men. Rather she writes:

35 > Instead of wondering why men resist women's struggle for a freer and healthier life, I began to wonder why men refrain from engaging in their own struggle. Why, despite a crescendo of random tantrums, have they offered no methodical, reasoned response to their predicament: Given the untenable and insulting nature of the demands placed on men to prove themselves in our culture, why don't men revolt? ... Why haven't men responded to the series of betrayals in their own lives—to the failures of their fathers to make good on their promises–with some thing coequal to feminism?

Note that Faludi does not dare risk either the ire of feminist females by suggesting that men can find salvation in feminist movement or rejection by potential male readers who are solidly antifeminist by suggesting that they have something to gain from engaging feminism.

So far in our nation visionary feminist movement is the only struggle for justice that emphasizes the need to end patriarchy. No mass body of women has challenged patriarchy and neither has any group of men come together to lead the struggle. The crisis facing men is not the crisis of masculinity; it is the crisis of patriarchal masculinity. Until we make this distinction clear, men will continue to fear that any critique of patriarchy represents a threat. Distinguishing political patriarchy, which he sees as largely committed to ending sexism, therapist Terrence Real makes clear that the patriarchy damaging us all is embedded in our psyches:

> Psychological patriarchy is the dynamic between those qualities deemed "masculine" and "feminine" in which half of our human traits are exalted while the other half is devalued. Both men and women participate in this tortured value system. Psychological patriarchy is a "dance of contempt," a perverse form of connection that replaces true intimacy with complex, covert layers of dominance and submission, collusion and manipulation. It is the unacknowledged paradigm of relationships that has suffused Western civilization generation after generation, deforming both sexes, and destroying the passionate bond between them.

By highlighting psychological patriarchy, we see that everyone is implicated and we are freed from the misperception that men are the enemy. To end patriarchy we must challenge both its psychological and its concrete manifestations in daily life. There are folks who are able to critique patriarchy but unable to act in an antipatriarchal manner.

40 To end male pain, to respond effectively to male crisis, we have to name the problem. We have to both acknowledge that the problem is patriarchy and work to end patriarchy. Terrence Real offers this valuable insight: "The reclamation of wholeness is a process even more fraught for men than it has been for women, more difficult and more profoundly threatening to the culture at large." If men are to reclaim the essential goodness of male being, if they are to regain the space of openheartedness and emotional expressiveness that is the foundation of well-being, we must envision alternatives to patriarchal masculinity. We must all change.

Credit

Bell Hooks, "Understanding Patriarchy" http://imaginenoborders.org/pdf/zines/UnderstandingPatriarchy.pdf

"Bros Before Hos": The Guy Code

MICHAEL KIMMEL

Whenever I ask young women what they think it means to be a woman, they look at me puzzled, and say, basically, "Whatever I want." "It doesn't mean anything at all to me," says Nicole, a junior at Colby College in Maine. "I can be Mia Hamm, I can be Britney Spears, I can be Madame Curie or Madonna. Nobody can tell me what it means to be a woman anymore."

For men, the question is still meaningful—and powerful. In countless workshops on college campuses and in high-school assemblies, I've asked young men what it means to be a man. I've asked guys from every state in the nation, as well as about fifteen other countries, what sorts of phrases and words come to mind when they hear someone say, "Be a man!"

The responses are rather predictable. The first thing someone usually says is "Don't cry," then other similar phrases and ideas—never show your feelings, never ask for directions, never give up, never give in, be strong, be aggressive, show no fear, show no mercy, get rich, get even, get laid, win—follow easily after that.

Here's what guys say, summarized into a set of current epigrams. Think of it as a "Real Guy's Top Ten List."

1. "Boys Don't Cry"
2. "It's Better to be Mad than Sad"
3. "Don't Get Mad—Get Even"
4. "Take It Like a Man"
5. "He Who has the Most Toys When he Dies, Wins"
6. "Just Do It," or "Ride or Die"
7. "Size Matters"
8. "I Don't Stop to Ask for Directions"
9. "Nice Guys Finish Last"
10. "It's All Good"

5 The unifying emotional subtext of all these aphorisms involves never showing emotions or admitting to weakness. The face you must show to the world insists that everything is going just fine, that everything is under control, that there's

nothing to be concerned about (a contemporary version of Alfred E. Neuman of *MAD* Magazine's "What, me worry?"). Winning is crucial, especially when the victory is over other men who have less amazing or smaller toys. Kindness is not an option, nor is compassion. Those sentiments are taboo.

This is "The Guy Code," the collection of attitudes, values, and traits that together composes what it means to be a man. These are the rules that govern behavior in Guyland, the criteria that will be used to evaluate whether any particular guy measures up. The Guy Code revisits what psychologist William Pollack called "the boy code" in his bestselling book *Real Boys*—just a couple of years older and with a lot more at stake. And just as Pollack and others have explored the dynamics of boyhood so well, we now need to extend the reach of that analysis to include late adolescence and young adulthood.

In 1976, social psychologist Robert Brannon summarized the four basic rules of masculinity:

1. "No Sissy Stuff!" Being a man means not being a sissy, not being perceived as weak, effeminate, or gay. Masculinity is the relentless repudiation of the feminine.
2. "Be a Big Wheel." This rule refers to the centrality of success and power in the definition of masculinity. Masculinity is measured more by wealth, power, and status than by any particular body part.
3. "Be a Sturdy Oak." What makes a man is that he is reliable in a crisis. And what makes him so reliable in a crisis is not that he is able to respond fully and appropriately to the situation at hand, but rather that he resembles an inanimate object. A rock, a pillar, a species of tree.
4. "Give 'em Hell." Exude an aura of daring and aggression. Live life out on the edge. Take risks. Go for it. Pay no attention to what others think.

Amazingly, these four rules have changed very little among successive generations of high-school and college-age men. James O'Neil, a developmental psychologist at the University of Connecticut, and Joseph Pleck, a social psychologist at the University of Illinois, have each been conducting studies of this normative definition of masculinity for decades. "One of the most surprising findings," O'Neil told me, "is how little these rules have changed."

Being a Man Among Men

Where do young men get these ideas? "Oh, definitely, my dad," says Mike, a 20-year-old sophomore at Wake Forest. "He was always riding my ass, telling me I had to be tough and strong to make it in this world."

10 "My older brothers were always on my case," says Drew, a 24-year-old University of Massachusetts grad. "They were like, always ragging on me, calling me a pussy, if I didn't want to play football or wrestle. If I just wanted to hang out and like play my Xbox, they were constantly in my face."

"It was subtle, sometimes," says Warren, a 21-year-old at Towson, "and other times really out front. In school, it was the male teachers, saying stuff about how explorers or scientists were so courageous and braving the elements and all that. Then, other times, it was phys-ed class, and everyone was all over everyone else talking about 'He's so gay' and 'He's a wuss.'"

"The first thing I think of is my coach," says Don, a 26-year-old former football player at Lehigh. "Any fatigue, any weakness, any sign that being hit actually hurt and he was like 'Waah! [fake crying] Widdle Donny got a boo boo. Should we kiss it guys?' He'd completely humiliate us for showing anything but complete toughness. I'm sure he thought he was building up our strength and ability to play, but it wore me out trying to pretend all the time, to suck it up and just take it."

The response was consistent: Guys hear the voices of the men in their lives—fathers, coaches, brothers, grandfathers, uncles, priests—to inform their ideas of masculinity.

This is no longer surprising to me. One of the more startling things I found when I researched the history of the idea of masculinity in America for a previous book was that men subscribe to these ideals not because they want to impress women, let alone any inner drive or desire to test themselves against some abstract standards. They do it because they want to be positively evaluated by other men. American men want to be a "man among men," an Arnold Schwarzenegger-like "man's man," not a Fabio-like "ladies' man." Masculinity is largely a "homosocial" experience: performed for, and judged by, other men.

15 Noted playwright David Mamet explains why women don't even enter the mix. "Women have, in men's minds, such a low place on the social ladder of this country that it's useless to define yourself in terms of a woman. What men need is men's approval." While women often become a kind of currency by which men negotiate their status with other men, women are for possessing, not for emulating.

The Gender Police

Other guys constantly watch how well we perform. Our peers are a kind of "gender police," always waiting for us to screw up so they can give us a ticket for crossing the well-drawn boundaries of manhood. As young men, we become relentless cowboys, riding the fences, checking the boundary line between masculinity and femininity, making sure that nothing slips over. The possibilities of being unmasked are everywhere. Even the most seemingly insignificant misstep can pose a threat or activate that haunting terror that we will be found out.

On the day the students in my class "Sociology of Masculinity" were scheduled to discuss homophobia, one student provided an honest and revealing anecdote. Noting that it was a beautiful day, the first day of spring after a particularly brutal Northeast winter, he decided to wear shorts to class. "I had this really nice pair of new Madras shorts," he recounted. "But then I thought to myself, these shorts have lavender and pink in them. Today's class topic is homophobia. Maybe today is not the best day to wear these shorts." Nods all around.

Our efforts to maintain a manly front cover everything we do. What we wear. How we talk. How we walk. What we eat (like the recent flap over "manwiches"—those artery-clogging massive burgers, dripping with extras). Every mannerism, every movement contains a coded gender language. What happens if you refuse or resist? What happens if you step outside the definition of masculinity? Consider the words that would be used to describe you. In workshops it generally takes less than a minute to get a list of about twenty terms that are at the tip of everyone's tongues: wimp, faggot, dork, pussy, loser, wuss, nerd, queer, homo, girl, gay, skirt, Mama's boy, pussy-whipped. This list is so effortlessly generated, so consistent, that it composes a national well from which to draw epithets and put-downs.

Ask any teenager in America what is the most common put-down in middle school or high school? The answer: "That's so gay." It's said about anything and everything—their clothes, their books, the music or TV shows they like, the sports figures they admire. "That's so gay" has become a free-floating put-down, meaning bad, dumb, stupid, wrong. It's the generic bad thing.

20 Listen to one of America's most observant analysts of masculinity, Eminem. Asked in an MTV interview in 2001 why he constantly used "faggot" in every one of his raps to put down other guys, Eminem told the interviewer, Kurt Loder,

> The lowest degrading thing you can say to a man when you're battling him is to call him a faggot and try to take away his manhood. Call him a sissy, call him a punk. "Faggot" to me doesn't necessarily mean gay people. "Faggot" to me just means taking away your manhood.

But does it mean homosexuality? Does it really suggest that you suspect the object of the epithet might actually be attracted to another guy? Think, for example, of how you would answer this question: If you see a man walking down the street, or meet him at a party, how do you "know" if he is homosexual? (Assume that he is not wearing a T-shirt with a big pink triangle on it, and that he's not already holding hands with another man.)

When I ask this question in classes or workshops, respondents invariably provide a standard list of stereotypically effeminate behaviors. He walks a certain way, talks a certain way, acts a certain way. He's well dressed, sensitive, and emotionally expressive. He has certain tastes in art and music—indeed, he has *any* taste in art and music! Men tend to focus on the physical attributes, women on the emotional. Women say they "suspect" a man might be gay if he's interested in what she's talking about, knows something about what she's talking about, or is sensitive and a good listener. One recently said, "I suspect he might be gay if he's looking at my eyes, and not down my blouse." Another said she suspects he might be gay if he shows no sexual interest in her, if he doesn't immediately come on to her.

Once I've established what makes a guy "suspect," I ask the men in the room if any of them would want to be thought of as gay. Rarely does a hand go up—despite the fact that this list of attributes is actually far preferable to the restrictive one that stands in the "Be a Man" box. So, what do straight men do to make sure that no one gets the wrong idea about them?

25 Everything that is perceived as gay goes into what we might call the Negative Playbook of Guyland. Avoid everything in it and you'll be all right. Just make sure that you walk, talk, and act in a different way from the gay stereotype; dress terribly; show no taste in art or music; show no emotions at all. Never listen to a thing a woman is saying, but express immediate and unquenchable sexual interest. Presto, you're a real man, back in the "Be a Man" box. Homophobia—the fear that people might *misperceive* you as gay—is the animating fear of American guys' masculinity. It's what lies underneath the crazy risk-taking behaviors practiced by boys of all ages, what drives the fear that other guys will see you as weak, unmanly, frightened. The single cardinal rule of manhood, the one from which all the other characteristics—wealth, power, status, strength, physicality—are derived is to offer constant proof that you are not gay.

Homophobia is even deeper than this. It's the fear *of* other men—that other men will perceive you as a failure, as a fraud. It's a fear that others will see you as weak, unmanly, frightened. This is how John Steinbeck put it in his novel *Of Mice and Men:*

> "Funny thing," [Curley's wife] said. "If I catch any one man, and he's alone, I get along fine with him. But just let two of the guys get together an' you won't talk. Jus' nothin' but mad." She dropped her fingers and put her hands on her hips. "You're all scared of each other, that's what. Ever'one of you's scared the rest is goin' to get something on you."

In that sense, homosexuality becomes a kind of shorthand for "unmanliness"—and the homophobia that defines and animates the daily conversations of Guyland is at least as much about masculinity as it is about sexuality.

But what would happen to a young man if he were to refuse such limiting parameters on who he is and how he's permitted to act? "It's not like I want to stay in that box," says Jeff, a first-year Cornell student at my workshop. "But as soon as you step outside it, even for a second, all the other guys are like, 'What are you, dude, a fag?' It's not very safe out there on your own. I suppose as I get older, I'll get more secure, and feel like I couldn't care less what other guys say. But now, in my fraternity, on this campus, man, I'd lose everything."

30 The consistency of responses is as arresting as the list is disturbing: "I would lose my friends." "Get beat up." "I'd be ostracized." "Lose my self-esteem." Some say they'd take drugs or drink. Become withdrawn, sullen, a loner, depressed. "Kill myself," says one guy. "Kill them," responds another. Everyone laughs, nervously. Some say they'd get mad. And some say they'd get even. "I dunno," replied Mike, a sophomore at Portland State University. "I'd probably pull a Columbine. I'd show them that they couldn't get away with calling me that shit."

Guys know that they risk everything—their friendships, their sense of self, maybe even their lives—if they fail to conform. Since the stakes are so enormous, young men take huge chances to prove their manhood, exposing themselves to health risks, workplace hazards, and stressrelated illnesses. Here's a revealing factoid. Men ages 19 to 29 are three times less likely to wear seat belts than women the same age. Before they turn nineteen though, young men are actually more likely to wear seat belts. It's as if they suddenly get the idea that as long as they're driving the car, they're completely in control, and therefore safe. Ninety percent of all driving offenses, excluding parking violations, are committed by men, and 93 percent of road ragers are male. Safety is emasculating! So they drink too much, drive too fast, and play chicken in a multitude of dangerous venues.

The comments above provide a telling riposte to all those theories of biology that claim that this definition of masculinity is "hard-wired," the result of millennia of evolutionary adaptation or the behavioral response to waves of aggression-producing testosterone, and therefore inevitable. What these theories fail to account for is the way that masculinity is coerced and policed relentlessly by other guys. If it were biological, it would be as natural as breathing or blinking. In truth, the Guy Code fits as comfortably as a straightjacket.

Boys' Psychological Development: Where the Guy Code Begins

Masculinity is a constant test—always up for grabs, always needing to be proved. And the testing starts early. Recently, I was speaking with a young black mother, a social worker, who was concerned about a conversation she had had with her husband a few nights earlier. It seems that her husband had taken their son to the barber, which, she explained to me, is a central social institution in the African-American community. As the barber prepared the boy's hair for treatment, using, apparently some heat and some painful burning chemicals, the boy began to cry. The barber turned to the boy's father and pronounced, "This boy is a wimp!" He went on, "This boy has been spending too much time with his mama! Man, you need to put your foot down. You have got to get this boy away from his mother!"

35 That evening the father came home, visibly shaken by the episode, and announced to his wife that from that moment on the boy would not be spending as much time with her, but instead would do more sports and other activities with him, "to make sure he doesn't become a sissy."

After telling me this story, the mother asked what I thought she should do. "Gee," I said, "I understand the pressures that dads feel to 'toughen up' their sons. But how old is your boy, anyway?"

"Three and a half," she said.

I tried to remind her, of course, that crying is the natural human response to pain, and that her son was behaving appropriately. But her story reminded me of how early this pressure starts to affect an emotionally impervious manly stoicism.

Ever since Freud, we've believed that the key to boys' development is separation, that the boy must switch his identification from mother to father in order to "become" a man. He achieves his masculinity by repudiation, dissociation, and then identification. It is a perilous path, but a necessary one, even though there is nothing inevitable about it—and nothing biological either. Throw in an overdominant mother, or an absent father, and we start worrying that the boy will not succeed in his masculine quest.

40 Boys learn that their connection to mother will emasculate them, turn them into Mama's Boys. And so they learn to act *as if* they have made that leap by pushing away from their mothers. Along the way they suppress all the feelings they associate with the maternal—compassion, nurturance, vulnerability, dependency. This suppression and repudiation is the origin of the Boy Code. It's what turns those happy, energetic, playful, and emotionally expressive 5-year-olds into sullen, withdrawn, and despondent 9-year-olds. In the recent spate of bestselling books about boys' development, psychologists like William Pollack, James Garbarino, Michael Thompson, Dan Kindlon, and others, argue that from an early age boys are taught to refrain from crying, to suppress their emotions, never to display vulnerability. As a result, boys feel effeminate not only if they *express* their emotions, but even if they *feel* them. In their bestseller, *Raising Cain,* Kindlon and Thompson describe a "culture of cruelty" in which peers force other boys to deny their emotional needs and disguise their feelings. It's no wonder that so many boys end up feeling emotionally isolated.

These books about boys map the inner despair that comes from such emotional numbness and fear of vulnerability. Pollack calls it the "mask of masculinity," the fake front of impervious, unemotional independence, a swaggering posture that boys believe will help them to present a stoic front. "Ruffled in a manly pose," the great Irish poet William Butler Yeats put it in his poem "Coole Park" (1929), "For all his timid heart."

The ruffling starts often by age 4 or 5, when he enters kindergarten, and it gets a second jolt when he hits adolescence. Think of the messages boys get: Stand on your own two feet! Don't cry! Don't be a sissy! As one boy in Pollack's book summarizes it: "Shut up and take it, or you'll be sorry." When I asked my 9-year-old son, Zachary, what he thought of when I said "be a man" he said that one of his friends said something about "taking it like a man. So," he explained, "I think it means acting tougher than you actually are."

Recently a colleague told me about a problem he was having. It seems his 7-year-old son, James, was being bullied by another boy on his way home from school. His wife, the boy's mother, strategized with her son about how to handle such situations in the future. She suggested he find an alternate route home, tell a teacher, or perhaps even tell the boy's parents. And she offered the standard "use your words, not your fists" conflict-reducer. "How can I get my wife to stop treating James like a baby?" my colleague asked. "How will he ever learn to stand up for himself if she turns him into a wimp?"

The Boy Code leaves boys disconnected from a wide range of emotions and prohibited from sharing those feelings with others. As they grow older, they feel disconnected from adults, as well, unable to experience the guidance towards maturity that adults can bring. When they turn to anger and violence it is because these, they believe, perhaps rightly, are the only acceptable forms of emotional expression allowed them. Just as the Boy Code shuts boys down, the Guy Code reinforces those messages, suppressing what was left of boyhood exuberance and turning it into sullen indifference.

45 No wonder boys are more prone to depression, suicidal behavior, and various other forms of out-of-control or out-of-touch behaviors than girls are. No wonder boys drop out of school and are diagnosed as emotionally disturbed four times more often as girls, get into fights twice as often, and are six times more likely than girls to be diagnosed with Attention Deficit and Hyperactivity Disorder (ADHD).

The Pressure to Conform

I often ask my students to imagine two American men—one, 75 years old, black, and gay, who lives in downtown Chicago, and the other, a 19-year-old white heterosexual farm boy living 100 miles south of Chicago. How might their ideas about masculinity differ? And what ideas about masculinity might they have in common, ideas that transcend class, race, age, and sexual or regional differences?

While the Guy Code isn't everywhere exactly the same, and while there are some variations by class or race or age or sexuality, the pressure to conform is so powerful a centripetal force that it minimizes differences, pushing guys into a homogenous, ill-fitting uniform. The sociologist Erving Goffman once described the dominant image of masculinity like this:

> In an important sense there is only one complete unblushing male in America: a young, married, white, urban, northern, heterosexual, Protestant, father, of college education, fully employed, of good complexion, weight, and height, and a recent record in sports ... Any male who fails to qualify in any one of these ways is likely to view himself—during moments at least—as unworthy, incomplete, and inferior.

This dynamic is critical. Every single man will, at some point in his life, "fail to qualify." That is, every single one of us will feel, at least at moments, "unworthy, incomplete, and inferior." It is from those feelings of inadequacy and inferiority that we often act recklessly—taking foolish risks, engaging in violence—all as an attempt to repair, restore, or reclaim our place in the sacred box of manhood.

50 It's equally true that guys express the Guy Code differently at different times of their lives. Even at different times of day! Even if he believes that to be a man is to always be in charge, to be aggressive and powerful, he is unlikely to express that around his coaches or teachers, let alone his parents. There are times when even the most manly of men must accept authority, obey orders, and shut up and listen.

This is especially true in Guyland, because this intermediate moment, poised between adolescence and adulthood, enables young men to be somewhat strategic in their expression of masculinity. They can be men when it suits them, when they want to be taken seriously by the world around them, and they can also be boys when it suits them, when they don't want to be held to account as adults for their actions, but simply want to get away with it.

Violence as Restoration

The Guy Code, and the Boy Code before it, demands a lot—that boys and young men shut down emotionally, that they suppress compassion, and inflate ambition. And it extracts compliance with coercion and fear. But it also promises so much as well. Part of what makes the Guy Code so seductive are the rewards guys think will be theirs if they only walk the line. If they embrace the Code, they will finally be in charge and feel powerful. And so, having dutifully subscribed, young men often feel cheated—and pissed off—when the rewards associated with power are not immediately forthcoming.

Violence is how they express all that disappointment. Rage is the way to displace the feelings of humiliation, to restore the entitlement. "The emotion of shame is the primary or ultimate cause of all violence," writes psychiatrist James Gilligan. "The purpose of violence is to diminish the intensity of shame and replace it as far as possible with its opposite, pride, thus preventing the individual from being overwhelmed by the feeling of shame." "It's better to be mad than sad," writes psychologist James Garbarino.

Virtually every male in America understands something about violence. We know how it works, we know how to use it, and we know that if we are perceived as weak or unmanly, it will be used against us. Each of us cuts his own deal with it.

55 It's as American as apple pie. Resorting to violence to restore one's honor from perceived humiliations has been around ever since one caveman chided another on the size of his club, but few modern societies have made violence such a cultural and psychological foundation. Cultural historian Richard Slotkin's history of the American frontier claims that our understanding of violence is regenerative: It enables us to grow. The great anthropologist Margaret Mead once commented that what made American violence stand out was our nearly obsessive need to legitimate the use of violence; ours is an aggression, she wrote, "which can never be shown except when the other fellow starts it" and which is "so unsure of itself that it had to be proved." Americans like to think that we don't start wars, we just finish them.

And what's true on the battlefield is also true on the playground. Watch two boys squaring off sometime. "You wanna start something?" one yells. "No, but if you start it, I'll finish it!" shouts the other. Adolescent male violence is so restorative that it's even been prescribed by generations of dads to enable their boys to stand up for themselves. And they've had plenty of support from experts, like J. Alfred Puffer, author of *The Boy and His Gang,* a child-rearing manual from the early twentieth century which offered this counsel:

> There are times when every boy must defend his own rights if he is not to become a coward and lose the road to independence and true manhood ... The strong willed boy needs no inspiration to combat, but often a good deal of guidance and restraint. If he fights more than, let us say, a half dozen times a week—except, of course, during his first week at a new school—he is probably over-quarrelsome and needs to curb. The sensitive, retiring boy, on the other hand, needs encouragement to stand his ground and fight.

In this bestseller, boys were encouraged to fight once a day, except during the first week at a new school, when it was presumed they would fight more often!

The contemporary Guy Code also descends from older notions of honor—a man had to be ready to fight to prove himself in the eyes of others. In the early nineteenth century, Southern whites called it "honor"; by the turn of the century it was called "reputation." Later in the century, "having a chip on your shoulder"—walking around mad, ready to rumble—were installed as fighting words in the American South, as a generation of boys were desperate to prove their manhood after the humiliating defeat in the Civil War. By the 1950s, blacks in the northern ghettos spoke of "respect," which has now been transformed again into not showing "disrespect," or "dissing." It's the same code, the same daring. And today that postbellum "chip on your shoulder" has morphed into what one gang member calls the "accidental bump," when you're walking down the street, "with your chest out, bumping into people and hoping they'll give you a bad time so you can pounce on them and beat 'em into the goddamn concrete."

60 Violence, or the threat of violence, is a main element of the Guy Code: Its use, legitimacy, and effectiveness are all well understood by most adolescent guys. They use violence when necessary to test and prove their manhood, and when others don't measure up, they make them pay.

The Three Cultures of Guyland

Practically every week we can read about a horrible hazing incident on campus, or an alcohol-related driving accident following a high-school prom, or allegations of a date rape at a party the previous weekend. Bullying is ubiquitous in middle schools and high schools across America, and not infrequently a case of bullying is so outrageous it becomes newsworthy. Rape on campus occurs with such alarming frequency that most colleges now incorporate sexual awareness training into their freshman orientation practices (apparently students not only must learn how to find their way around campus and how to use a library, but they must also learn how not to rape their classmates).

Every single emergency room in every single hospital adjoining or near a college campus stocks extra supplies on Thursday nights—rape kits for the sexual assault victims, IV fluids for those who are dehydrated from alcohol-induced vomiting, blood for drunk driving accidents. On many campuses, at least one party gets "out of hand" each week, and someone is seriously injured: A group of guys stage a "train" or a "ledge party," or someone gets so sick from drinking that they need to be hospitalized. And that's just the more "routine" weekend events. Newspaper and magazine stories, alarmist television exposés, and campus crusaders typically focus on the extreme cases—the fatal drunk driving accidents, the murder-by-hazing.

Though it may not be possible to read these headlines without a shudder of horror, most adults among us, particularly those of us with sons and daughters who live in Guyland, are nonetheless often able to convince ourselves that these stories are not about *our* kids. We might even think the media is a bit hysterical. Our sons aren't rapists. They don't tie cinderblocks to each other's penises and then throw those blocks off the roof, for crying out loud. They don't drink and drive, or get in fistfights, or paint swastikas on each other's passed-out drunken bodies. They're good kids. We believe these stories are anomalies, that the perpetrators are deviants, bad apples who otherwise don't represent the majority of guys. We look to psychology to explain these rare occurrences: bad parenting, most likely, or the cumulative negative effects of media consumption. We treat these as individual cases, not as a social and cultural phenomenon that impacts all guys, including the ones we know and love.

And, as I've argued, for the most part that's true. Most guys *are* good guys, but that doesn't lessen the reality of the violence that surrounds them, or the ways that they, and we, collaborate by turning a blind eye. If we really want to help guide our sons to manhood, it's imperative that we, as a society, look at their world with eyes wide open. We must be willing to ask the hard questions. How do such events happen? And what do such extreme cases tell us about the dynamics of Guyland, the operations of the Guy Code in action?

65 Guyland rests on three distinct cultural dynamics: a culture of entitlement, a culture of silence, and a culture of protection. Taken together, these cultures do more than make these more extreme cases the actions of a small group of predatory thugs. They suggest the ways in which we, too, are implicated. Why? Because if we really want to help these guys, then we must know the world they live in.

The Culture of Entitlement

Many young men today have a shockingly strong sense of male superiority and a diminished capacity for empathy. They believe that the capacity for empathy and compassion has to be suppressed, early on, in the name of achieving masculinity. That this is true despite the progress of the women's movement, parents who are psychologically aware and moral, stunning opportunities for men and women, is disappointing at best. But there is no way around it:

Most young men who engage in acts of violence—or who watch them and do nothing, or who joke about them with their friends—fully subscribe to traditional ideologies about masculinity. The problem isn't psychological; these guys aren't deviants. If anything, they are overconforming to the hyperbolic expressions of masculinity that still inform American culture.

This culture of entitlement is the reward for subscribing to the Guy Code. As boys they may have felt powerless as they struggled heroically to live up to impossible conventions of masculinity. As William Pollack argues, "it's still a man's world, but it's not a boys' world." But *someday it would be*. Someday, if I play my cards right, if I follow all the rules, the world will be mine. Having worked so hard and sacrificed so much to become a man—it'll be my turn. Payback. I'm entitled.

It's facile to argue about whether or not young men "have" power: Some do, some don't. Some are powerful in some settings, but not in others. Besides, power isn't a possession, it's a relationship. It's about the ability to do what you want in the world. Few *people* feel that sort of power even as adults: Most of us "have to" work, we are weighed down by family and workplace obligations. But even when they feel powerless, unlike women, men feel *entitled* to power.

This sense of entitlement is crucial for understanding Guyland—and the lives of young men as they pass into adulthood. Here is another example. Not long ago, I appeared on a television talk show opposite three "angry white males" who felt they had been the victims of workplace discrimination. They were in their late twenties and early thirties— just on the other side of the Guyland divide. The show's title, no doubt to entice a large potential audience was "A Black Woman Stole My Job." Each of the men described how he was passed over for jobs or promotions for which all believed themselves qualified. Then it was my turn to respond. I said I had one question about one word in the title of the show. I asked them about the word "my." Where did they get the idea it was "their" job? Why wasn't the show called "A Black Woman Got *a* Job," or "A Black Woman Got *the* Job"? These men felt the job was "theirs" because they felt entitled to it, and when some "other" person—black, female—got the job, that person was really taking what was "rightfully" theirs.

70 Another example of entitlement appeared in an Anna Quindlen column in the *New York Times*. "It seems like if you're a white male you don't have a chance," commented a young man who attended a college where 5 percent of his classmates were black. By way of explanation, Quindlen commented

> What the kid really meant is that he no longer has the edge, that the rules of a system that may have served his father will have changed. It is one of those good-old-days constructs to believe it was a system based purely on merit, but we know that's not true. It is a system that once favored him, and others like him. Now sometimes—just sometimes—it favors someone different.

Young men feel like Esau, that sad character in the Bible who sold his birthright for a bowl of lentils and never felt whole again. From that moment, everything belonged to Jacob, and we never hear of Esau again. And, like Esau, young men often feel that they've been tricked out of it, in Esau's case by a pair of hairy arms offered to his blind father, and in the case of guys today, by equally blind fathers who have failed to pass down to them what was "rightfully" supposed to be theirs.

The Culture of Silence

If thwarted entitlement is the underlying cause of so much of the violence in Guyland, and if violence is so intimately woven into the fabric of the Guy Code as to be one of its core elements, how come no one says anything about it?

Because they're afraid. They're afraid of being outcast, marginalized, shunned. Or they're afraid that the violence just might be turned against them if they voice their opposition too vehemently. So they learn to keep their mouths shut, even when what they're seeing goes against everything they know to be good. The Guy Code imposes a "code of silence on boys, requiring them to suffer without speaking of it and to be silent witnesses to acts of cruelty to others," write Dan Kindlon and Michael Thompson. Boys and men learn to be silent in the face of other men's violence. Silence is one of the ways boys *become* men.

75 They learn not to say anything when guys make sexist comments to girls. They learn not to say anything when guys taunt or tease another guy, or start fights, or bully or torment a classmate or a friend. They scurry silently if they're walking down the street and some guys at a construction site—or, for that matter, in business suits—start harassing a woman. They learn not to tell anyone about the homoerotic sadism that is practiced on new kids when they join a high-school or college athletic team, or the school band, or a fraternity. Or when they hear that a bunch of guys gang raped a classmate. They tell no parents, no teachers, no administrators. They don't tell the police. And they certainly don't confront the perpetrators.

A friend recently wrote to me about his experience leading a workshop for high-school kids in the frozen Yukon Territories of Canada. From the stories of their teachers, it was clear that the school had a tough and aggressive boy culture. He was surprised, then, when the boys opened up, and spoke with candor and honesty. During a break, though, he heard them talking about the fighting that went on each week at their school. A circle would form around a fight as it began. And the boys would cheer with glee.

He was taken aback. Suddenly these same boys, who minutes earlier had been earnest and caring, were now gleefully recounting blow-by-blow descriptions of the fights. Apparently without effort, they had shifted into masculine performance mode, each trying to outdo the other with shows of verbal bravado.

He interrupted them. "Wait a minute," he said. "I've spent the past day and a half with you guys, hearing you talk about your lives. I know you don't like that fighting. I know you don't like having to prove you're a real man. So how come you're going on about how great these fights are? Why do you stand in that circle and cheer the others on?"

The group went deadly silent. No one met his eyes. No one smirked or glanced that conspiratorial look that young people often share when an adult is challenging them. Finally, one boy looked up.

80 "So why do you cheer the fights?" my friend asked.

"Because if you don't, they'll turn on you. Because if you don't, you'll be the next one inside the ring."

If they're quiet, they believe, if they hide in the mass, if they disappear, maybe the bullies will ignore them, pick on someone else.

The silence is not limited to boys. Girls, too, know about the Guy Code, know how weaker guys are targeted, bullied, battered, and they keep quiet also. "We know that it's wrong," Ellen, a sophomore at the University of Illinois told me. "But we know that if we go along with it, the cool guys will like us. No big deal. It isn't like they're hitting *us,* is it?"

That silence, though, is what gives the perpetrators and the victims the idea that everyone supports the Guy Code. It's what gives everyone a mark of shame. And it's what keeps it going—even when so many guys are aching to change it, or eliminate it altogether. The first rule of the Guy Code is that you can express no doubts, no fears, no vulnerabilities. No questions even. As they might say in Las Vegas: What happens in Guyland stays in Guyland.

The Culture of Protection

85 By upholding the culture of silence, guys implicitly support the criminals in their midst who take that silence as tacit approval. And not only does that silence support them, it also protects them. It ensures that there will be no whistleblowers and, as we'll see, that there will be no witnesses when, and if, the victims themselves come forward. Nobody knows anything, nobody saw anything, nobody remembers anything.

Yet it's one thing for the guys themselves to protect one another— as we've seen, there's a tremendous amount at stake for them, and the pressure is high to conform—it's another thing entirely when the entire community that surrounds these guys also protects them. When the parents, teachers, girlfriends, school administrators, and city officials make the decision to look the other way, to dismiss these acts of violence as "poor judgment" or "things getting a little out of hand." I call this protective bubble of community support that surrounds Guyland the *culture of protection*. Communities rally around "their" guys, protecting the criminals and demeaning their victims. This shields the participants from taking full responsibility for their actions and often provides a cushion of support between those who feel entitled and the rest of the world.

It's natural for parents to want to protect their children. Parents work hard to keep their children safe—we immunize them, try to get them into the best schools, and intercede on their behalf if they are victimized or bullied. But sometimes this natural instinct to protect children may also infantalize them, may keep them from accepting responsibility for their actions, or confronting the negative consequences of their mistakes. And sometimes, parents' efforts to protect and defend their young adults may actually enable them to transgress again, or even to escalate the severity of their actions to the point where they are trying to get away with something truly criminal.

Not only do parents' responses characterize this culture of protection, but the entire community's response may shield them as well. From teachers, coaches, and school administrators who look the other way, as long as it didn't happen on school property, to the community determined to maintain the illusion that theirs is an ideal community in which to live and raise children, it's often neighbors and friends who exacerbate the problem by siding with the perpetrators against the victims.

The culture of silence and the culture of protection sustain many of guys' other excessive behaviors—from Justin Volpe and his police friends who sodomized Abner Louima, to the military brass who looked the other way when cadets at the Air Force Academy were routinely sexually assaulting female cadets, to the codes of silence on campus following any number of hazing deaths. And those who do stand up and challenge the culture of male entitlement—the whistleblowers—are often so vilified, ostracized from their communities, and threatened with retaliation that they might as well join the Witness Protection Program. Parents who stick up for their victimized kids can find themselves shunned by their neighbors and former friends; administrators who try and discipline perpetrators often face a wall of opposition and lawsuits—especially if the perpetrators happen to be athletes on winning teams.

"Our Guys"

90 A startling—and extreme—example of how these three cultures play out in Guyland is the infamous sexual assault in Glen Ridge, New Jersey, in 1989. It is well documented in the bestselling book *Our Guys* by Bernard Lefkowitz and also in a made-for-TV movie. I use this example, and others like it, not because the crime itself is typical—thankfully it is not—but because the cultural dynamics that enable the most extreme and egregious offenses in Guyland are equally present even in the more everyday aspects of guys' lives. We need to take a close look at the kind of culture that allows this to happen even once. Sociologists often point to extreme examples of phenomena, as if to say: If we can see such processes at work even here, then surely we can see them at work in more quotidian events. And, indeed, the response—by the criminals, their peers, and the larger community—was typical of the social dynamics that sustain and support Guyland as a whole.

In the spring of 1989, thirteen high-status athletes at Glen Ridge High School lured a 17-year-old "slightly retarded" girl into one of the guys' basement. Chairs had been arranged, theater style, around a sofa in the middle of the room. Most of the boys arranged themselves on the chairs, while a few led the girl to the sofa and got her to perform oral sex on one of the highest-status boys.

As the event began to unfold, one sophomore noticed "puzzlement and confusion" in the girl's eyes, and turned to his friend and said, "Let's get out of here." Another senior baseball player, age 17, said he started to "feel queasy" and thought to himself, "I don't belong here." He and another baseball player got up to leave. On the way out, he said to another guy, "It's wrong. C'mon with me." But the other guy stayed. In all, six of the young men left the scene, while seven others—six seniors and one junior—remained in the basement. All of them were 17 or 18 years old.

As the girl was forced to continue giving oral sex to the boy, the other boys laughed, yelled encouragement to their friends, and derisively shouted, "You whore!" One guy got a baseball bat, which he forced into her vagina. As he did this (and followed with a broom handle), the girl heard one boy say, "Stop. You're hurting her." But another voice chimed in, "Do it more."

Later, the girl remembered that the boys were all laughing, while she was crying. When they finished, they warned her not to tell anyone and she left the house. The event concluded with an athletic ritual of togetherness as the boys stood in a circle, clasping "one hand on top of the other," Lefkowtiz writes, "all their hands together, like a basketball team on the sidelines at the end of a time-out."

95 In the eyes of their friends, their parents, and their community, these guys were not pathological deviants. They were all high-status athletes, well respected in their schools and in their communities. They were not crazed psychotics, they were regular guys. Our guys.

So, too, were the football players at Wellington C. Mepham High School, a well-funded, well-heeled high school in a relatively affluent Long Island neighborhood, who participated in another extreme example. When students returned from vacation in the fall of 2004, they were confronted by rumors of a terrifying hazing incident that had taken place during the summer. While away at a training camp in Pennsylvania in August, three varsity members of Mepham's football team sexually abused three young teammates in a hazing ritual. According to the police report, the boys were sodomized with pine cones, broom handles, and golf balls, all of which had been coated with Mineral Ice, a Ben-Gay–like cream that produces intense menthol-induced coolness, and is typically used to treat sore muscles. When applied to moist or broken skin, or used internally, it causes severe pain. Thirteen other players watched, but did nothing.

Once again, the perpetrators were respected members of the community—good boys, Boy Scouts, pillars of the tight-knit community. Just regular guys.

When I've described the sexual assaults in Glen Ridge to young men around the country, they instantly and steadfastly agree: those guys who actually did it are thugs, and their behavior is indefensible. "C'mon, man," said one, "they should be charged with criminal assault and go to jail. QED." And they show equal contempt for the guys who stayed, watched, and did nothing. "What is up with that?" another said. "It's just wrong."

When we consider the guys who left, many of the guys I've spoken with assure me that they too would have left at the first sign of the assault. Self-congratulation comes easily and quickly. "No way am I staying there," one guy said. "At the first sign of trouble, I'm gone," said another. Other guys readily agree. All seem to identify with the guys who left, who refused to participate. And they're all feeling pretty good about it until a female student invariably asks, "Yeah, but did they call the police? Did they tell anybody?"

100 No. No one called the police. No one told a teacher or an administrator. No one told their parents. No one told *anybody.*

And the next day, *everyone* at Glen Ridge High School knew what had happened. Everyone knew, that is, that a bunch of guys had "had sex with" that particular girl and other guys had watched. And she let them! And that next day not one student told their parents, their teachers, their administrators. Not one student—male or female—called the police to report the assault.

In fact, it wasn't until two weeks later that the girl herself finally told her parents what had happened to her, and why she was crying all the time, unable to sleep and eat, and why she was so bruised and sore "down there."

In the Mepham case, the assault was perpetrated by three guys while thirteen other players watched. They did not intervene to stop this cruel and horrific assault on their teammates. They did not tell the coaches, their parents, school administrators, or the police. They did nothing. "Of course, we heard about it instantly," one Mepham graduate told me. "Everybody did. Man, it was like the only thing everyone was talking about the next day. 'Hey, did you hear what went down at the football camp?'"

It's those *other* guys who illustrate the second cultural dynamic of Guyland—the *culture of silence.* And not only did none of the bystanders in Glen Ridge or Mepham intervene, but none told a parent or a teacher, or reported the assault to the police. As the case played out in Glen Ridge for six whole years the guys consistently refused to "turn" on their friends and provide incriminating evidence.

105 The motto of Guyland is "Bros Before Hos." One remains steadfastly loyal to your guy friends, your bros, and one never even considers siding with women, the hos, against a brother. It is the guys to whom your primary allegiance must always be offered, and for many that may even extend to abetting a crime. Anything less is a betrayal of Guyland.

No one is immune to the culture of silence. Every single kid is culpable. If you still don't think this has anything to do with you, ask yourself what you would have done. If you think this has nothing to do with your son, ask him what he would do if he heard about such a thing. Then ask him when was the last time he actually *did* hear about such a thing.

The culture of silence is the culture of complicity. The bystanders may think that they withdraw their support—by turning away, leaving the scene, or just standing stoically by—but their silence reinforces the behaviors anyway. It's as strong an unwritten code as the police department's famed "blue wall of silence," or the Mafia's infamous rule of "omerta," or the secret rituals of the Masons. Breaking the silence is treason, worse, perhaps, than the activities themselves.

The relationship between perpetrators and bystanders is crucial in Guyland. Peer loyalty shields the perpetrators, and helps us explain the question of numbers. Despite the fact that the overwhelming majority of guys do not sexually assault their teammates, gang rape college women at fraternity parties, or indulge in acts of unspeakable cruelty, they also do nothing to stop it.

Most bystanders are relatively decent guys. But they are anything but "innocent." The bystander comforts himself with the illusion "this isn't about me. I've never bullied anyone." This is similar to the reaction of white people when confronted with discussions of racism or sexism on campus. "It's not about me! My family didn't own slaves." Or "I never raped anyone. These discussions about sexual violence are not about me."

110 It *is* about them. The perpetrators could not do what they do without the amoral avoidance and silence of the bystanders. In a way, the violence is done *for* them—and so it is most definitely *about* them.

When the story about the Mepham football hazing broke, and the national media descended on sleepy Bellmore, Long Island, the community reacted as one—it defended the players and the coaches who denied any responsibility. Parents of the boys who had been abused were threatened with death if they pressed charges. "It's simple," read one letter to a victim's parents. "Keep your mouth shut and nothing will happen to your family." Campus rallies were held for the team, both the coaches and the players.

When the school administration took the drastic (and courageous) step of canceling the entire football season, Mepham students felt that *they* had been victimized by an overzealous superintendent. "I don't see why we should all be penalized for the actions of a few football players," commented one girl.

Not everyone participates in this culture of protection, of course. Recall the case of Spur Posse a few years ago. The Southern California clique of young men kept tallies of the girls they had had sex with (many of the girls, some as young as 11, had been coerced). When the boys were exposed as sexual predators and rapists, their fathers seemed almost proud. "That's my boy!" said one. "If these girls are going to give it away, my boy is going to take it," said another. The mothers, however, were surprised, even shocked. They wanted to talk to their sons, find out how such a thing was possible. So the culture of protection is not uniform; there are gender gaps—and these gaps between mothers and fathers will form a crucial part of our discussion of what we, as a society, can do to make Guyland a more hospitable place.

The Guy Code keeps young men from venturing beyond the borders of Guyland. The good guys are silenced and the predators and bullies are encouraged. What we need, of course, is exactly the reverse—to empower the silent guys to disable the predators, to facilitate young men's entry into an adulthood propelled by both energy and ethics, and animated by both courage and compassion.

115 Now that we have a sense of the philosophical principles that underlie Guyland, we need to see the way the Guy Code operates in the lives of young men in America today. The next few chapters will explore the spaces they call home much as an anthropologist might explore a different culture—examining its terrain, its economy, its rites and rituals, its belief systems and cultural practices, and the behaviors and attitudes that support and sustain it.

The Other America

REV. MARTIN LUTHER KING, JR.

Grosse Pointe High School—March 14, 1968

1 Dr. Meserve, Bishop Emrich, my dear friend Congressman Conyers, ladies and gentlemen.

I need not pause to say how very delighted I am to be here tonight and to have the great privilege of discussing with you some of the vital issues confronting our nation and confronting the world. It is always a very rich and rewarding experience when I can take a brief break from the day-to-day demands of our struggle for freedom and human dignity and discuss the issues involved in that struggle with concerned people of good will all over our nation and all over the world, and I certainly want to express my deep personal appreciation to you for inviting me to occupy this significant platform.

I want to discuss the race problem tonight and I want to discuss it very honestly. I still believe that freedom is the bonus you receive for telling the truth. Ye shall know the truth and the truth shall set you free. And I do not see how we will ever solve the turbulent problem of race confronting our nation until **there** is an honest confrontation with it and a willing search for the truth and a willingness to admit the truth when we discover it. And so I want to use as a title for my lecture tonight, "The Other America." And I use this title because there are literally two Americas. Every city in our country has this kind of dualism, this schizophrenia, split at so many parts, and so every city ends up being two cities rather than one. There are two Americas. One America is beautiful for situation. In this America, millions of people have the milk of prosperity and the honey of equality flowing before them. This America is the **habitat** of millions of people who have food and material necessities for their bodies, culture and education for their minds, freedom **and** human dignity for their spirits. In this America children grow up in the sunlight of opportunity. But there is another America. This other America has a daily ugliness about it that transforms the buoyancy of hope into the fatigue of despair. In this other America, thousands and thousands of people, men in particular walk the streets in search for jobs that do not exist. In this other America, millions of people are forced to live in vermin-filled, distressing housing conditions where they do not have the privilege of having wall-to-wall carpeting, but all too often, they end up with wall-to-wall rats and roaches. Almost forty percent of the Negro families of America live in sub-standard housing conditions. In this other America, thousands of young people are deprived of an opportunity to get an adequate education. Every year thousands finish high school reading at a seventh, eighth and sometimes ninth grade level. Not because they're dumb, not because they don't have the native intelligence, but because the schools are so inadequate, so over-crowded, so devoid of quality, so segregated if you will, that the best in these minds can never come out. Probably the most critical problem in the other America is the economic problem. There are so many other people in the other America who can never make ends meet because their incomes are far too low if they have incomes, and their jobs are so devoid of quality. And so in this other America, unemployment is a reality and under-employment is a reality. (I'll just wait until our friend can have her say) (applause). I'll just wait until things are restored and … everybody talks about law and order. (applause)

Now before I was so rudely interrupted … (applause), and I might say that it was my understanding that we're going to have a question and answer period, and if anybody disagrees with me, you will have the privilege, the opportunity to raise a question if you think I'm a traitor, then you'll have an opportunity to ask me about my traitorness and we will give you that opportunity.

5 Now let me get back to the point that I was trying to bring out about the economic problem. And that is one of the most critical problems that we face in America today. We find in the other America unemployment constantly rising to astronomical proportions and black people generally find themselves living in a literal depression. All too often when there is mass unemployment in the black community, it's referred to as a social problem and when there is mass unemployment in the white community, it's referred to as a depression. But there is no basic difference. The fact is, that the negro faces a literal depression all over the U.S. The unemployment rate on the basis of statistics from the labor department is about 8.8 percent in the black community. But these statistics only take under consideration individuals who were once in the labor market, or individuals who go to employment offices to seek employment. But they do not take under consideration the thousands of people who have given up, who have lost motivation, the thousands of people who have had so many doors closed in their faces that they feel defeated and they no longer go out and look for jobs, the thousands who've come to feel that life is a long and desolate corridor with no exit signs. These people are considered the discouraged and when you add the discouraged to the individuals who can't be calculated through statistics in the unemployment category, the unemployment rate in the negro community probably goes to 16 or 17 percent. And among black youth, it is in some communities as high as 40 and 45 percent. But the problem of unemployment is not the only problem. There is the problem of under-

employment, and there are thousands and thousand, I would say millions of people in the negro community who are poverty stricken—not because they are not working but because they receive wages so low that they cannot begin to function in the main stream of the economic life of our nation. Most of the poverty stricken people of America are persons who are working every day and they end up getting part-time wages for full-time work. So the vast majority of negroes in America find themselves perishing on a lonely island of poverty in the midst of a vast ocean of material prosperity. This has caused a great deal of bitterness. It has caused a great deal of agony. It has caused ache and anguish. It has caused great despair, and we have seen the angered expressions of this despair and this bitterness in the violent rebellions that have taken place in cities all over our country. Now I think my views on non-violence are pretty generally known. I still believe that non-violence is the most potent weapon available to the negro in his struggle for justice and freedom in the U.S.

Now let me relieve you a bit. I've been in the struggle a long time now, (applause) and I've conditioned myself to some things that are much more painful than discourteous people not allowing you to speak, so if they feel that they can discourage me, they'll be up here all night.

Now I wanted to say something about the fact that we have lived over these last two or three summers with agony and we have seen our cities going up in flames. And I would be the first to say that I am still committed to militant, powerful, massive, non-violence as the most potent weapon in grappling with the problem from a direct action point of view. I'm absolutely convinced that a riot merely intensifies the fears of the white community while relieving the guilt. And I feel that we must always work with an effective, powerful weapon and method that brings about tangible results. But it is not enough for me to stand before you tonight and condemn riots. It would be morally irresponsible for me to do that without, at the same time, condemning the contingent, intolerable conditions that exist in our society. These conditions are the things that cause individuals to feel that they have no other alternative than to engage in violent rebellions to get attention. And I must say tonight that a riot is the language of the unheard. And what is it America has failed to hear? It has failed to hear that the plight of the negro poor has worsened over the last twelve or fifteen years. It has failed to hear that the promises of freedom and justice have not been met. And it has failed to hear that large segments of white society are more concerned about tranquility and the status quo than about justice and humanity.

Now every year about this time, our newspapers and our televisions and people generally start talking about the long hot summer ahead. What always bothers me is that the long hot summer has always been preceded by a long cold winter. And the great problem is that the nation has not used its winters creatively enough to develop the program, to develop the kind of massive acts of concern that will bring about a solution to the problem. And so we must still face the fact that our nation's summers of riots are caused by our nations winters of delay. As long as justice is postponed we always stand on the verge of these darker nights of social disruption. The question now, is whether America is prepared to do something massively, affirmatively and forthrightly about the great problem we face in the area of race and the problem which can bring the curtain of doom down on American civilization if it is not solved. And I would like to talk for the next few minutes about some of the things that must be done if we are to solve this problem.

The first thing I would like to mention is that there must be a recognition on the part of everybody in this nation that America is still a racist country. Now however unpleasant that sounds, it is the truth. And we will never solve the problem of racism until there is a recognition of the fact that racism still stands at the center of so much of our nation and we must see racism for what it is. It is the nymph of an inferior people. It is the notion that one group has all of the knowledge, all of the insights, all of the purity, all of the work, all of the dignity. And another group is worthless, on a lower level of humanity, inferior. To put it in philosophical language, racism is not based on some empirical generalization which, after some studies, would come to conclusion that these people are behind because of environmental conditions. Racism is based on an ontological affirmation. It is the notion that the very being of a people is inferior. And their ultimate logic of racism is genocide. Hitler was a very sick man. He was one of the great tragedies of history. But he was very honest. He took his racism to its logical conclusion. The minute his racism caused him to sickly feel and go about saying that there was something innately inferior about the Jew he ended up killing six million Jews. The ultimate logic of racism is genocide, and if one says that one is not good enough to have a job that is a solid quality job, if one is not good enough to have access to public accommodations, if one is not good enough to have the right to vote, if one is not good enough to live next door to him, if one is not good enough to marry his daughter because of his race. Then at that moment that person is saying that that person who is not good to do all of this is not fit to exist or to live. And that is the ultimate logic of racism. And we've got to see that this still exists in American society. And until it is removed, there will be people walking the streets of live and living in their humble dwellings feeling that they are nobody, feeling that they have no dignity and feeling that they are not respected. The first thing that must be on the agenda of our nation is to get rid of racism.

10 Secondly, we've got to get rid of two or three myths that still pervade our nation. One is the myth of time. I'm sure you've heard this notion. It is the notion that only time can solve the problem of racial injustice. And I've heard it from many sincere people. They've said to the negro and/to his allies in the white community you should slow up, you're pushing things too fast, only time can solve the problem. And if you'll just be nice and patient and continue to pray, in a hundred or two hundred years the problem will work itself out. There is an answer to that myth. It is the time is neutral. It can be used either constructively or destructively. And I'm sad to say to you tonight I'm absolutely convinced that the forces of ill will in our nation, the forces on the wrong side in our nation, the extreme righteous of our nation have often used time much more effectively than the forces of good will and it may well be that we may have to repent in this generation not merely for the vitriolic words of the bad people who will say bad things in a meeting like this or who will bomb a church in Birmingham, Alabama, but for the appalling silence and indifference of the good people who sit around and say wait on time. Somewhere we must come to see that human progress never rolls in on the wheels of inevitability, it comes through the tireless efforts and the persistent work of dedicated individuals who are willing to be co-workers with God and without this hard work time itself becomes an ally of the primitive forces of social stagnation. And so we must always help time and realize that the time is always right to do right.

Now there is another myth and that is the notion that legislation can't solve the problem that you've got to change the heart and naturally I believe in changing the heart. I happen to be a Baptist preacher and that puts me in the heart changing business and Sunday after Sunday I'm preaching about conversion and the need for the new birth and re-generation. I believe that there's something wrong with human nature. I believe in original sin not in terms of the historical event but as the mythological category to explain the universality of evil, so I'm honest enough to see the gone-wrongness of human nature so naturally I'm not against changing the heart and I do feel that that is the half truth involved here, that there is some truth in the whole question of changing the heart. We are not going to have the kind of society that we should have until the white person treats the negro right—not because the law says it but because it's natural because it's right and because the black man is the white man's brother. I'll be the first to say that we will never have a truly **integrated** society, a truly colorless society until men and women are obedient to the unenforceable. But after saying that, let me point out the other side. It may be true that morality cannot be legislated, but behavior can be regulated. It may be true that the law cannot change the heart but it can restrain the heartless. It may be true that the law can't make a man love me, but it can restrain him from lynching me, and I think that's pretty important also.

And so while legislation may not change the hearts of men, it does change the habits of men when it's vigorously enforced and when you change the habits of people pretty soon attitudes begin to be changed and people begin to see that they can do things that fears caused them to feel that they could never do. And I say that there's a need still for strong civil rights legislation in various areas. There's legislation in Congress right now dealing with the whole question of housing and equal administration of justice and these things are very important **for** I submit to you tonight that there is no more dangerous development in our nation than the constant building up of predominantly negro central cities ringed by white suburbs. This will do nothing but invite social disaster. And this problem has to be dealt with—some through legislation, some through education, but it has to be dealt with in a very concrete and meaningful manner.

Now let me get back to my point. I'm going to finish my speech. I've been trying to think about what I'm going to preach about tomorrow down to Central Methodist Church in the Lenten series and I think **I'll** use as the text, "Father forgive them for they know not what they do."

I want to deal with another myth briefly which concerns me and I want to talk about it very honestly and that is over-reliance on the bootstrap philosophy. Now certainly it's very important for people to engage in self-help programs and do all they can to lift themselves by their own bootstraps. Now I'm not talking against that at all. I think there is a great deal that the black people of this country must do for themselves and that nobody else can do for them. And we must see the other side of this question. I remember the other day I was on a plane and a man starting talking with me and he said I'm sympathetic toward what you're trying to do, but I just feel that you people don't do enough for yourself and then he went on to say that my problem is, my concern is, that I know of other ethnic groups, many of the ethnic groups that came to this country and they had problems just as negroes and yet they did the job for themselves, they lifted themselves by their own bootstraps. Why is it that negroes can't do that? And I looked at him and I tried to talk as understanding as possible but I said to him, it does not help the negro for unfeeling, sensitive white people to say that other ethnic groups that came to the country maybe a hundred or a hundred and fifty years voluntarily have gotten ahead of them and he was brought here in chains involuntarily almost three hundred and fifty years ago. I said it doesn't help him to be told that and then I went on to say to this gentlemen that he failed to recognize that no other ethnic group has been enslaved on American soil. Then I had to go on to say to him that you failed to realize that America made the black man's color a stigma. Something that he couldn't change. Not only was the color a stigma, but even linguistic then stigmatic conspired against the black man so that his color was thought of as something very evil. If you open Roget's Thesaurus and notice the synonym for black you'll find about a hundred and twenty and most of them represent something dirty, smut, degrading, low, and when you turn to the synonym for white, about one hundred and thirty, all of them represent something high, pure, chaste. You go right down that list. And so in the language a white life is a little better than a black life. Just follow. If somebody goes wrong in the family, we don't call him a white sheep we call him a black sheep. And then if you block somebody from getting somewhere you don't say they've been whiteballed, you say they've been blackballed. And just go down the line. It's not whitemail it's blackmail. I tell you this to seriously say that the nation made the black man's color a stigma and then I had to say to my friend on the plane another thing that is often forgotten in this country. That nobody, no ethnic group has completely lifted itself by it own bootstraps. I can never forget that the black man was free from the bondage of physical slavery in 1863. He wasn't given any land to make that freedom meaningful after being held in slavery 244 years. And it was like keeping a man in prison for many many years and then coming to see that he is not guilty of the crime for which he was convicted. Alright good night and God bless you.

15 And I was about to say that to free, to have freed the negro from slavery without doing anything to get him started in life on a sound economic footing, it was almost like freeing a man who had been in prison many years and you had discovered that he was unjustly convicted of, that he was innocent of the crime for which he was convicted and you go up to him and say now you're free, but you don't give him any bus fare to get to town or you don't give him any money to buy some clothes to put on his back or to get started in life again. Every code of jurisprudence would rise up against it. This is the very thing that happened to the black man in America. And then when we look at it even deeper than this, it becomes more ironic. We're reaping the harvest of this failure today.

While America refused to do anything for the black man at that point, during that very period, the nation, through an act of Congress, was giving away millions of acres of land in the west and the mid-west, which meant that it was willing to under gird its white peasants from Europe with an economic floor. Not only did they give the land, **they** built land grant colleges for them to learn how to farm. Not only that it provided county agents to further their expertise in farming and went beyond this and came to the point of providing low interest rates for these persons so that they could mechanize their farms, and today many of these persons are being paid millions of dollars a year in federal subsidies not to farm and these are so often the very people saying to the black man that he must lift himself by his own bootstraps. I can never think … Senator Eastland, incidentally, who says this all the time gets a hundred and twenty-five thousand dollars a year, not to farm on various areas of his plantation down in Mississippi. And yet he feels that we must do everything for ourselves. Well that appears to me to be a kind of socialism for the rich and rugged hard individualistic capitalism for the poor.

Now let me say two other things and I'm going to rush on. One, I want to say that if we're to move ahead and solve this problem we must re-order our national priorities. Today we're spending almost thirty-five billion dollars a year to fight what I consider an unjust, ill-considered, evil, costly, unwinable war at Viet Nam. I wish I had time to go into the dimensions of this. But I must say that the war in Viet Nam is playing havoc with our Domestic destinies. That war has torn up the Geneva accord, it has strengthened, it has substituted.. . (interruption) … alright if you want to speak, I'll let you come down and speak and I'll wait. You can give your Viet Nam speech now listen to mine. Come right on.

Speaker: Ladies and gentlemen, my name is Joseph McLawtern, communications technician, U.S. Navy, United States of America and I fought for freedom I didn't fight for communism, traitors and I didn't fight to be sold down the drain. Not by Romney, Cavanagh, Johnson—nobody, nobody's going to sell me down the drain.

Alright, thank you very much. I just want to say in response to that, that there are those of us who oppose the war in Viet Nam. I feel like opposing it for many reasons. Many of them are moral reasons but one basic reason is that we love our boys who are fighting there and we just want them to come back home. But I don't have time to go into the history and the development of the war in Viet Nam. I happen to be a pacifist but if I had had to make a decision about fighting a war against Hitler, I may have temporarily given up my pacifism and taken up arms. But nobody is to compare what is happening in Viet Nam today with that. I'm convinced that it is clearly an unjust war and it's doing so many things—not only on the domestic scene, it is carrying the whole world closer to nuclear annihilation. And so I've found it necessary to take a stand against the war in Viet Nam and I appreciate Bishop Emrich's question and I must answer it by saying that for me the tuitus cannot be divided. It's nice for me to talk about … it's alright to talk about integrated schools and integrated lunch counters which I will continue to work for, but I think it would be rather absurd for me to work for integrated schools and not be concerned about the survival of the world in which to integrate.

The other thing is, that I have been working too long and too hard now against segregated public accommodations to end up at this stage of my life segregating my moral concern. I must make it clear. For me justice is indivisible. Injustice anywhere is a threat to justice everywhere.

20 Now for the question of hurting civil rights. I think the war in Viet Nam hurt civil rights much more than my taking a stand against the war. And I could point out so many things to say that … a reporter asked me sometime ago when I first took a strong stand against the war didn't I feel that I would have to reverse my position because so many people disagreed, and people who once had respect for me wouldn't have respect, and he went on to say that I hear that it's hurt the budget of your organization and don't you think that you have to get in line more with the administration's policy … and of course those were very lonely days when I first started speaking out and not many people were speaking out but now I have a lot of company and it's not as lonesome now. But anyway, I had to say to the reporter, I'm sorry sir but you don't know me. I'm not a consensus leader and I do not determine what is right and wrong by looking at the budget of the Southern Christian Leadership Conference or by kind of taking a look at a gallop poll and getting the expression of the majority opinion. Ultimately, a genuine leader is not a succor for consensus but a mold of consensus. And on some positions cowardice ask the question is it safe? Expediency asks the question is it politics? Vanity asks the question is it popular? The conscience asks the question is it right? And there comes a time when one must take a position that is neither safe nor politics nor popular but he must do it because conscience tells him it is right.

Now the time is passing and I'm not going to … I was going into the need for direct action to dramatize and call attention to the gulf between promise and fulfillment. I've been searching for a long time for an alternative to riots on the one hand and timid supplication for justice on the other and I think that alternative is found in militant massive non-violence. I'll wait until the question period before going into the Washington campaign. But let me say that it has been my experience in these years that I've been in the struggle for justice, that things just don't happen until the issue is dramatized in a massive direct-action way. I never will forget when we came through Washington in 1964, in December coming from Oslo. I stopped by to see President Johnson. We talked about a lot of things and we finally got to the point of talking about voting rights. The President was concerned about voting, but he said Martin, I can't get this through in this session of Congress. We can't get a voting rights bill, he said because there are two or three other things that I feel that we've got to get through and they're going to benefit negroes as much as anything. One was the education bill and something else. And then he went on to say that if I push a voting rights bill now, I'll lose the support of seven congressmen that I sorely need for the particular things that I had and we just can't get it. Well, I went on to say to the President that I felt that we had to do something about it and two weeks later we started a movement in Selma, Alabama. We started dramatizing the issue of the denial of the right to vote and I submit to you that three months later as a result of that Selma movement, the same President who said to me that we could not get a voting rights bill in that session of Congress was on the television singing through a speaking voice "we shall overcome" and calling for the passage of a voting rights bill and I could go on and on to show … and we did get a voting rights bill in that session of Congress. Now, I could go on to give many other examples to show that it just doesn't come about without pressure and this is what we plan to do in Washington. We aren't planning to close down Washington, we aren't planning to close down Congress. This isn't anywhere in our plans. We are planning to dramatize the issue to the point that poor people in this nation will have to be seen and will not be invisible.

Now let me finally say something in the realm of the spirit and then I'm going to take my seat. Let me say finally, that in the midst of the hollering and in the midst of the discourtesy tonight, we got to come to see that however much we dislike it, the destinies of white and black America are tied together. Now the races don't understand this apparently. But our destinies are tied together. And somehow, we must all learn to live together as brothers in this country or we're all going to perish together as fools. Our destinies are tied together. Whether we like it or not culturally and otherwise, every white person is a little bit negro and every negro is a little bit white. Our language, our music, our material prosperity and even our food are an amalgam of black and white, so there can be no separate black path to power and fulfillment that does not intersect white routes and there can ultimately be no separate white path to power and fulfillment short of social disaster without recognizing the necessity of sharing that power with black aspirations for freedom and human dignity. We must come to see … yes we do need each other, the black man needs the white man to save him from his fear and the white man needs the black man to free him from his guilt.

John Donne was right. No man is an island and the tide that fills every man is a piece of the continent, a part of the main. And he goes on toward the end to say, "any man's death diminishes me because I'm involved in mankind. Therefore, it's not to know for whom the bell tolls, it tolls for thee." Somehow we must come to see that in this pluralistic, interrelated society we are all tied together in a single garment of destiny, caught in an inescapable network of mutuality. And by working with determination and realizing that power must be shared, I think we can solve this problem, and may I say in conclusion that our goal is freedom and I believe that we're going to get there. It's going to be more difficult from here on in but I believe we're going to get there because however much she strays away from it, the goal of America is freedom and Our destiny is tied up with the destiny of America. Before the Pilgrim fathers landed at Plymouth we were here. Before Jefferson etched across the pages of history the majestic words of the Declaration of Independence we were here. Before the beautiful words of the Star Spangled Banner were written we were here. And for more than two centuries our forbearers labored here without wages. They made cotton King, they built the homes of their masters in the midst of the most humiliating and oppressive conditions and yet out of a bottomless vitality they continued to grow and develop and if the inexpressible cruelties of slavery couldn't stop us, the opposition that we now face including the white backlash will surely fail.

We are going to win our freedom because both the sacred heritage of our nation and the eternal will of the Almighty God are embodied in our echoing demands. So however difficult it is during this period, however difficult it is to continue to live with the agony and the continued existence of racism, however difficult it is to live amidst the constant hurt, the constant insult and the constant disrespect, I can still sing we shall overcome. We shall overcome because the arc of the moral universe is long but it bends towards justice.

25 We shall overcome because Carlisle is right. "No lie can live forever." We shall overcome because William Cullen Bryant is right. "Truth crushed to earth will rise again." We shall overcome because James Russell Lowell is right. "Truth forever on the scaffold, wrong forever on the throne." Yet that scaffold sways the future. We shall overcome because the Bible is right. "You shall reap

what you sow." With this faith we will be able to hew out of the mountain of despair, a stone of hope. With this faith we will be able to transform the jangling discords of our nation into a beautiful symphony of brotherhood. With this faith we will be able to speed up the day when all of God's children all over this nation—black men and white men, Jews and Gentiles, Protestants and Catholics will be able to join hands and sing in the words of the old negro spiritual, "Free at Last, Free at Last, Thank God Almighty, We are Free At Last."

Credit

"The Other America" Speech by Rev. Martin Luther King, Jr. Grosse Pointe High School, March 14, 1968.

Learning to Read

MALCOLM X

It was because of my letters that I happened to stumble upon starting to acquire some kind of a homemade education.

I became increasingly frustrated at not being able to express what I wanted to convey in letters that I wrote, especially those to Mr. Elijah Muhammad. In the street, I had been the most articulate hustler out there—I had commanded attention when I said something. But now, trying to write simple English, I not only wasn't articulate, I wasn't even functional. How would I sound writing in slang, the way I would *say* it, something such as, "Look, daddy, let me pull your coat about a cat, Elijah Muhammad—"

Many who today hear me somewhere in person, or on television, or those who read something I've said, will think I went to school far beyond the eighth grade. This impression is due entirely to my prison studies.

It had really begun back in the Charlestown Prison, when Bimbi first made me feel envy of his stock of knowledge. Bimbi had always taken charge of any conversations he was in, and I had tried to emulate him. But every book I picked up had few sentences which didn't contain anywhere from one to nearly all of the words that might as well have been in Chinese. When I just skipped those words, of course, I really ended up with little idea of what the book said. So I had come to the Norfolk Prison Colony still going through only book-reading motions. Pretty soon, I would have quit even these motions, unless I had received the motivation that I did.

5 I saw that the best thing I could do was get hold of a dictionary—to study, to learn some words. I was lucky enough to reason also that I should try to improve my penmanship. It was sad. I couldn't even write in a straight line. It was both ideas together that moved me to request a dictionary along with some tablets and pencils from the Norfolk Prison Colony school.

I spent two days just riffling uncertainly through the dictionary's pages. I'd never realized so many words existed! I didn't know *which* words I needed to learn. Finally, just to start some kind of action, I began copying.

In my slow, painstaking, ragged handwriting, I copied into my tablet everything printed on that first page, down to the punctuation marks.

I believe it took me a day. Then, aloud, I read back, to myself, everything I'd written on the tablet. Over and over, aloud, to myself, I read my own handwriting.

I woke up the next morning, thinking about those words—immensely proud to realize that not only had I written so much at one time, but I'd written words that I never knew were in the world. Moreover, with a little effort, I also could remember what many of these words meant. I reviewed the words whose meanings I didn't remember. Funny thing, from the dictionary first page right now, that "aardvark" springs to my mind. The dictionary had a picture of it, a longtailed, long-eared, burrowing African mammal, which lives off termites caught by sticking out its tongue as an anteater does for ants.

10 I was so fascinated that I went on—I copied the dictionary's next page. And the same experience came when I studied that. With every succeeding page, I also learned of people and places and events from history. Actually the dictionary is like a miniature encyclopedia. Finally the dictionary's A section had filled a whole tablet—and I went on into the B's. That was the way I started copying what eventually became the entire dictionary. It went a lot faster after so much practice helped me to pick up handwriting speed. Between what I wrote in my tablet, and writing letters, during the rest of my time in prison I would guess I wrote a million words.

I suppose it was inevitable that as my word-base broadened, I could for the first time pick up a book and read and now begin to understand what the book was saying. Anyone who has read a great deal can imagine the new world that opened. Let me tell you something: from then until I left that prison, in every free moment I had, if I was not reading in the library, I was reading on my bunk. You couldn't have gotten me out of books with a wedge. Between Mr. Muhammad's teachings, my correspondence, my visitors, ... and my reading of books, months passed without my even thinking about being imprisoned. In fact, up to then, I never had been so truly free in my life.

The Norfolk Prison Colony's library was in the school building. A variety of classes was taught there by instructors who came from such places as Harvard and Boston universities. The weekly debates between inmate teams were also held in the school building. You would be astonished to know how worked up convict debaters and audiences would get over subjects like "Should Babies Be Fed Milk?"

Available on the prison library's shelves were books on just about every general subject. Much of the big private collection that Parkhurst[1] had willed to the prison was still in crates and boxes in the back of the library—thousands of old books. Some of them looked ancient: covers faded, oldtime parchment-looking binding. Parkhurst ... seemed to have been principally interested in history and religion. He had the money and the special interest to have a lot of books that you wouldn't have in a general circulation. Any college library would have been lucky to get that collection.

As you can imagine, especially in a prison where there was heavy emphasis on rehabilitation, an inmate was smiled upon if he demonstrated an unusually intense interest in books. There was a sizable number of well-read inmates, especially the popular debaters. Some were said by many to be practically walking encyclopedias. They were almost celebrities. No university would ask any student to devour literature as I did when this new world opened to me, of being able to read and *understand.*

15 I read more in my room than in the library itself. An inmate who was known to read a lot could check out more than the permitted maximum number of books. I preferred reading in the total isolation of my own room.

When I had progressed to really serious reading, every night at about ten P.M. I would be outraged with the "lights out." It always seemed to catch me right in the middle of something engrossing.

Fortunately, right outside my door was a corridor light that cast a glow into my room. The glow was enough to read by, once my eyes adjusted to it. So when "lights out" came, I would sit on the floor where I could continue reading in that glow.

At one-hour intervals at night guards paced past every room. Each time I heard the approaching footsteps, I jumped into bed and feigned sleep. And as soon as the guard passed, I got back out of bed onto the floor area of that light-glow, where I would read for another fifty-eight minutes until the guard approached again. That went on until three or four every morning. Three or four hours of sleep a night was enough for me. Often in the years in the streets I had slept less than that.

The teachings of Mr. Muhammad stressed how history had been "whitened"—when white men had written history books, the black man simply had been left out. Mr. Muhammad couldn't have said anything that would have struck me much harder. I had never forgotten how when my class, me and all of those whites, had studied seventh-grade United States history back in Mason, the history of the Negro had been covered in one paragraph, and the teacher had gotten a big laugh with his joke, "'Negroes' feet are so big that when they walk, they leave a hole in the ground."

20 This is one reason why Mr. Muhammad's teachings spread so swiftly all over the United States, among *all* Negroes, whether or not they became followers of Mr. Muhammad. The teachings ring true—to every Negro. You can hardly

show me a black adult in America—or a white one, for that matter—who knows from the history books anything like the truth about the black man's role. In my own case, once I heard of the "glorious history of the black man," I took special pains to hunt in the library for books that would inform me on details about black history.

I can remember accurately the very first set of books that really impressed me. I have since bought that set of books and I have it at home for my children to read as they grow up. It's called *Wonders of the World.* It's full of pictures of archeological finds, statues that depict, usually, non-European people.

I found books like Will Durant's *Story of Civilization.* I read H. G. Wells' *Outline of History. Souls of Black Folk* by W. E. B. Du Bois gave me a glimpse into the black people's history before they came to this country. Carter G. Woodson's *Negro History* opened my eyes about black empires before the black slave was brought to the United States, and the early Negro struggles for freedom.

J. A. Rogers' three volumes of *Sex and Race* told about race-mixing before Christ's time; and Aesop being a black man who told fables; about Egypt's Pharaohs; about the great Coptic Christian Empire;[2] about Ethiopia, the earth's oldest continuous black civilization, as China is the oldest continuous civilization.

Mr. Muhammad's teaching about how the white man had been created led me to *Findings in Genetics,* by Gregor Mendel. (The dictionary's G section was where I had learned what "genetics" meant.) I really studied this book by the Austrian monk. Reading it over and over, especially certain sections, helped me to understand that if you started with a black man, a white man could be produced; but starting with a white man, you never could produce a black man—because the white chromosome is recessive. And since no one disputes that there was but one Original Man, the conclusion is clear.

25 During the last year or so, in the *New York Times,* Arnold Toynbee used the word "bleached" in describing the white man. His words were: "White (i.e., bleached) human beings of North European origin ..." Toynbee also referred to the European geographic area as only a peninsula of Asia. He said there was no such thing as Europe. And if you look at the globe, you will see for yourself that America is only an extension of Asia. (But at the same time Toynbee is among those who have helped to bleach history. He has written that Africa was the only continent that produced no history. He won't write that again. Every day now, the truth is coming to light.)

I never will forget how shocked I was when I began reading about slavery's total horror. It made such an impact upon me that it later became one of my favorite subjects when I became a minister of Mr. Muhammad's. The world's most monstrous crime, the sin and the blood on the white man's hands, are almost impossible to believe. Books like the one by Frederick Olmsted opened my eyes to the horrors suffered when the slave was landed in the United States. The European woman, Fanny Kemble, who had married a Southern white slaveowner, described how human beings were degraded. Of course I read *Uncle Tom's Cabin.* In fact, I believe that's the only novel I have ever read since I started serious reading.

Parkhurst's collection also contained some bound pamphlets of the Abolitionist Anti-Slavery Society of New England. I read descriptions of atrocities, saw those illustrations of black slave women tied up and flogged with whips; of black mothers watching their babies being dragged off, never to be seen by their mothers again; of dogs after slaves, and of the fugitive slave catchers, evil white men with whips and clubs and chains and guns. I read about the slave preacher Nat Turner, who put the fear of God into the white slave master. Nat Turner wasn't going around preaching pie-in-the-sky and "non-violent" freedom for the black man. There in Virginia one night in 1831, Nat and seven other slaves started out at his master's home and through the night they went from one plantation "big house" to the next, killing, until by the next morning 57 white people were dead and Nat had about 70 slaves following him. White people, terrified for their lives, fled from their homes, locked themselves up in public buildings, hid in the woods, and some even left the state. A small army of soldiers took two months to catch and hang Nat Turner. Somewhere I have read where Nat Turner's example is said to have inspired John Brown to invade Virginia and attack Harpers Ferry nearly thirty years later, with thirteen white men and five Negroes.

I read Herodotus, "the father of History," or, rather, I read about him. And I read the histories of various nations, which opened my eyes gradually, then wider and wider, to how the whole world's white men had indeed acted like devils, pillaging and raping and bleeding and draining the whole world's non-white people. I remember, for instance, books such as Will Durant's *The Story of Oriental Civilization,* and Mahatma Gandhi's accounts of the struggle to drive the British out of India.

Book after book showed me how the white man had brought upon the world's black, brown, red, and yellow peoples every variety of the suffering of exploitation. I saw how since the sixteenth century, the so-called "Christian trader" white man began to ply the seas in his lust for Asian and African empires, and plunder, and power. I read, I saw, how the white man never has gone among the non-white peoples bearing the Cross in the true manner and spirit of Christ's teachings—meek, humble, and Christlike.

30 I perceived, as I read, how the collective white man had been actually nothing but a piratical opportunist who used Faustian machinations[3] to make his own Christianity his initial wedge in criminal conquests. First, always "religiously," he branded "heathen" and "pagan" labels upon ancient non-white cultures and civilizations. The stage thus set, he then turned upon his non-white victims his weapons of war.

I read how, entering India—half a *billion* deeply religious brown people—the British white man, by 1759, through promises, trickery, and manipulations, controlled much of India through Great Britain's East India Company. The parasitical British administration kept tentacling out to half of the sub-continent. In 1857, some of the desperate people of India finally mutinied—and, excepting the African slave trade, nowhere has history recorded any more unnecessary bestial and ruthless human carnage than the British suppression of the non-white Indian people.

Over 115 million African blacks—close to the 1930's population of the United States—were murdered or enslaved during the slave trade. And I read how when the slave market was glutted, the cannibalistic white powers of Europe next carved up, as their colonies, the richest areas of the black continent. And Europe's chancelleries for the next century played a chess game of naked exploitation and power from Cape Horn to Cairo.

Ten guards and the warden couldn't have torn me out of those books. Not even Elijah Muhammad could have been more eloquent than those books were in providing indisputable proof that the collective white man had acted like a devil in virtually every contact he had with the world's collective non-white man. I listen today to the radio, and watch television, and read the headlines about the collective white man's fear and tension concerning China. When the white man professes ignorance about why the Chinese hate him so, my mind can't help flashing back to what I read, there in prison, about how the blood forebears of this same white man raped China at a time when China was trusting and helpless. Those original white "Christian traders" sent into China millions of pounds of opium. By 1839, so many of the Chinese were addicts that China's desperate government destroyed twenty thousand chests of opium. The first Opium war[4] was promptly declared by the white man. Imagine! Declaring *war* upon someone who objects to being narcotized! The Chinese were severely beaten, with Chinese-invented gunpowder.

The Treaty of Nanking made China pay the British white man for the destroyed opium; forced open China's major ports to British trade; forced China to abandon Hong Kong; fixed China's import tariffs so low that cheap British articles soon flooded in, maiming China's industrial development.

35 After a second Opium War, the Tientsin Treaties legalized the ravaging opium trade, legalized a British-French-American control of China's customs. China tried delaying that Treaty's ratification; Peking was looted and burned.

"Kill the foreign white devils!" was the 1901 Chinese war cry in the Boxer Rebellion.[5] Losing again, this time the Chinese were driven from Peking's choicest areas. The vicious, arrogant white man put up the famous signs, "Chinese and dogs not allowed."

Red China after World War II closed its doors to the Western white world. Massive Chinese agricultural, scientific, and industrial efforts are described in a book that *Life* magazine recently published. Some observers inside Red China have reported that the world never has known such a hate-white campaign as is now going on in this non-white country where, present birth-rates continuing, in fifty more years Chinese will be half the earth's population. And it seems that some Chinese chickens will soon come home to roost, with China's recent successful nuclear tests.

Let us face reality. We can see in the United Nations a new world order being shaped, along color lines—an alliance among the non-white nations. America's U.N. Ambassador Adlai Stevenson complained not long ago that in the United Nations "a skin game" was being played. He was right. He was facing reality. A "skin game" is being played. But Ambassador Stevenson sounded like Jesse James accusing the marshal of carrying a gun. Because who in the world's history ever has played a worse "skin game" than the white man?

Mr. Muhammad, to whom I was writing daily, had no idea of what a new world had opened up to me through my efforts to document his teachings in books.

40 When I discovered philosophy, I tried to touch all the landmarks of philosophical development. Gradually, I read most of the old philosophers, Occidental and Oriental. The Oriental philosophers were the ones I came to prefer; finally, my impression was that most Occidental philosophy had largely been borrowed from the Oriental thinkers. Socrates, for instance, traveled in Egypt. Some sources even say that Socrates was initiated into some of the Egyptian mysteries. Obviously Socrates got some of his wisdom among the East's wise men.

I have often reflected upon the new vistas that reading opened to me. I knew right there in prison that reading had changed forever the course of my life.

As I see it today, the ability to read awoke inside me some long dormant craving to be mentally alive. I certainly wasn't seeking any degree, the way a college confers a status symbol upon its students. My homemade education gave me, with every additional book that I read, a little bit more sensitivity to the deafness, dumbness, and blindness that was afflicting the black race in America. Not long ago, an English writer telephoned me from London, asking questions. One was, "What's your alma mater?" I told him, "Books." You will never catch me with a free fifteen minutes in which I'm not studying something I feel might be able to help the black man.

Yesterday I spoke in London, and both ways on the plane across the Atlantic I was studying a document about how the United Nations proposes to insure the human rights of the oppressed minorities of the world. The American black man is the world's most shameful case of minority oppression. What makes the black man think of himself as only an internal United States issue is just a catch-phrase, two words, "civil rights." How is the black man going to get "civil rights" before first he wins his *human* rights? If the American black man will start thinking about his *human* rights, and then start thinking of himself as part of one of the world's great peoples, he will see he has a case for the United Nations.

I can't think of a better case! Four hundred years of black blood and sweat invested here in America, and the white man still has the black man begging for what every immigrant fresh off the ship can take for granted the minute he walks down the gangplank.

But I'm digressing. I told the Englishman that my alma mater was books, a good library. Every time I catch a plane, I have with me a book that I want to read—and that's a lot of books these days. If I weren't out here every day battling the white man, I could spend the rest of my life reading, just satisfying my curiosity—because you can hardly mention anything I'm not curious about. I don't think anybody ever got more out of going to prison than I did. In fact, prison enabled me to study far more intensively than I would have if my life had gone differently and I had attended some college. I imagine that one of the biggest troubles with colleges is there are too many distractions, too much panty-raiding, fraternities, and boola-boola and all of that. Where else but in a prison could I have attacked my ignorance by being able to study intensely sometimes as much as fifteen hours a day?

Credit

On Being a Refugee, an American—and a Human Being

VIET THANH NGUYEN

The Pulitzer Prize-winning novelist and Vietnam War refugee reflects on American identity.

1 I am a refugee, an American, and a human being, which is important to proclaim, as there are many who think these identities cannot be reconciled. In March 1975, as Saigon was about to fall, or on the brink of liberation, depending on your point of view, my humanity was temporarily put into question as I became a refugee.

My family lived in Ban Me Thuot, famous for its coffee and for being the first town overrun by communist invasion. My father was in Saigon on business and my mother had no way to contact him. She took my 10-year-old brother and four-year-old me and we walked 184km to the nearest port in Nha Trang (I admit to possibly being carried). At least it was downhill. At least I was too young, unlike my brother, to remember the dead paratroopers hanging from the trees. I am grateful not to remember the terror and the chaos that must have been involved in finding a boat. We made it to Saigon and reunited with my father, and, a month later, when the communists arrived, repeated the mad scramble for our lives. That summer we arrived in America.

I came to understand that in the United States, land of the fabled American dream, it is un-American to be a refugee. The refugee embodies fear, failure, and flight. Americans of all kinds believe that it is impossible for an American to become a refugee, although it is possible for refugees to become Americans and in that way be elevated one step closer to heaven.

To become a refugee means that one's country has imploded, taking with it all the things that protect our humanity: a functional government, a mostly non-murderous police force, a reliable drinking water and food supply, an efficient sewage system (do not underestimate how important a sewage system is to your humanity; refugees know that their subhuman status as the waste of nations is confirmed by having to live in their own waste).

5 I was luckier than many refugees, but I still remain scarred by my experience. After I arrived in the refugee camp set up at Fort Indiantown Gap, Pennsylvania, at four years old, I was taken away from my parents and sent to live with a white

sponsor family. The theory, I think, was that my parents would have an easier time of working if they didn't have to worry about me. Or maybe there was no sponsor willing to take all of us. Regardless, being taken away from my family was simply another sign of how my life was no longer in my hands, or those of my parents. My life was in the hands of strangers, and I was fortunate that they were kind, even if to this day I still remember howling as I was taken from my parents.

Like the homeless, refugees are living embodiments of a disturbing possibility: that human privileges are quite fragile, that one's home, family, and nation are one catastrophe away from being destroyed. As the refugees cluster in camps; as they dare to make a claim on the limited real estate of our conscience—we deny we can be like them and many of us do everything we can to avoid our obligations to them.

The better angels of our nature have always told us that morality means opening our doors, helping the helpless, sharing our material wealth. The reasons we come up with to deny doing such things are rationalizations. We have wealth to share with refugees, but we would rather spend it on other things. We are capable of living with foreigners and strangers, but they make us uncomfortable, and we do not want to be uncomfortable. We fear that strangers will kill us, so we keep them out.

Our fate as refugees is controlled by the strategies of the men who command the bombers. In my case, the US dropped more bombs on Vietnam, Laos, and Cambodia during the Vietnam war than it did all of Europe during the Second World War. This played a role in creating refugees, and because of American guilt and anticommunist feeling, the US government took in 150,000 Vietnamese refugees in 1975. It authorized the admission of several hundred thousand more, and other Southeast Asian refugees, in the subsequent decade. What the US did exceeded what Southeast Asian countries did, which was to deny entry to the "boat people" or contain them in camps until they could find a host country like the United States. Accepting these refugees was proof that the US was paying its debt to its South Vietnamese allies, and the refugees became reminders that life under communism was horrible. We were expected to be grateful for our rescue from such a life, and many of us were and are thankful.

"But I was also one of those unfortunate cases who could not help but wonder whether my need for American charity was due to my having first been the recipient of American aid," or so I wrote in my novel *The Sympathizer.* I am a bad refugee, you see, who can't help but see that my good fortune is a stroke of bureaucratic luck and the racial politics of the United States, where Asians are considered model minorities. If I was Haitian in the 1970s and 1980s, I would not have been admitted as a refugee, because I was black and poor. If I was Central American today, I would not be admitted as a refugee, even though the US has destabilized the region in the past through supporting dictatorial regimes and creating the conditions for the drug economy and drug wars. I am a bad refugee because I insist on seeing the historical reasons that create refugees and the historical reasons for denying refugee status to certain populations.

10 Central Americans are categorized instead by the United States as immigrants, which suspends questions over the influence of American policy on their countries of origin. The immigrant is that foreigner who has proceeded through the proper channels. The immigrant is the one who wants to come, unlike the refugee, who is forced to come. The immigrant, as contrasted to the refugee, is awesome. The immigrant, in turn, makes America awesome. Or great. I forget the right word. In any case, here are the famous words on the Statue of Liberty:

"Give me your tired, your poor,
Your huddled masses yearning to
breathe free,
The wretched refuse of your
teeming shore.
Send these, the homeless, tempest-tost
to me,
I lift my lamp beside the golden door!"

Except that this has not always been true. The current xenophobia in American society that is directed against refugees and their cousins, undocumented immigrants, and even against legal immigrants, has deep roots. Inasmuch as America has been built by immigrants and is welcoming to foreigners, it has also been built on genocide, slavery, and colonialism.

These two aspects of America are contradictory but both are true at the same time, as they are true of the other liberal democracies of the west. So it is that in the US, where 51 per cent of billion-dollar start-ups were founded by immigrants, and all of the 2016 Nobel Prize winners are immigrants, the country has periodically turned on its immigrants. Beginning in 1882, the United States banned Chinese immigrants. The excuse was that the Chinese were an economic, moral, sexual, and hygienic threat to white Americans. In retrospect, these reasons seem ridiculous, particularly given how well Chinese Americans have integrated into American society. These reasons should make us aware of how laughable contemporary fears about Muslims are—these fears are as irrational as the racism directed against the Chinese. Various other legal acts effectively ended non-white immigration to the country by 1924, and while the door would slowly creak open with the repeal of the Chinese Exclusion Act in 1943 (when 105 Chinese were permitted to enter annually), the United States would not embrace open immigration until 1965's Immigration Act.

The contemporary US has been defined by that act, with large numbers of Asian and Latino immigrants coming in and reshaping what America is (and for the better; without immigration from non-white countries, American food would be as terrible as that of pre-immigration England). But the prejudice remains. It emerges in the feeling against undocumented immigrants. Those who oppose them say we should give preference to documented immigrants, but I suspect that once the undocumented have been kicked out, these rational people will start speaking about how there are too many immigrants in general.

In truth, my own family is an example of the model minority that could be used to rebut such an argument. My parents became respectable merchants. My brother went to Harvard seven years after arriving in the States with no English. I won the Pulitzer Prize. We could be put on a poster touting how refugees make America great. And we do. But it shouldn't take this kind of success to be welcomed. Even if refugees, undocumented immigrants, and legal immigrants are not all potential billionaires, that is no reason to exclude them. Even if their fate is to be the high-school dropout and the fast-food cashier, so what? That makes them about as human as the average American, and we are not about to deport the average American (are we?).

15 The average American, or European, who feels that refugees or immigrants threaten their jobs does not recognize that the real culprits for their economic plight are the corporate interests and individuals that want to take the profits and are perfectly happy to see the struggling pitted against each other. The economic interests of the unwanted and the fearful middle class are aligned—but so many can't see that because of how much they fear the different, the refugee, the immigrant. In its most naked form, this is racism. In a more polite form, it takes the shape of defending one's culture, where one would rather remain economically poor but ethnically pure. This fear is a powerful force, and I admit to being afraid of it.

Then I think of my parents, who were younger than me when they lost nearly everything and became refugees. I can't help but remember how, after we settled in San Jose, California, and my parents opened a Vietnamese grocery store in the rundown downtown, a neighboring store put a sign up in its window: "Another American driven out of business by the Vietnamese." But my parents did not give in to fear, even though they must have been afraid. And I think of my son, nearly the age I was when I became a refugee, and while I do not want him to be afraid, I know he will be. What is important is that he have the strength to overcome his fear. And the way to overcome fear is to demand the America that should be, and can be, the America that dreams the best version of itself.

Credit

FT FINANCIAL TIMES

A Time to Hole Up and a Time to Kick Ass: Reimagining Activism as a Million Different Ways to Fight

LEAH LAKSHMI PIEPZNA-SAMARASINHA

I stopped being an activist right after September 11. A U.S.-born and -raised Sri Lankan living in Toronto by way of central Massachusetts and Brooklyn, I was a little bit out of the fray of American flags and foaming mouths, but not by that much. I refused to feel guilty about it, and it wasn't hard—nobody in my friendship circle tried to make me continue being an activist. In fact, they were all doing the same thing.

Who were we? Some privileged-ass girls who could sit in a bubble and not care? Hell no. We were brown immigrant girls—no, mostly not wearing *hijab*, but still caught up in the web of stares, glares, hate crimes, and feelings of being completely freaked out and terrified by anyone who could maybe possibly be Arab or Muslim in the aftermath of 9/11. In 2001 and 2002, every South Asian, Arab, North African, and Muslim I knew lived in constant fear of physical violence, and many dealt with it as a reality. Five of my friends in New York, all of them queer and trans people of color, were physically attacked that year. As temples and mosques were torched, and a wave of violence swept over South Asian, North African, and Arab America, some of us helped organize the hate-crime hotlines and patrols outside the temples; some of us huddled up. Some of us did both. The reasons behind those choices are a complicated indictment of how and why mainstream activist strategies don't work: don't work period, and definitely did not work for those of us trying to organize in the belly of the beast against forces that place faces like ours on the "wanted" list.

A week after the attacks, I remember thinking, *This is messed-up but maybe this will finally make people get their shit together.* I don't think I have to tell you this was wishful thinking. I went to the first citywide meeting in Toronto called after the attacks and walked out when it dissolved into chaos. All the Lefties who'd been fighting with each other for the past decade showed up and decided to not let the drama drop just yet. The meeting had been called by four young organizers, all women of color, including Helen Luu and Pauline Hwang from the Colours of Resistance network. The organizers began the meeting by saying that because they'd heard so many people say they felt isolated, like they were the only people anywhere who had a critical stance on what was happening, they wanted to start the meeting by getting everyone to find a partner and just talk for a few minutes about what they'd been feeling. A member of a socialist splinter group yelled, "We're here to take action, not to be a fucking encounter group!" and pandemonium ensued. Similar yells of protest came up when the organizers asked for there to be two open mics—one open to everyone and one for people of color only—in response to meetings in other cities where the open mic had been completely dominated by white guys. The screaming about reverse racism made me wonder if we were back in 1991, not 2001. Despite a Huge Bad Thing going down, despite it being 2001, it looked like too many white Leftists still didn't know how to respect the leadership of young women of color as organizers.

Regardless of my disappointment with the first meeting, I went to the next one to plan the response demos and actions. I was trying to hang in there. I spent a big chunk of that meeting chain-smoking outside with my girl Amandeep and a bunch of other *desis* (South Asians). Amandeep's parents lived in Hamilton, Ontario, a small auto-factory city two hours outside Toronto. They're Sikh, and *gurdwaras* had been burning all over the place. The Hamilton Jain temple had just been torched (you know, the people who respect life so much they brush the grass with a broom before they walk on it so they don't kill any insects), and Amandeep's mother wasn't leaving the house. My coworker Barinder's mother also wasn't leaving her house, and in slow times at the women's crisis line where we worked, Barinder told me she had made wills for herself and her partner so that if anything happened, her son would be taken care of. Earlier that week, a bus refused to stop for me, the only person at the bus stop; in another incident, I realized that everybody was silent and staring at me when I bought halal food at the supermarket. We stood around stubs of smokes and looked into each other's eyes. We had no words.

5 During that second meeting, the argument continued through a longass speakers' list over the protest route. It had already been decided—somewhere, somehow—before this meeting that the march's final destination would be the U.S. consulate in downtown Toronto. This was totally not okay with any of the South Asians and Arabs present. If we didn't feel safe on the bus, why the hell would we want to walk in a circle in front of the U.S. consulate for a couple of hours? Other people argued that the route had already been decided, it'd already been printed on posters. If we changed it now, people would be confused. "If people of color don't feel safe protesting, our duty is to go out and protest for them!" one white guy yelled out. Well-intentioned, maybe, but I couldn't think up anything better in terms of strategy at the moment. I didn't go to that march, or most of the ones after it. I wanted to go fuck shit up so

bad—with a bunch of other rad people of color, working-class and poor people, people with style, queer and trans POC, and immigrants. But those people weren't there, and I was paranoid about immigration calling as soon as I tried to organize anything close to what I was envisioning. I wanted to stop traffic, stop business as usual, shut down the financial district the way people would in the Bay Area in 2003. I wanted to take risks, too. If I had been organizing those marches and rallies, the meetings would have had good food and tokens, and we would have taken care of the kids; or there would have been no meetings at all, I would have just hung out on my stoop and talked to my neighbors until we organized something.

What did I do instead? Worked at the women's crisis line giving out info about hate crimes, immigration rights, and the Canadian Arab Federation. Went out sticker-bombing at night with my girls. Performed at a poetry reading benefit for the huge shut-down-the-city protests that had been in the works for six months, which got raided midway through by undercovers who said that the antiterrorism bill hadn't passed yet—but once it did, this would be illegal, and could they see our email list? Cooked potatoes the night before the demos for thousands of people who showed up at the rallying points at five o'clock in the morning. Instead of being there with them, went to bail court for my friend who had been picked up the night before on charges of stealing the new standardized test for all of Ontario.

What else? Hung out with my new lover. Had lots of sex. Stayed inside. Slept a lot. I would have felt terrified if I hadn't felt numb. Made big Sri Lankan meals of *mallung,* curry chicken, okra with coconut and rice. Made bitter jokes with my best friend. Stopped reading the newspaper. Felt sick all the time. Felt scared to try and cross the border. Took the train to New York anyway for a book launch and watched the train get searched twice at each border crossing (U.S. and Canadian immigration came onboard with dogs and U.S. marshals). Cried when the United States started bombing Afghanistan and got told to stop freaking out—that we had to be strong—by a then-friend. Wrote and performed poetry. Didn't go to demos because I was afraid I would get arrested and then get deported. Signed petitions and sent letters.

This is what it felt like to try and do traditional activism when you're so physically and emotionally attached to the subject matter and so physically and emotionally vulnerable to attack, arrest, and deportation. It meant running smack into a wall of many things that were wrong with activism pre-9/11: leadership and organizing models dominated by white or straight men (and women) that were stuck in the kind of old-school activism that Aya de León describes as "an endless series of meetings where people sit on their butt, get stiff backs, feel hungry, have to go to the bathroom, get dehydrated, and stay up in their heads." "Movements are traumatizing," a friend said to me. A lot of the ways in which mainstream activism is set up makes it impossible to take part in if you're broke, have kids, have a disability, or just have a job or two you have to work. For a lot of people it meant staying and getting burned out, questioning the whole way the organizing was set up, and trying to create new models of organizing that worked for us as busy, exhausted, freaked-out brown queer folks. But before we got there, it meant some time on the couch.

Bad Activist!

The whole time I was staying inside, watching cable, rolling around with my girl, and feeling despair (about the war, not about our sex lives), I was also beating myself over the head. I should be at that meeting! I was just lazy. It wasn't like I had kids or anything really stopping me from going there. I would feel much better if I went. (Is this starting to sound like someone's internal dialogue about why she's not going to the gym?) Activism was the cure for depression, right? I *should* go. But, hey, it was cold out, and it was *ER* night. Maybe next week.

10 Too much of the time, the choice was: Either do formulaic activism that doesn't keep you safe and is not imagined with your needs in mind, or stay home and do whatever you want. Either do activism where the message is, "We're warriors—the Zapatistas/Palestinians/Iraqis/fill in your favorite objectified revolutionary group—so we don't have the privilege to have emotions or be tired," or stay home with your girls who will allow you to feel sad. Which would you choose?

What counts as activism? Why didn't the kind of emotional self-care me and my girls were doing—talking to each other about all the fucked-up shit we were going through as brown girls—count? Why didn't my best friend driving her elderly East African mother to the doctor and negotiating her way through all the layers of the racist, sexist, condescending bullshit medical system count as activism? Did staying alive count as activism? Did relearning Tamil, one of my Sri Lankan family's languages, count? Did cooking good Sri Lankan food and learning how to cook those recipes I didn't have female family members around to teach me count? As a South Asian femme immigrant who was having a shitty week, did stopping at the MAC counter and finding the perfect shade of fuchsia lip gloss for my milk-tea skin count?

In the year after 9/11, I decided my activism was the kind of activism women of color do on a daily basis. Everything I did to keep myself alive—from holding down my job to painting my toenails to building and using my altar to cooking up big pots of sweet potato curry with my best girlfriends before we watched *The Siege* (with irony)—I decided to count as activism. That was badass. But it still nagged at me: Was building an altar enough if I wasn't taking the street? Just what does it take to make massive change happen—to defeat the war machine?

In February 2003, I paid a visit to New York. I didn't have a gig. I just had two hundred bucks, for once, and I wanted to jump on the bus to go see peeps I love and a city I had fled when I'd left the United States five years prior. All my people were going through rough times. One had just had an ovary removed without health insurance. Others were surviving being jumped, mugged, and otherwise targeted for hate post-9/11. All were brown, queer, and struggling. After a year in which my activism had increasingly been defined as staying inside the house and cooking good food for my friends and lover, and us trying to hold each other up in the face of brutal times, their work was eye-opening.

The people I loved were a mile from Ground Zero, had been beat down for being brown post-9/11, and they were forming POC squads to march in the protests. They were making antiwar stickers and going out and slapping them up all over Brooklyn, making bomb-ass poetry and writing in the face of death and fascism, cooking rice and beans, fucking around on the PlayStation, throwing open-mic jams. Whether as part of Operation Homeland Resistance, three days of POC-led civil disobedience, sit-ins, and media events to shut down the Department of Homeland Security in New York, sticking up DO NOT BOMB IRAQ stickers that matched the DO NOT HOLD DOORS signs in the subway, they were using their activism—on their own terms—as an opportunity to get into conversations with people about the war, 9/11, and the upcoming invasion of Iraq. They were creating their own space as queers and trans people of color, brokeass folks, disabled folks, immigrant folks, to make resistance in their own image. I saw that my fears were real, but that there is a time for holing up, and a time for kicking ass.

15 After New York, I compiled, edited, and distributed a zine entitled *Letters from the war years: some notes on love and struggle in times of war.* Letters included emails in the days leading up to the first U.S. bombing of Iraq exchanged between myself and those New York City friends; position papers about racism in the antiwar movement; coverage of Homeland Resistance actions; and poetry, prose, and artwork by authors Lauren Jade Martin, Marian Yalini Thmabynayagam, Bianca Ortiz, and myself. Much of our writing focused on the rage and despair we were feeling as we marched and organized, and our struggle to stay active against the urge to hibernate, cocoon, change the channel. I wanted to create a zine that would capture a variety of writing and thinking about POC antiwar organizing that would talk about how the ways in which we were personally affected were key parts of our organizing.

In "Notes on Despair," a piece Lauren Jade Martin published in *Letters,* she writes, "There is present not only an overwhelming despair, but also a huge sense of failure. What am I supposed to do with the knowledge that even though millions and millions of people worldwide protested on February 15, 2003, it did not do one lick of good, it did not stop anything? Fucking hopeless. Yet there must still be some sliver of hope, because then what else is it that propels us to keep on protesting?" I was so glad to hear LJ speaking out loud what everyone I knew was grappling with—the building up of hope in the days leading up to the war deadline, the hope that the historically massive antiwar protest in thousands of cities and towns on the planet would actually have an effect. If that level of mobilizing didn't get Bush to pull back, what would? The disappointment and, yes, despair I felt when Shock and Awe happened anyway was overwhelming. Almost two years later, LJ wrote a follow-up piece, "On the Eve of a New Year, Reflections on 'Notes on Despair,'" in which she was able, from a bit more distance, to talk about how post-traumatic stress had affected her activism and her responses to 9/11 and the impending Iraq War. In her piece, she talks about how she hates herself for giving in to despair and not being able to mobilize, as a year and a half after the historic February 15 protests, war still rages in Iraq and mass resistance in the West is on the decline.

In 2005, I talked with a friend, a genderqueer South Asian writer and activist, who said he felt ashamed, in a way, of the writing and work he had done back then. He, too, had done a lot of work organizing against deportations and special registration in a South Asian immigrant community, and also writing and speaking about his own fears of being targeted. He had felt ashamed that nothing he went through really compared to what that mostly Pakistani immigrant community had gone through. And I understood. I am not Muslim. I am an immigrant to Canada, but not from one of the hot-listed countries. I do not wear *hijab.* I am not an Arab or South Asian man. Yet, I did experience the harassment, and the harassment I was afraid I would get was bad enough to stop me from mobilizing the way I wanted to. Back in 2001 or 2003, I didn't know how to go beyond the wave of nausea and despair I felt when I opened up my email or watched the news. More than ever, what I saw made me feel like actions were futile.

What I am trying to do now, instead of getting stuck in despair, getting stuck in feeling hopeless, is to use my experiences as lessons. To ask: How do I feel fear and move forward? What kinds of political resistance can I make in which it's okay to talk about feeling nauseated and terrified? Where I can strategize with other queer POC, immigrant, and disabled folks, and/or folks who get it or are willing to get it? What kinds of organizing can I do on the way home, when I'm tired from my nine-to-five job, when my hips and ass are sore from my fibromyalgia and walking is hard, while I'm waiting for the bus? What are the new ways of organizing we can create that can move me through and out of despair? Where is there space to acknowledge that, yeah, it is totally fucking depressing that the public said no to war and the government did it anyway? How should we move now?

Some other things I think: All that lipstick buying and hanging with my girls is definitely resistance. But there is also a need for organized resistance—a kind that is sustainable, caring, open to listening, and created with our needs in the center—not some other model that doesn't work. Taking your mom to the doctor is resistance. Talking with all the other kids with their moms in the doctor's office about the crappy conditions there, and maybe trying to create a new clinic, is also resistance. But it's organized.

20 In the organizing we do, we need to make room for us to cry and freak out, and we also need to create ways to move past and through those feelings. And not in a cheesy "turning tears into guns" way, but in a way that sits with what really happens when a whole community is deported or jailed, what it specifically feels like to organize and protest and then watch satellite-beamed images of destruction of the countries we are fighting for. I don't want every political project to be an encounter group, but unless we figure out ways to take care of each other, the whole thing will self-destruct. In her recent memoir of the contra war, *Blood on the Border,* Roxanne Dunbar-Ortiz talks about being in Nicaragua right after the revolution and seeing how alcoholism and depression were rampant, how people had no place to deal with having seen so many people die in the revolution. Throughout her memoir, she writes about how her own struggles with alcoholism over four decades of radical feminist, Native, and anti-imperialist work were directly tied to having no place to process her grief over failed revolutions she'd been in the center of, and about the intense emotions that come out of working in movements that use armed struggle.

Maybe we should be asking, as a friend asked me: "What do you like about organizing? What do you hate about it? What do you get out of it? What do you have to offer in terms of time and energy?" Well, I like taking the street. I like working with everyday folks to transform our lives—like I really wanted to go into the Celebrity Inn and work with the women who were on immigration hold there, but I was also really worried 'cause I know that work takes a hell of a lot of time and energy and I wasn't sure I'd be able to hold on to it. I like creating culture, whether it's journalism or throwing a spoken-word night or performing or teaching a writing and activism workshop. My friend nodded and said, "I think about what I can offer and also what I can get out of it. With the writing group I'm teaching to the South Asian domestic workers group, I'm giving out stuff but I'm also learning how to teach with a translator. I know how much time I need to spend making money, and then I have choices about what I do with the rest of my time: Some of it needs to be for sleeping and eating, some of it needs to be for friends, some of it needs to be for making art, and some of it needs to be for organizing. I have choices about where I think my energy can best be used in political action. Whatever group I work with absolutely can't dis my creative work or tell me that eating or sleeping are luxuries."

In "The Revolution Will Not Be Funded," *Left Turn* magazine's special issue on INCITE!'s "The Revolution Will Not Be Funded: Beyond the Nonprofit Industrial Complex" conference,[1] most writers call for a return to grassroots movement building, and mostly I agree with them. However, Makani Themba-Nixon reminds us that "the whole sellout theory crowds out the discussion of burnout." She points out that many people left revolutionary parties and collectives out of exhaustion at the internal political processes and abuses of authority within them. "Women in particular needed a way to get away from the sexism, the exploitation, the rough stuff … to do smart work, practical work, in a way that allowed you to survive."[2]

What do I believe now'? Cooking Sri Lankan food, hanging with my girls, painting my toenails, praying, fucking, loving the size of my ass and my girlfriends are all forms of resistance. The only activism I am interested in is the type that sees all the different ways we resist as legitimate because they change ourselves and the world. We also need to find some ways to create big, macro organizing projects that are antiburnout and sustainable over the long haul. We need ways of organizing that allow us to name our despair. We need movements that acknowledge our feelings of grief and mourning when our homelands, or the homelands of people who are family, get bombed. We need movements that acknowledge that our feelings are not distractions from the struggle, but that they are damn well why we start or stop struggling in the first place. We need movements that do creative organizing and come up with innovative, fun strategies around how to keep immigrants, trans folks, disabled folks, and anybody who does not feel safe to take part in Big Demo culture to feel safer. We need to have big demos that are fierce and also look at all the million and one other organizing strategies there are. To have emotion and action wedded as part of one movement. To rest when we need to, and to pick up a rock when we need to, and to have the support team ready. To claim a million different ways to fight.

Further Reading

INCITE! Women of Color Against Violence: www.incite-national.org.

How to Get Stupid White Men out of Office: The Anti-Politics, Unboring Guide to Power, edited by Adrienne Maree Brown and William Upski Wimsatt (New York: Soft Skull Press, 2004).

Letters from Young Activists, edited by Dan Berger, Chesa Boudin, and Kenyon Farrow (New York: Nation Books, 2005).

"Notes on Despair" and "Reflections on Notes on Despair," revised, by Lauren Martin at www.theyellowperil.com.

Some of Us Did Not Die, collected essays by June Jordan (New York: Basic Books, 2003).

Colonize This!: Young Women of Color on Today's Feminism, edited by Daisy Hernández and Bushra Rehman (Emeryville, CA: Seal Press, 2002).

Medicine Stories, by Aurora Levins Morales (Boston: South End, 1999).

De Colores Means All of Us, by Elizabeth Martínez (Boston: South End, 1997).

Credit

Reading Games: Strategies for Reading Scholarly Sources

KAREN ROSENBERG

If at First You Fall Asleep …

During my first year in college, I feared many things: calculus, cafeteria food, the stained, sweet smelling mattress in the basement of my dorm.* But I did not fear reading. I didn't really think about reading at all, that automatic making of meaning from symbols in books, newspapers, on cereal boxes. And, indeed, some of my coziest memories of that bewildering first year involved reading. I adopted an overstuffed red chair in the library that enveloped me like the lap of a department store Santa. I curled up many evenings during that first, brilliant autumn with my English homework: Toni Morrison's *The Bluest Eye,* Gloria Naylor's *Mama Day*, Sandra Cisneros' *The House on Mango Street*. I'd read a gorgeous passage, snuggle deeper into my chair, and glance out to the sunset and fall leaves outside of the library window. This felt deeply, unmistakably collegiate.

But English was a requirement—I planned to major in political science. I took an intro course my first semester and brought my readings to that same chair. I curled up, opened a book on the Chinese Revolution, started reading, and fell asleep. I woke up a little drooly, surprised at the harsh fluorescent light, the sudden pitch outside. Not to be deterred, I bit my lip and started over. I'd hold on for a paragraph or two, and then suddenly I'd be thinking about my classmate Joel's elbows, the casual way he'd put them on the desk when our professor lectured, sometimes resting his chin in his hands. He was a long limbed runner and smelled scrubbed—a mixture of laundry detergent and shampoo. He had black hair and startling blue eyes. Did I find him sexy?

Crap! How many paragraphs had my eyes grazed over while I was thinking about Joel's stupid elbows? By the end of that first semester, I abandoned ideas of majoring in political science. I vacillated between intense irritation with my assigned readings and a sneaking suspicion that perhaps the problem was me—I was too dumb to read academic texts. Whichever it was—a problem with the readings or with me—I carefully chose my classes so that I could read novels, poetry, and plays for credit. But even in my English classes, I discovered, I had to read dense scholarly articles. By my Junior year, I trained myself to spend days from dawn until dusk hunkered over a carrel in the library's basement armed with a dictionary and a rainbow of highlighters. Enjoying my reading seemed hopelessly naïve—an indulgence best reserved for beach blankets and bathtubs. A combination of obstinacy, butt-numbingly hard chairs, and caffeine helped me survive my scholarly reading assignments. But it wasn't fun.

Seven years later I entered graduate school. I was also working and living on my own, cooking for myself instead of eating off cafeteria trays. In short, I had a life. My days were not the blank canvas they had been when I was an undergraduate and could sequester myself in the dungeon of the library basement. And so, I finally learned how to read smarter, not harder. Perhaps the strangest part of my reading transformation was that I came to *like* reading those dense scholarly articles; I came to crave the process of sucking the marrow from the texts. If you can relate to this, if you also love wrestling with academic journal articles, take joy in arguing with authors in the margins of the page, I am not writing for you.

5 However, if your reading assignments confound you, if they send you into slumber, or you avoid them, or they seem to take you *way* too long, then pay attention. Based on my experience as a frustrated student and now as a teacher of reading strategies, I have some insights to share with you designed to make the reading process more productive, more interesting, and more enjoyable.

Joining the Conversation[1]

Even though it may seem like a solitary, isolated activity, when you read a scholarly work, you are participating in a conversation. Academic writers do not make up their arguments off the top of their heads (or solely from creative inspiration). Rather, they look at how others have approached similar issues and problems. Your job—and one for which you'll get plenty of help from your professors and your peers—is to locate the writer and yourself in this larger conversation. Reading academic texts is a deeply social activity; talking with your professors and peers about texts can not only help you understand your readings better, but it can push your thinking and clarify your own stances on issues that really matter to you.

In your college courses, you may have come across the term "rhetorical reading."[2] Rhetoric in this context refers to how texts work to persuade readers—a bit different from the common connotation of empty, misleading, or puffed up speech. Rhetorical reading refers to a set of practices designed to help us understand how texts work and to engage more deeply and fully in a conversation that extends beyond the boundaries of any particular reading. Rhetorical reading practices ask us to think deliberately about the role and relationship between the writer, reader, and text.

When thinking about the writer, we are particularly interested in clues about the writer's motivation and agenda. If we know something about what the writer cares about and is trying to accomplish, it can help orient us to the reading and understand some of the choices the writer makes in his or her work.

As readers, our role is quite active. We pay attention to our own motivation and agenda for each reading. On one level, our motivation may be as simple as wanting to do well in a class, and our agenda may involve wanting to understand as much as necessary in order to complete our assignments. In order to meet these goals, we need to go deeper, asking, "Why is my professor asking me to read this piece?" You may find clues in your course syllabus, comments your professor makes in class, or comments from your classmates. If you aren't sure why you are being asked to read something, ask! Most professors will be more than happy to discuss in general terms what "work" they want a reading to do—for example, to introduce you to a set of debates, to provide information on a specific topic, or to challenge conventional thinking on an issue.

10 Finally, there is the text—the thing that the writer wrote and that you are reading. In addition to figuring out *what* the text says, rhetorical reading strategies ask us to focus on *how* the text delivers its message. In this way of thinking about texts, there is not one right and perfect meaning for the diligent reader to uncover; rather, interpretations of the reading will differ depending on the questions and contexts readers bring to the text.

Strategies for Rhetorical Reading

Here are some ways to approach your reading that better equip you for the larger conversation. First, consider the **audience.** When the writer sat down to write your assigned reading, to whom was he or she implicitly talking? Textbooks, for the most part, have students like you in mind. They may be boring, but you've probably learned what to do with them: pay attention to the goals of the chapter, check out the summary at the end, ignore the text in the boxes because it's usually more of a "fun fact" than something that will be on the test, and so on. Magazines in the checkout line at the supermarket also have you in mind: you can't help but notice headlines about who is cheating or fat or anorexic or suicidal. Writers of scholarly sources, on the other hand, likely don't think much about you at all when they sit down to write. Often, academics write primarily for other academics. But just because it's people with PhDs writing for other people with PhDs doesn't mean that you should throw in the towel. There's a formula for these types of texts, just like there's a formula for all the *Cosmo* articles that beckon with titles that involve the words "hot," "sex tips," "your man," and "naughty" in different configurations.

It's just that the formula is a little more complicated.

The formula also changes depending on the flavor of study (physics, management, sociology, English, etc.) and the venue. However, if you determine that the audience for your reading is other academics, recognize that you are in foreign territory. You won't understand all of the chatter you hear on street corners, you may not be able to read the menus in the restaurants, but, with a little practice, you will be able to find and understand the major road signs, go in the right direction, and find your way.

How can you figure out the primary audience? First, look at the publication venue. (Here, to some extent, you can judge a book by its cover). If the reading comes from an academic journal, then chances are good that the primary audience is other academics. Clues that a journal is academic (as opposed to popular, like *Time* or *Newsweek*) include a citation format that refers to a volume number and an issue number, and often this information appears at the top or bottom of every page. Sometimes you can tell if a reading comes from an academic journal based on the title—e.g., do the *Journal for Research in Mathematics Education or Qualitative Research in Psychology* sound like they are written for a popular audience? What if you're still not sure? Ask your reference librarians, classmates, your instructor, or friends and family who have more experience with these types of readings than you do.

15 There are two implications that you should be aware of if you are not the primary audience for a text. First, the author will assume prior knowledge that you likely don't have. You can expect sentences like "as Durkheim has so famously argued …" or "much ink has been spilled on the implications of the modernization hypothesis" where you have no idea who Durkheim is or what the modernization hypothesis says. That's OK. It might even be OK to not look these things up at all and still get what you need from the reading (but you won't know that yet). In the first reading of an article, it's smart to hold off on looking too many things up. Just be prepared to face a wall of references that don't mean a whole lot to you.

Second, if you're not the primary audience, don't be surprised if you find that the writing isn't appealing to you. Whereas a novelist or a magazine writer works hard to draw us in as readers, many academic authors don't use strategies to keep us hooked. In fact, many of these strategies (use of sensory language, suspense, etc.) would never get published in academic venues. By the same token, you'll use very different strategies to read these scholarly texts.

You may be wondering, if you're not the intended audience for the text, why do you have to read it in the first place? This is an excellent question, and one that you need to answer before you do your reading. As I mentioned earlier in the discussion of the role of the reader, you may need to do a little sleuthing to figure this out. In addition to the suggestions I provided earlier, look to your course notes and syllabus for answers. Often professors will tell you why they assign specific readings. Pay attention—they will likely offer insights on the context of the reading and the most important points. If after all of this, you still have no idea why you're supposed to read six articles on the history of Newtonian physics, then ask your professor. Use the answers to help you focus on the really important aspects of the texts and to gloss over the parts that are less relevant to your coursework. If you remain confused, continue to ask for clarification. Ask questions in class (your classmates will be grateful). Go to office hours. Most faculty love the opportunity to talk about readings that they have chosen with care.

Once you have an idea who the intended audience is for the article and why you are assigned to read it, don't sit down and read the article from start to finish, like a good mystery. Get a lay of the land before you go too deep. One way to do this is to study the architecture of the article. Here are some key components to look for:

The title. As obvious as it sounds, pay attention to the title because it can convey a lot of information that can help you figure out how to read the rest of the article more efficiently. Let's say that I know my reading will be about the Russian Revolution. Let's say I even know that it will be about the role of music in the Russian Revolution. Let's say the title is "'Like the beating of my heart': A discourse analysis of Muscovite musicians' letters during the Russian Revolution." This tells me not only the subject matter of the article (something about letters Russian musicians wrote during the Revolution) but it also tells me something about the methodology, or the way that the author approaches the subject matter. I might not know exactly what discourse analysis is, but I can guess that you can do it to letters and that I should pay particular attention to it when the author mentions it in the article. On the other hand, if the title of the article were "Garbage cans and metal pipes: Bolshevik music and the politics of proletariat propaganda" I would know to look out for very different words and concepts. Note, also, that the convention within some academic disciplines to have a pretty long title separated by a colon usually follows a predictable pattern. The text to the left of the colon serves as a teaser, or as something to grab a reader's attention (remember that the author is likely not trying to grab your attention, so you may not find these teasers particularly effective—though it is probably packed with phrases that would entice someone who already studies the topic). The information to the right of the colon typically is a more straightforward explanation of what the article is about.

20 **The abstract.** Not all of your readings will come with abstracts, but when they do, pay close attention. An abstract is like an executive summary. Usually one paragraph at the beginning of an article, the abstract serves to encapsulate the main points of the article. It's generally a pretty specialized summary that seeks to answer specific questions. These include: the main problem or question, the approach (how did the author(s) do the work they write about in the article?), the shiny new thing that this article does (more on this later, but to be published in an academic journal you often need to argue that you are doing something that has not been done before), and why people who are already invested in this field should care (in other words, you should be able to figure out why

another academic should find the article important). The abstract often appears in database searches, and helps scholars decide if they want to seek out the full article.

That's a whole lot to accomplish in one paragraph.

As a result, authors often use specialized jargon to convey complex ideas in few words, make assumptions of prior knowledge, and don't worry much about general readability. Abstracts, thus, are generally dense, and it's not uncommon to read through an abstract and not have a clue about what you just read. This is a good place to re-read, highlight, underline, look up what you don't know. You still may not have a firm grasp on everything in the abstract, but treat the key terms in the abstract like parts of a map when you see them in the main text, leading you to treasure: understanding the main argument.

The introduction. The introduction serves some of the same functions as the abstract, but there is a lot more breathing room here. When I started reading academic texts, I'd breeze through the introduction to get to the "meat" of the text. This was exactly the wrong thing to do. I can't remember how many times I'd find myself in the middle of some dense reading, perhaps understanding the content of a particular paragraph, but completely unable to connect that paragraph with the overall structure of the article. I'd jump from the lily pad of one paragraph to the next, continually fearful that I'd slip off and lose myself in a sea of total confusion (and I often did slip).

If the author is doing her/his job well, the introduction will not only summarize the whole piece, present the main idea, and tell us why we should care, but it will also often offer a road map for the rest of the article. Sometimes, the introduction will be called "introduction," which makes things easy. Sometimes, it's not. Generally, treat the first section of an article as the introduction, regardless if it's explicitly called that or not.

25 There are times where your reading will have the introduction chopped off. This makes your work harder. The two most common instances of introduction-less readings are assigned excerpts of articles and lone book chapters. In the first case, you only have a portion of an article so you cannot take advantage of many of the context clues the writer set out for readers. You will need to rely more heavily on the context of your course in general and your assignment in particular to find your bearings here. If the reading is high stakes (e.g., if you have to write a paper or take an exam on it), you may want to ask your

professor how you can get the whole article. In the second case, your professor assigns a chapter or two from the middle of an academic book. The chapter will hopefully contain some introductory material (and generally will include much more than the middle of a journal article), but you will likely be missing some context clues that the author included in the introduction to the whole book. If you have trouble finding your footing here, and it's important that you grasp the meaning and significance of the chapter, seek out the book itself and skim the introductory chapter to ground you in the larger questions that the author is addressing. Oddly, even though you'll be doing more reading, it may save you time because you can read your assigned chapter(s) more efficiently.

Roadmaps included in the introduction are often surprisingly straightforward. They often are as simple as "in the first section, we examine … in the second section we argue …" etc. Search for these maps. Underline them. Highlight them. Go back to them when you find your comprehension slipping.

Section headings. A section heading serves as a title for a particular part of an article. Read all of these to get a sense of the trajectory of the text before delving into the content in each section (with the exception of the introduction and the conclusion which you should read in detail). Get a passing familiarity with the meanings of the words in the section headings—they are likely important to understanding the main argument of the text.

Conclusion. When writing papers, you've likely heard the cliché "in the introduction, write what you will say, then say it, then write what you just said." With this formula, it would seem logical to gloss over the conclusion, because, essentially, you've already read it already. However, this is not the case. Instead, pay close attention to the conclusion. It can help you make sure you understood the introduction. Sometimes a slight re-phrasing can help you understand the author's arguments in an important, new way. In addition, the conclusion is often where authors indicate the limitations of their work, the unanswered questions, the horizons left unexplored. And this is often the land of exam and essay questions … asking you to extend the author's analysis beyond its own shores.

At this point, you have pored over the title, the introduction, the section headings, and the conclusion. You haven't really read the body of the article yet. Your next step is to see if you can answer the question: what is the **main argument or idea** in this text?

30 Figuring out the main argument is *the* key to reading the text effectively and efficiently. Once you can identify the main argument, you can determine how much energy to spend on various parts of the reading. For example, if I am drowning in details about the temperance movement in the United States in the 19th Century, I need to know the main argument of the text to know if I need to slow down or if a swift skim will do. If the main argument is that women's organizing has taken different forms in different times, it will probably be enough for me to understand that women organized against the sale and consumption of alcohol. That might involve me looking up "temperance" and getting the gist of women's organizing. However, if the main argument were that scholars have misunderstood the role of upper class white women in temperance organizing in Boston from 1840–1865, then I would probably need to slow down and pay closer attention.

Unless the reading is billed as a review or a synthesis, the only way that an academic text can even get published is if it claims to argue something new or different. However, unlike laundry detergent or soft drinks, academic articles don't advertise what makes them new and different in block letters inside cartoon bubbles. In fact, finding the main argument can sometimes be tricky. Mostly, though, it's just a matter of knowing where to look. The abstract and the introduction are the best places to look first. With complicated texts, do this work with your classmates, visit your campus writing center (many of them help with reading assignments), or drag a friend into it.

Once you understand the different parts of the text and the writer's main argument, use this information to see how and where you can enter the conversation. In addition, keep your own agenda as a reader in mind as you do this work.

Putting It All Together

Collectively, these suggestions and guidelines will help you read and understand academic texts. They ask you to bring a great deal of awareness and preparation to your reading—for example, figuring out who the primary audience is for the text and, if you are not that audience, why your professor is asking you to read it anyway. Then, instead of passively reading the text from start to finish, my suggestions encourage you to pull the reading into its constituent parts—the abstract, the introduction, the section headings, conclusion, etc.—and read them unevenly and out of order to look for the holy grail of the main argument. Once you have the main argument you can make wise decisions about which parts of the text you need to pore over and which you can blithely skim. The final key to reading smarter, not harder is to make it social. When you have questions, ask. Start conversations with your professors about the reading. Ask your classmates to work with you to find the main arguments. Offer a hand to your peers who are drowning in dense details. Academics write to join scholarly conversations. Your professors assign you their texts so that you can join them too.

Works Cited

Norgaard, Rolf. *Composing Knowledge: Readings for College Writers*. Boston: Bedford/St. Martin's, 2007. Print.

Rounsaville, Angela, Rachel Goldberg, Keith Feldman, Cathryn Cabral, and Anis Bawarshi, eds. *Situating Inquiry: An Introduction to Reading, Research, and Writing at the University of Washington*. Boston: Bedford/St. Martin's, 2008. Print.

Credit

Rosenberg, Karen. "Reading Games: Strategies for Reading Scholarly Sources." *Writing Spaces: Readings on Writing, Vol. 2*. Eds. Charles Lowe and Pavel Zemiliansky. Anderson, SC: Parlor Press, 2011. 210–220. Used with author's permission.

The Case

TIM SEIBLES

White people don't know they're white.

Newspaper. Coffee. Gosh-whataday!

Not everyone doesn't admire them. In fact,
a lot of people like their *time-for-the-news* TV voices.

It's not that they're not beautiful. Just check out a beach.
Oh, they're beautiful all right.

Sometimes though, if you're not white
and a lot of other people are—
but they don't know it:

Well, it can make you feel like you need to be somewhere
way far away.

And if you go to the supermarket and look
at the magazine racks you might start getting
that "uh-oh" feeling.

Most of the time you just laugh, that's all—you just
have to laugh and probably shake lots of hands.

Once a woman I worked with said
I never even ***think*** *of you as black.*

She was being un- pre- ju- diced.

You shouldn't get angry about stuff though.

I know some brothers, they see a white face
and their whole bodies sneer—

even if everything was going perfect that day, even
if the white face never did anything,
never said nothin'.

And then, of course, there are the Nazi-like skinheads
and the other etceteras

who wannabe all about whiteness—hating the gooks,
the spics, and all the geronimos et cetera.

Oh, they're white enough all right.

Credit

Queer Characters in Comic Strips

EDWARD H. SEWELL, JR.

"Gay and lesbian readers," Matthew Pustz says, "have felt that their experience has ... been marginalized by the [comics] industry, prompting the production of titles such as *Gay Comix, Dykes to Watch Out For,* and *Hothead Paisan, Homicidal Lesbian Terrorist* that might better speak to this audience" (Pustz, 1999, p. 101).

This chapter explores the role of queer[1] characters in comic strips found in both dominant mainstream newspapers and in alternative queer publications or on the Internet.[2] After a discussion of opposing points of view within critical/queer theory and the foundational arguments they suggest for our critique, a few examples of comic strips with queer characters from both mainstream dominant culture newspapers and from alternative queer sources are examined in light of a queer theory perspective.

Within the critical theory community, there is a less-than-friendly debate about what ideological approach can provide the best framework for reading, understanding, and interpreting queer texts (see for example Abelove, 1995; Dilley, 1999; Fuss, 1991; Gamson, 1995, 2000; Honeychurch, 1996; Jagose, 1996; Seidman, 1993, 1996; Slagle, 1995).

Seidman provides a simple explanation of the implications of a queer theory perspective:

5 Queer theory is suggesting that the study of homosexuality should not be a study of a minority—the making of the lesbian/gay/bisexual subject—but a study of those knowledges and social practices that organize "society" as a whole by sexualizing—heterosexualizing or homosexualizing—bodies, desires, acts, identities, social relationships, knowledges, culture, and social institutions. (Seidman, 1996, pp. 12–13)

Some critical scholars argue that the queer, while marginal in the dominant culture, can be tolerated in, if not openly accepted into, that culture. Many queer theory scholars argue, however, that toleration and marginalization are not acceptable goals or even options for queers. Abelove, based on the experiences self-identified queer students have shared in class, clearly presents the queer sense of "place" when he says:

> ... they [students who call themselves queer] do not typically experience their own subjectivity as marginal, even at those moments when they feel more oppressed by homophobic and heterosexist discourses and institutions.

> Marginalization isn't their preferred trope. It doesn't seem to them to be cogent as a narrative device for organizing the telling of their own lives or, for that matter, of their history. What these queers prefer to say and believe or try to believe instead is that they are both present and at the center. (Abelove, 1995, p. 48)

The popular "gay" slogan of the 1970s, "We are everywhere," contrasts with the 1990s slogan of Queer Nation, "We are here. We are queer. Get used to it."

"The queer movement," Slagle points out, "is unique in that it avoids essentialism on two separate levels. First, while liberationists have argued for years that gay men, lesbians, and bisexuals are essentially no different from heterosexuals, the new activists argue that queers are different but that marginalization is not justified on the basis of these differences. Second, queer activists avoid essentializing strategies within the movement itself." (Slagle, 1995, p. 87)

10 One important aspect of queer theory is the performative function of being queer. Halperin argues that performative functions of sexual identity are more related to a location of identity than abstract identity:

> [T]o come out is precisely to expose oneself to a different set of dangers and constraints, to make oneself into a convenient screen onto which straight people can project all the fantasies they routinely entertain about gay people ... coming out puts into play a different set of political relations and alters the dynamics of personal and political struggle. *Coming out is an act of freedom, not in the sense of liberation but in the sense of resistance* [emphasis in the original]. (Halperin, 1995, p. 30)

While coming out is an event with major personal implications, being queer is primarily a performative function defining how the queer acts once s/he has decided to live their queerness in a straight world. This performative function is the most common focus of media treatments of the queer community as demonstrated by how queer guests are portrayed on television talk shows (Gamson, 1998) hosted by presumably straight hosts for dominant heterosexual audiences where only the extreme queer caricature is presented as normative.

The rift between assimilation into the dominant heterosexual culture and separation from it also is evident in the treatments of queer characters in mainstream newspaper comic strips and those run in alternative queer publications and on the Internet. Queer characters in mainstream comic strips are well integrated into heterosexual society in that they look and act "straight" before coming out as queer, and they look and act in a manner appropriate to the dominant heterosexual culture after coming out. They can quickly blend back into their pre-coming out comfortable context in which they may be "gay" and marginal, but still are quite acceptable to those with whom they must interact on a daily basis. There is no homophobic-induced harassment or violence, no offensive remarks about them being a "faggot," and no gay-bashing. They come out and fade back in rather quickly with no lasting consequences.

Lawrence Grossberg (1993, 1996) argues that cultural studies needs to move from essentialist models based on identity differences without separation to models based on articulation, singularity, and otherness. The logic of difference leads to negativity while the logic of otherness leads to positivity. Marginality is replaced by a sense of effectively belonging in which "agency involves relations of participation and access, the possibilities of moving into particular sites of activity and power, and of belonging to them in such a way as to be able to enact their powers" (Grossberg, 1996, p. 99). Thus, in terms of comic strips, rather than simply being different and marginal in a dominant social context, the queer character should be presented in a context that permits a sense of being unique and "other" from the dominant heterosexual culture. Queers need their own "space" in which they can acknowledge their own values, be authentic, and be powerful as individuals and not be simply seen as people with a variant "lifestyle" or "agenda."

15 Queer characters have not been completely absent in mainstream comic strips. Indeed, several early comic strips appearing in major newspapers made oblique references to queer characters. Milt Caniff's *Terry and the Pirates* introduced a gay male character (Papa Pyzon) in 1936 and a lesbian character (Sanjak) in 1939 (Applegate, 1994). In an interview for *The Comics Journal,* issue no. 108, Caniff said of Papa Pyzon: "People just thought he was a sissy. The idea of any kind of sexual deviation didn't even enter into peoples' minds in those days." Likewise, he said of Sanjak that "in those days the word 'lesbian' simply wouldn't have been understood by half your audience, and the other half would have resented it" (cited in Applegate, 1994). Mark Burstein suggested in *The Fort Mudge Post,* issue no. 32 (March 1993) that Howland Owl and Churchy LeFemme, two characters in Walt Kelly's *Pogo* comic strip, may have been gay lovers. According to Applegate (1994) "[Burstein's] suggestion based on sight gags and lines taken out of context, generated outraged protests and the conclusion that Kelly may have been engaging in whimsy, but that he certainly didn't seriously intend for readers to infer that Churchy and Howland were gay."

Given these oblique or coded references to queer characters in the comic strips before the 1970s, it was not until February 11, 1976, that Garry Trudeau in the *Doonesbury* comic strip introduced the first openly gay male character

(Trudeau, 1978, n.p.). Andy Lippincott was a regular character living successfully in a tolerant but heterosexual world. He was dating Joanie Caucus and there was even the assumption that they might get married. Then, one day, Andy announces that he is gay (Figure 11.1).

Figure 11.1. Andy Lippincott comes out. From Trudeau, G. B. (1976, February 9–10). Doonesbury. DOONESBURY © G. B. Trudeau. Reprinted with permission of UNIVERSAL PRESS SYNDICATE. All rights reserved.

There is nothing to visually distinguish Andy from any other character in the strip. Indeed, when Joanie hints to a mutual friend that the relationship between she and Andy is not going to go anywhere, the friend assumes she is the queer party in the relationship.

There is no argument, no recrimination, no strong negative reaction to Andy's "coming out" of the closet. There are no homophobic remarks, no gay-bashing. What Trudeau did by introducing a gay character was admirable. It took a great deal of courage and went against all the accepted standards of the comic strips page. Andy's sexual orientation, however, basically disappears from the strip for 7 years until September 1982 when Lacey Davenport, an older female character who had been a regular in the comic strip, is running for political office in San Francisco. At a meeting of the Bay Area Gay Alliance, Andy reappears as one of the leaders in the organization. There still is nothing about his character to identify him as queer other than the context—a queer meeting—in which the reader encounters him.

While Lacey tries to understand her new gay constituency, she lacks basic knowledge about some key characteristics of what it means to be queer as illustrated in a conversation with two of the men:

20 "But have you really tried, I mean, REALLY tried, dating girls your own age?" Lacey asks.

> "It doesn't quite work that way, ma'am," one of the men answers.
>
> "I must say, dears, this little chat has been most enlightening. I had no idea the gay community was facing so many problems. As you can imagine, this is all new ground for me. We never had any gays among our family and friends. Well, actually, that's not true. Dick's Uncle Orville came out of the closet last year. He's a federal judge in Chicago."
>
> "That's great! What made him do it?" interrupts one of the men.
>
> "High interest rates," Lacey says, "His butler tried to blackmail him, and he couldn't afford it."

Trudeau, though heterosexual, demonstrates some clear insights into the queer community as he focuses our attention on stereotypes common within the dominant culture that represent the standard cultural caricature of queers.

Lacey wins the election and some time passes until March 27, 1989, when Trudeau introduces into the strip a discussion of AIDS. Once again, Lacey Davenport is the vehicle for discussing the queer community in relationship to what was at the time being described as a national epidemic, and once again common misconceptions and humor work in tandem to make a positive point. While the queer community suffers devastating losses, the dominant culture represented by Lacey finds it difficult to even say the word AIDS when speaking to a queer gathering.

The next time Andy is mentioned in the strip is on June 2, 1990, after he has died of AIDS. The world-view of the dominant culture and the queer community in this episode are not congruent, as a conversation between Joanie and a young queer at the funeral aptly demonstrates. Joanie has just delivered a eulogy for Andy, and as she sits down, an exchange with a young man seated behind her ensues:

> "Excuse me? That was a lovely eulogy!"
>
> "Oh ... thank you," Joanie responds.

"Would you mind if I asked you a personal question?" the young man asks, "Are you a transvestite?"

"No, I'm a mother of two," she answers.

"A mother of two?" he says, "Wow ... Andy sure knew some interesting people!"

25 Between 1976 and 1990, *Doonesbury* included 27 panels related to queer characters and issues. During this same time period, no other mainline newspaper comic strip talked about queers or AIDS.[3]

Trudeau "outed" a second queer character in September 1993. Mark Slackmeyer, a disc jockey, has a dream in which Andy, or his ghost, appears and plants the idea in Mark's mind that he might be gay. Mark, of course, denies the possibility at first, thinks about it, and finally goes to his friend Mike Doonesbury to talk about it:

"I'm scared, Mike," Mark confesses, "Being gay in this culture is too damn hard. I'd rather continue to be a sexual agnostic."

"What's going on out there?" J.J. [Mike's wife], calls from another room.

"It's Mark, J.J.—He thinks he might be gay," responds Mike.

"Of course he's gay. I've known that for years."

J.J., who has "lots of gay friends," offers to introduce them to Mark who says, "I don't think so, J.J., I'm not quite there yet ... " J.J., though in the dominant heterosexual culture, appears to be very familiar with the queer community and actually thinks she can help Mark become a part of this marginal subculture in which she, though an outsider, feels quite comfortable.

In December 1993, Mark tells his father he is gay; in January 1994, he outs himself on National Public Radio; and in May 1994, he comes out to his mother. While there are some initial negative responses and questions, in each episode Mark is accepted and quickly assimilated back into heterosexual culture. Mark, along with his partner and co-disc jockey Chase, continues to regularly introduce gay topics into *Doonesbury* through their radio show. Commenting on congressional and presidential actions related to gay marriage, for example, Mark says:

30 ... and Clinton's failure to veto the anti-gay marriage bill was a new low in election-year gutlessness! What were Clinton and Congress thinking? That their official censure would cause gays to rethink their sexual orientation? Does the family-values crowd believe in the value of commitment or don't they? Here's the irony, gang—come the election, conservatives should be prepared to accept full credit for promoting unstable, irresponsible gay relationships! (Trudeau, 1998, p. 77)

During an on-air interview with presidential candidate George W. Bush, Mark asks, "Why not unburden yourself right now so you won't be tempted to lie later?" Bush replies, "Yeah, right, why don't *you*?" Mark accepts the challenge: "Okay, I ducked the draft, smoked pot, and I'm gay. Your turn." "Um ..." says Bush, "Gotta run" (Trudeau, 1999, p. 64).

Each time Trudeau introduced a queer theme in *Doonesbury,* some newspapers chose not to run the comic strip, some dropped it altogether, and some moved it from the comics page to the editorial page. Both characters who came out as gay had been regular characters in the strip before Trudeau "outed" them. They had established significant roles within the context of the heterosexual culture in which they lived and worked before coming out. After revealing their sexual orientation, followed by a brief time of adjustment without any strongly negative attitudes, behavior, or lasting effect from the homosexual culture, they returned to their previously established role in the dominant culture status quo.

Readers of newspaper comics learned over the years to expect socially controversial topics in *Doonesbury,* which was not the "typical" family-oriented comic strip. When Lawrence, a regular character in Lynn Johnston's *For Better or For Worse,* came out as gay in 1993, there was a quick public response, both negative and positive (Lawlor, et al., 1994). The syndicate management warned newspaper editors about the potentially controversial content that was going to be presented so they could plan their course of action.

On March 26, 1993, Lawrence, while having a typical casual teenage conversation with his best friend Michael about a new puppy that Lawrence's mother loves dearly, says:

35 "I can't get over how much my mom loves that dog, man,"

> "Yeah," responds Michael, "Know what she told my mom? She said the puppy would keep her happy 'til you had children!"
>
> "What?" asks Lawrence with a surprised look. "Then that puppy better live a long time, Mike, because I'm probably never gonna *have* children."
>
> "Hey, how do you know?" asks Michael.
>
> "... 'cause I'm probably never going to get married. Ever," replies Lawrence.
>
> "I don't get what you're saying, man! If you, you know—fall in love?"
>
> "I have fallen in love," says Lawrence," ... but it's not with a girl."

The physical expressions on each boy's face and their body reactions clearly suggest apprehension about the topic's unexpected turn and development. The conversation continues and Lawrence comes out to Michael (see the conversation in Figure 11.2).

Figure 11.2. Lawrence comes out. From Johnston, L. (1993, March 26–27). *For Better or for Worse.* FOR BETTER OR FOR WORSE © UFS. Reprinted by permission. All rights reserved.

Michael is angry with Lawrence, but with time and thought, he decides to remain friends with him. He even convinces Lawrence to tell his mom he is gay. The conversation between Lawrence and his mom goes like this:

> "This isn't going to be easy," Lawrence begins.
>
> "Don't worry, honey," Mom says, "Whatever it is, we'll handle it together—calmly and sensibly."
>
> "I'm gay," Lawrence says with an apprehensive look.
>
> "Don't be RIDICULOUS!" his mom exclaims, "I don't believe you!"
>
> "It's the truth, mom," Lawrence says.
>
> "It's a phase," Mom says, "You'll pass through it!"
>
> "It isn't a phase, mom!" Lawrence says, "I've always been gay! It's the way I AM!!"

> "It's my fault," Mom says, "I was too protective! I should have pushed you harder."

Lawrence's father throws him out of the house and his mom calls Michael's mom in panic about her missing son. A search is undertaken and Lawrence is found. In the end Lawrence is accepted and assimilated back into the dominant culture of his family and friends.

40 According to reports in *Editor & Publisher* (Astor, 1993a, 1993b), at least 18 newspapers cancelled *For Better or For Worse,* while about 50 ran an alternate comic strip in place of the controversial episode. Newspapers and trade magazines ran major articles on the controversy, and many newspapers received volumes of letters to the editor on both sides of the issue (Kramer, 1993; Neal, 1993).

Since his initial "coming out" experience, Lawrence continues to appear from time to time in the strip. In one sequence he took his boyfriend, Ben, to the prom. In August 1997, Johnston again angered some readers and newspaper editors when she ran an episode in which Ben, now Lawrence's partner, considers moving to Paris to study piano, and Lawrence has to decide whether to go with him. Each time Lawrence appeared in an episode, some newspapers canceled the strip or replaced it with reruns of earlier episodes (Murray, 1997; Friess, 1997).

Lynn Johnston recalls the event and her reaction:

> Lawrence has been Michael Patterson's close friend and neighbor for many years. He has always been "the kid next door." For the longest time, he appeared consistently with Michael and his friends—but a few years ago, I began to find it harder and harder to bring Lawrence into the picture. Somehow, his life had taken a different turn and I couldn't quite understand why he wasn't still part of the gang. I began to concentrate on him, see his room, his things, his life.
>
> I know all these people so well. I know where their houses are, what their furniture's like, where they work. I know their voices and their mannerisms, their thoughts are open to me ... and yet, I couldn't connect with Lawrence.
>
> After "being" with him for some time, I realized that the reason he was having so much trouble communicating with Michael and his friends was because Lawrence, now in his late teens, was different. Lawrence was gay. (Johnston, 1994, p. 106)

As was the case with Trudeau, it is clear that Johnston knows something about the queer community, but she is not a part of it. She writes: "It [Lawrence's story] was written for my friend Michael Vade-Boncoeur, a comedy writer, performer, and childhood friend for whom my son [Michael] and the character in the strip were named. It was written under the guidance of my husband's brother, Ralph Johnston … who, when he came out, gave me the honor of trusting me first" (Johnston, 1999, p. 75).

45 Although many readers protested the inclusion of a gay character in *For Better or For Worse,* the endings are always happy. Lawrence is not beaten up. After the initial negative reaction from his dad, he is accepted back into the family. There are no offensive names directed toward Lawrence, and as Johnston says of Lawrence, " … he works at Lakeside Landscaping, where he excels in design. He is faithful to his partner, Ben, who is presently studying composition in Paris. He keeps in touch with the Patterson's, who are almost his family, and even though he says he's different … he really hasn't changed at all" (Johnston, 1999, p. 76).

Many in the queer community cannot understand or accept that the process of "coming out" in a heterosexual culture can happen with such calmness and peaceful acceptance. Only a person who is part of the dominant cultural point of view, some queer theorists would argue, could create a world where coming out as queer could have a "fairy tale" ending.

These examples clearly illustrate the acceptable narrative script for queer characters when the comic strip creator is, as far as readers know, heterosexual. Assimilation is normal and easy, being different clearly has its limits, and everyone "lives happily ever after." The world portrayed in the mainstream comic strip does not correlate well with the experiences of people who, in their real lives in the dominant culture, "come out" and identify themselves as queer.

In the 1960s, in response to an ad in the *New York Times* that read "Gay cartoonist wanted," Al Shapiro created *Harry Chess, The Man from A.U.N.T.I.E.* under the pen name A. Jay. This was the first gay comic strip, and it played on the James Bond/*Man from U.N.C.L.E.* theme that was current at the time (Triptow, 1989; Streitmatter, 1995b, pp. 98, 104). Other strips from the 1960s and 1970s included Joe Johnson's *Miss Thing,* Trina Robbins' *Sandy Comes Out,* Roberta Gregory's *Dynamite Damsels,* Howard Cruse's *Barefootz,* and Alison Bechdel's *The Crush.*[5]

Robert Triptow (1989) says of the audiences for these early comic strips: "There are a lot of similarities between comics fandom and the gay subculture. The average comics reader, usually a teenage 'fanboy,' is acquainted with the oppression of conformist society—as is the average gay person. Gay life is often looked down upon as (at best) trivial and self-indulgent …" (p. 4). Gerard Donelan describes his experience as a queer cartoonist:

50 > Hasn't everyone at one time had the urge to cut out a cartoon because "That's me!"? That's what I wanted to do with my cartoons for the gay community. I wanted to do what Joe Johnston's *Miss Thing* in the early days of The Advocate had done for me when I was first coming out. I wanted some fairy to see one of my cartoons, say, "That's me!" and realize that there are others who do what "I" do, feel as "I" feel. I wanted to help show other gay people that "we" have a validity, a sense of humor and a sense of community. (Donelan, 1987, preface, n.p.)

Some queer newspapers in major urban centers include comic strips in their weekly editions. The *Washington (DC) Blade,* for example, runs comic strips each week including Alison Bechdel's *Dykes to Watch Out For,* Eric Orner's *The Unfabulous Social Life of Ethan Green,* John Anderson's *Honestly Ethel,* Glen Hanson and Allan Neuwirth's *Chelsea Boys,* Paige Braddock's *Jane's World,* and Noreen Stevens' *Chosen Family.* It can be argued, however, that these newspapers more and more represent a "niche" publication rather than an "alternative" one (Streitmatter 1995a, 1995b; Fejes & Lennon, 2000). Fred Fejes and Ron Lennon conclude: "The developing lesbian/gay niche media have acquired the legitimacy and the authority to define and speak for the community. Yet in doing so they run the risk again of marginalizing, and making invisible groups who have already suffered and been stigmatized because of their sexual and cultural differences" (Fejes & Lennon, 2000, p. 40).

Alison Bechdel, probably the most widely known queer cartoonist, talks about the effect of a niche market attitude in terms of editorial standards and changes: "[A] comic strip is pretty much editorial proof. Newspapers can't delete, add, or rearrange anything I do. I'm in complete control." She quickly corrects herself, however: "Actually, I lied when I said newspapers can't change anything I do. The *Washington Blade* doesn't permit swearing or reference to certain body parts in their newspaper, so I provide them with a self-bowdlerized alternative when one of my strips contains naughty words" (Bechdel, 1998, p 185). Books based on her strip are available in mainstream bookstores and thus are readily available to a much wider non-queer audience as would be expected of a "niche" publication.

Universal Press Syndicate even approached Bechdel at a meeting of the National Lesbian and Gay Journalists Association conference about syndicating her strip, but the terms were unacceptable (Fitzgerald, 1994). One change that would have been required before syndication, according to Lee Salem of Universal Press, was that "the title would have to go [to appeal] to a mainstream audience." Other stipulations Salem said in included that the strip could not be too political, and that of the four or six characters, only two could be lesbians and they would have to be nonpartisan (cited in Fitzgerald, 1994, p. 14). "I'm not interested in writing for a mainstream audience," Bechdel said: "I'm really happy. I can draw naked people. I can write about politics. I mean, papers are still suspending episodes of *Doonesbury*. I'm not interested in making those kind of compromises" (cited in Fitzgerald, 1994, p. 14). What would a queer comic strip in a mainstream newspaper look like? "I imagine it would be like a lot of the African-American strips," said Bechdel, "like *Jump Start,* which is a nice strip but all the characters are kind of assimilated. The strip would be about straight and gay people living together, maybe. Well, I don't know, but it just wouldn't have any controversy" (cited in Fitzgerald, 1994, p. 15).

Our focus is on comic strips that move beyond the niche market and are directed toward a specifically identified queer audience. Queer comic strips that do not fit into the "niche" category are printed by small alternative presses or are self-published. They are available only at queer bookstores[4] or on the Internet.

The first example is from *XY Magazine,* which is targeted at a young queer population and runs a comic strip as a regular feature. In 1997, the comic strip by Abby Denson, *Tough Love,* featured a high school sophomore, Brian, who talces a martial arts class taught by a "cute" guy named Chris. Brian dreams of taking Chris to the prom, but he doesn't know if Chris is gay. Julie, a straight friend, has been pressuring Brian to take her to the prom until he tells her he is gay. They remain friends since she is "okay" with his sexual orientation. At school, Brian encounters Chris, half-naked, in the locker room. Brian blushes, and Chris invites him over to watch Kung Fu movies. In the course of conversation, Brian discovers that Chris did have a Chinese boyfriend, but when Li's parents discovered he was queer, they sent him back to China "to make him straight." Brian and Chris go to bed together.

Back at school, word has gotten out about Brian's sexual orientation. Some "jocks" discover that Brian is queer, find him alone in the gym and begin to bully him (Figure 11.3). As the encounter continues, the language gets more explicit when one of the jocks says, "He probably went through our lockers for underwear and shit, what a pervert!" They are interrupted when Chris arrives and uses his martial arts skills to rescue Brian. They spend the night together. Chris asks Brian if he's out to his parents, and when Brian says no, Chris asks, "Brian, are you going to tell her [Brian's mother] you're gay?" "Yes ... not now ... eventually," Brian replies, "I want to, but I'm afraid .... Chris, I know you're right. But I need some time. Please be patient with me on this."

Figure 11.3. Brian is bullied by "jocks." From Denson, A. (1997, July). *Tough Love,* 6(8), p. 45. © 1997 Abby Denson, *XY Magazine.* Reprinted by permission. All rights reserved.

It is clear that the story is written for teenagers who are dealing with their own sexuality and sexual orientation. It addresses basic experiences in the language typical of teenagers, especially those who have been labeled as gay, queer, or fag. There is little question about whether this is a "family" cartoon appropriate for a mainstream newspaper comic strips page. The only "straight" male characters are homophobic bullies who enjoy bashing queers. The experience it narrates is clearly different from that portrayed in either *Doonesbury* or *For Better or For Worse.*

Club Survival 101 by Joe Phillips, another comic strip from *XY Magazine,* ran in 1999. The main character is a college guy, Camron (Cam to his friends), who, is somewhat "out" but who has not made the transition from straight to queer culture. The strip follows him as he goes to the gay club for the first time, where his friend, Trevor, sees him:

> "My God! I can't believe you actually made it! Your first time in a gay club! I'm so proud!"
>
> "Whatever … I don't see what the big deal is," Cam says, "Trevor, tell me why everybody is hugging each other like they're goin' off to war."
>
> "Oh relax," Trevor says, "Um … Cam? Who told you to dress like a confused straight boy? I take my eyes off you for two minutes and you leave the house lookin' like beach trade."

60 The dialogue is filled with queer jargon that at times may be quite difficult for non-queer readers to understand completely. Trevor introduces the idea that there is something about the way a person dresses that identifies him or her as queer, at least in a queer environment. A stranger comes up behind Cam, puts his hand on Cam's shoulder, and says: "Oh no she didn't! Yer wearin' A+F after sundown! What in gay hell is wrong with you, Mary? This ain't no rave!" The stranger leads Cam into a back room where a complete transformation takes place. Including a change in the style of his clothes, Cam, now restyled and recreated into an appropriately queer image that fits into the queer club scene, returns to the dance floor. Trevor sees the transformation and says: "Oh, there you … who the hell are you now, the queer formerly known as trade?" (Figure 11.4). They watch the male dancers and mingle with the young gay crowd.

The story continues as the young college guy transitions from straight to queer culture. He meets a wide range of characters and behaves in a manner appropriate to the gay club scene. All the characters in the strip are queer. The role of clothing as a defining characteristic in the queer culture that distinguishes it from the dominant culture is emphasized when at the bottom of the last page of the strip is the notice: "Character clothing and merchandise can be found at http://www.xgear.com."

Figure 11.4. Cam is transformed. From Phillips, J. (1999, March). *Club Survival 101,* 1(17), p. 42. © 1999 Joe Phillips, *XY Magazine.* Reprinted by permission. All rights reserved.

Kyle's Bed & Breakfast by Greg Fox is an on-line comic strip[5] about a queer man who owns a bed and breakfast. Its focus is the lives and experiences of several men who live there or who are friends of the owner. Each character in the strip is modeled after "typical" queer personality types. Kyle, the owner of the B&B, is a 30-something single man. Brad Steele, a 19-year-old minor league baseball player who is still "in the closet" when in the "straight" world, is just beginning to come to terms with being queer. He lives at the B&B and works as a handyman in exchange for his rent. Richard Rubin is a 24-year-old part-time club deejay, gossip, and fashion disaster. Richard means well but lacks basic social skills. Lance Powers, a 28-year-old African-American advertising executive, has just been relocated from LA to New York. Eduardo Vasquez is an 18-year-old high school senior whose parents threw him out when he came out to them. A Hispanic, he is portrayed as young and foolish. There is one female character who makes cameo appearances, but the story centers almost entirely on male characters who clearly represent some diversity within the queer community.

One of the early episodes revolves around a new baseball player, Jeff Olsen, who has been traded to the minor league baseball team on which Brad plays. One of the men on the team says to Brad, "Well ... he's supposed to be an awesome catcher, but, um ... he's a little 'light in the cleats'." "Huh?" Brad interjects. The teammate continues:, "He's a *FAG*. Least that's what the rumor is. He's been bounced around between five teams this season. Good catchers don't get bounced around that much ... unless there's a *reason*."

When Brad and Jeff encounter one another in the locker room, Brad makes it clear that he does not want to be associated with anyone who may even be suspected of being a queer (Figure 11.5). Jeff is harassed by the men on the team and is quickly traded to a new team, but before leaving, he and Brad have a confrontation. Kyle and Jeff are talking when Brad comes into the room and the conversation escalates into an argument centered on what it means for a man to remain in the closet rather than being honest about his sexual orientation (Figure 11.6).

65 The action in *Kyle's Bed & Breakfast* does not take place within the dominant heterosexual culture. It does not present a majority of straight characters. The endings are not always happy. The characters use a jargon and language that step well outside the boundaries of the dominant culture. There is little question that this comic strip is created by a queer artist/writer, about queer characters, and for a queer audience.

Figure 11.5. Brad learns Jeff is queer. From Fox, G. (1999). *Kyle's Bed and Breakfast,* 1(5). © 1999 Greg Fox. Reprinted by permission of the publisher. All rights reserved.

Figure 11.6. Brad and Jeff argue. From Fox, G. (1999). *Kyle's Bed and Breakfast,* 1(6).

Conclusion

Heterosexual cartoonists may introduce queer characters into their comic strips, they may be sympathetic in their treatment, and they may even encounter negative reactions from readers and newspaper editors about their openness and empathy. They live, however, in the dominant heterosexual culture and are an integral part of it in their socialization and thinking. The queer character does not have any clear distinguishing characteristics to differentiate him (so far all the queer characters in mainstream comic strips have been men) from the dominant culture. He is different in a non-obvious, non-threatening way so he can be easily and thoroughly assimilated. He seems to look like everyone else, talk like everyone else, think like everyone else, and behave like all the other heterosexual characters.

Queer cartoonists, on the other hand, tend to include only queer characters or perhaps a small set of heterosexual characters who provide the necessary protagonist needed to create a good narrative. The focus is not on assimilation into a dominant culture, but rather on the creation of a thoroughly queer culture that often is in opposition, if not direct conflict, with the dominant heterosexual culture. Queer individuals often look different, certainly think and act different, and generally feel "out of place" or they have the need to hide their queerness when working within the "straight" world environment. Characters who cannot or will not face up to being queer, such as Brad in *Kyle's Bed & Breakfast,* have internal battles as well as external confrontations about their unwillingness to explore and possibly further own up to their sexual orientation or queerness.

The Internet provides a welcoming environment for queer comic strips. Smaller audiences can access a strip with a clearly defined focus without consideration of issues such as cost of publication, distribution, or editorial oversight—all issues that tend to thwart, if not kill, diversity on the comics pages of dominant culture newspapers.

Will an authentically queer comic strip, by an openly queer cartoonist, appear on the comics pages of your local newspaper? Perhaps the time will come. It happened with African-American and Hispanic comic strips. Queer characters must be allowed to live in a queer world doing queer things with the dominant culture playing a marginalized role. The Queer Nation slogan might be rephrased for queer comic strips as "We're here. We're queer. Give us our queer space!"

Works Cited

Abelove, H. (1995). The queering of lesbian/gay history. *Radical History Review, 62,* 44–57.

Applegate, D. (1994, Fall). Coming out in the comic strips. *Hogan's Alley,* 1, pp. 75–78.

Astor, D. (1993a, April 3). Comic with gay character is dropped by some newspapers. *Editor & Publisher,* p. 32.

Astor, D. (1993b, April 10). More papers cancel controversial comic. *Editor & Publisher,* pp. 34–35.

Bechdel, A. (1998). *The indelible Alison Bechqel: Confessions, comix, and miscellaneous dykes to watch out for.* Ithaca, NY: Firebrand Books.

Dilley, P. (1999). Queer theory: Under construction. *Qualitative Studies in Education,* 12, 457–472.

Donelan, G. P. (1987). *Drawing on the gay experience.* Los Angeles, CA: Liberation Publications.

Fejes, F., & Lennon, R. (2000). Defining the lesbian/gay community? Market research and the lesbian/gay press. *Journal of Homosexuality,* 39, 25–42.

Fitzgerald, M. (1994, October 15). The biggest closet in newspapering. *Editor & Publisher,* pp. 14–15.

Friess (1997, Fall). Syndicate warns papers about gay-themed comic strip. *Alternatives* [newsletter of the National Lesbian & Gay Journalists Assoctiation].

Fuss, D. (1991). Inside/out. In D. Fuss (Ed.), *Inside/out: Lesbian theories, gay theories* (pp. 1–12). New York: Routledge.

Gamson, J. (1995). Must identity movements self-destruct? A queer dilemma. *Social Problems,* 42, 390–407.

Gamson, J. (1998). *Freaks talk back: Tabloid talk shows and sexual nonconformity.* Chicago, IL: University of Chicago Press.

Gamson, J. (2000). Sexualities, queer theory, and qualitative research. In N. K. Denzin & Y. S. Lincoln (Eds.), *Handbook of qualitative research,* second edition (pp. 347–365). Thousand Oaks, CA: Sage.

Grossberg, L. (1993). Cultural studies and new worlds. In C. McCarthy & W. Crichlow (Eds.), *Race, identity and representation* (pp. 89–105). New York: Routledge.

Grossberg, L. (1996). Identity and cultural studies: Is that all there is? In S. Hall & P. duGay (Eds.), *Questions of cultural identity* (pp. 87–107). Thousand Oaks, CA: Sage.

Halperin, D. (1995). *Saint Foucault: Toward a gay hagiography.* New York: Oxford University Press.

Honeychurch, K. G. (1996). Researching dissident subjectivities: Queering the grounds of theory and practice, *Harvard Educational Review,* 66, 339–355.

Jagose, A. (1996). *Queer theory: An introduction.* New York: New York University Press.

Johnston, L. (1994). *It's the thought that counts* .... Kansas City, MO: Andrews & McMeel.

Johnston, L. (1999). *The lives behind the lines.* Kansas City, MO: Andrews & McMeel.

Kramer, S. D. (I 993, April 13). 'Coming out.' *The Washington Post,* B5.

Lawlor, S. D., Sparkes, A., & Wood, J. (1994, July). *When Lawrence came out: Taking the funnies seriously.* Paper presented at the International Communication Association. Sydney, Australia.

Murray, J. (1997, August 25). Cartoon carries message of tolerance. *The Gazette* (Montreal), B3.

Neal, J. (1993, April 23). Family-oriented comic strip character says he's gay. *Comics Buyer's Guide.*

Pustz, M. J. (1999). *Comic book culture: Fanboys and true believers.* Jackson, MS: University Press of Mississippi.

Rotella, G. (2000, August 15). The word that failed. *The Advocate,* p. 112.

Sabin, R. (1996). *Comics, comix & graphic novels.* London: Phaidon.

Seidman, S. (1993). Identity and politics in a "postmodern" gay culture: Some historical and conceptual notes. In M. Warner (Ed.), *Fear of a queer planet: Queer politics and social theory* (pp. 105–142). Minneapolis, MN: University of Minnesota Press.

Seidman, S. (1996). Introduction. In S. Seidman (Ed.), *Queer theory/sociology* (pp. 1–29). Cambridge, MA: Blackweli.

Slagle, A. (1995). In defense of Queer Nation: From identity politics to a politics of difference. *Western Journal of Communication,* 59, 85–102.

Streitmatter, R. (1995a). Creating a venue for the "Love that dare not speak its name": Origins of the gay and lesbian press. *Journalism and Mass Communication Quarterly,* 72, 436–447.

Streitmatter, R. (1995b). *Unspeakable: The rise of the gay and lesbian press in America.* Boston: Faber and Faber.

Triptow, R. (1989). *Gay comics.* New York: New American Library.

Trudeau, G. B. (1978). *Doonesbury's greatest hits.* NY: Henry Holt.

Trudeau, G. B. (1998). *The bundled Doonesbury: A pre-millennial anthology.* Kansas City, MO: Andrews & McMeel.

Trudeau, G. B. (1999). *Buck wild Doonesbury.* Kansas City, MO: Andrews & McMeel.

Credit

"God Don't Never Change": Black English from a Black Perspective

GENEVA SMITHERMAN

Ain nothin in a long time lit up the English teaching profession like the current hassle over Black English. One finds beaucoup socio-linguistic research studies and language projects for the "disadvantaged" on the scene in nearly every sizable Black community in the country.[1] And educators from K through grad. school bees debating whether: 1) Blacks should learn and use only standard white English (hereafter referred to as WE); 2) Blacks should command both dialects, i.e., be bidialectal (hereafter BD); 3) Blacks should be allowed (??????????) to use standard Black English (hereafter BE or BI, for Black Idiom, a more accurate term). The appropriate choice having everything to do with American political reality, which is usually ignored, and nothing to do with the educational process, which is usually claimed. I say without qualification that we cannot talk about BI apart from Black Culture and the Black Experience. Nor can we specify educational goals for Blacks apart from considerations about the structure of white American society.

Both Black and white critics of American society have dealt extensively with the rather schizophrenic nature of the American politico-social sensibility, caused by the clash of the emphasis on class flexibility and individualism with the concomitant stress on class conformity and group status. It is interesting to note the way this class consciousness neurosis is reflected in the area of language.

A quick look at the tradition of schoolroom grammars and the undergirding ideology of early English grammarians reveals that the current "national mania for correctness" has been around a long time. You see, from the Jump, the English language itself, didn't command no respect, for Latin was the lingo of the elite. (Outside thought: if WE wasn't given no propers, you know BI wouldn't be given any.) What those grammarians did was to take note of the actual usage of English only for the purpose of denouncing and reforming that usage. Clearly these grammarians was comin from a position that English could and must be subjected to a process of regularizing, based on a Latin/Classical model On the British side, there was Bishop Robert Lowth *(Short Introduction to English Grammar,* 1763), who conceptualized his grammar in terms of giving "order and permanence" to the "unruly, barbarous" tongue of the AngloSaxons:

"The English language, as it is spoken by the politest part of the nation, and as it stands in the writings of our most approved authors, often offends against every part of Grammar." The continuity of this line of thinking in the American sensibility is best exemplified by Lindley Murray *(English Grammar,* 1795). Now Murray was really a deep dude cause, see, his book, was not gon simply introduce the proper method of English usage among the young, but inculcate in them all the morals and virtues commensurate with correct English. Dig it, now, here what he say:

> The author of the following work [referring to himself, like they always did, in the ridiculous third person] wishes to promote the cause of virtue as well as of learning; and with this view, he has been studious, through the whole of the work, not only to avoid every example and illustration, which might have an improper effect on the minds of youth, but also to introduce on many occasions such as have a moral and religious tendency.

By the Twentieth Century, the individual norm had been replaced by a group norm. According to Charles C. Fries *(American English Grammar,* 1940), the job of the public schools was to teach

> the type of English used by the socially acceptable of most of our communities [since] in the matter of the English language, it is clear that any one who cannot use the language habits in which the major affairs of the country are conducted, the language habits of the socially acceptable of most of our communities, would have a serious handicap.

Obviously this didn't make things no better for the common folk. It was just substituting one linguistic authority for another—the individual Latinate standards of a Lowth or Murray for the group Anglican standards of middle America. Both authorities and norms is based on race and class position and is simply attempts to make the "outsiders" talk like the "insiders." This superimposition of a dialect norm has little to do with language power, linguistic versatility, or variety of expression and everything to do with making what one grammarian labeled the "depraved language of common people" *(The Art of Speaking,* 1668), and by extension, the common people themselves, conform to white, middle-class society. Thus nowadays, "nonstandard" dialect is that which "deviates" from the collective language of the majority culture. For example, it is now all right to use the contracted form (which offended the idiosyncratic sensibilities of those early grammarians like crazy), so it is acceptable to say *It's that way* for *It is that way.* Similarly, we can, without causing too much consternation, use the objective case after copula, as *It is me* for *It is I.* The point is that both examples represent forms regularly used by middle-class and white Americans. But dig now, in no way, do the new language pacesetters accept *It bees that way* (a popular BI statement; an expression of Black existentialist reflection and thought; used by Nina Simone as the title of a hit recording). See, an idiomatic phrase like this comes from a "lower-class" dialect (and a people) that is given no respect.

On the one hand, then, the denigration of BI is but a manifestation of white America's class anxiety. After all, as Baldwin says, in a country where everybody has status, it is possible that nobody has status. So Americans, lacking a fixed place in the society, don't know where they be in terms of social and personal identity. For this reason, it has been useful to have nigguhs around, so at least they always knows where the *bottom* bees. On the other hand, then, the pejorative attitude toward BI is a manifestation of white America's racism (undergirded by or coupled with class elitism). I shall cite three examples reflecting racism in the area of linguistics.

5 Toward the end of the last century, Ambrose Gonzales collected stories from the Gullah (or, as we called it down in Tennessee, "Geechee") region of the Carolina Coast and published these in *Black Border*. Speaking about the language of the Gullah Black folk, Gonzales contended:

> The [Gullah] words are, of course, not African, for the African brought over or retained only a few words of his jungle-tongue, and even these few are by no means authenticated as part of the original scant baggage of the negro slaves ... Slovenly and careless of speech, these Gullahs seized upon the peasant English used by some of the early settlers and by the white servants of the wealthier colonists, wrapped their clumsy tongues about it as well as they could, and, enriched with certain expressive African words, it issued through their flat noses and thick lips as so workable a form of speech that it was gradually adopted by the other slaves and became in time the accepted Negro speech of the lower districts of South Carolina and Georgia. With characteristic laziness, these Gullah Negroes took short cuts to the ears of their auditors, using as few words as possible, sometimes making one gender serve for three, one tense for several, and totally disregarding singular and plural numbers.

(Outside thought: such absurd nonsense was validly challenged by Black historian-turned-linguist Lorenzo Dow Turner in his *Africanisms in the Gullah Dialect*, 1949.)

In 1924, in an article titled "The English of the Negro," and again in 1925, in his *English Language in America,* George Philip Krapp discussed Black speech patterns throughout the South. (Outside thought: his discussion is appropriately titled by his last name.) In reconstructing the evolution of this dialect, Krapp argued that there were "no African elements ... in the English of negroes [sic]";

rather this dialect reflected "archaic survivals" of English which had lingered because the "negro, being socially backward, has held onto many habits which the white world has left behind." Finally, Krapp dismissed Black speech by concluding that "negro English ... is merely a debased dialect of English, learned by the negroes from the whites."

Well, even though Gonzales and Krapp were writing in what my fifteen-year-old son terms the "olden days," ain't nothin changed. In a recent record, *The Dialect of Black Americans,* distributed for educational purposes by Western Electric, we are told of Joseph, a recent Black high school graduate, who was refused a job because "his speech carries no respect. In fact it generates negative attitudes, and the middle-class Black must be careful of the language he uses—or which language he uses." Sound familiar? Sure, just another variation on the linguistic purist/class anxiety theme of Lowth, Murray, and Fries; and the linguistic ethnocentricism and rampant racism of Gonzales and Krapp. (Outside thought: still at 1763 and it's 1973.)

In conceptualizing linguistic performance models for Black students, our contemporary objectives must be informed by such historical socio-political realities as I have touched upon here. They must also be informed by accurate, comprehensive descriptions of BI. Both kinds of information are so highly interrelated as to be virtually inseparable. Let me proceed, then, to discuss this latter point in some detail.

Most linguists and educators currently belaboring the "problem" of what has come to be popularly termed "Black English" have conceptualized the dialect in very narrow, constricting, and ultimately meaningless terms. Depending on the "scholarship" consulted or the rap sessions overheard in teachers' lounges, one finds 8–10 patterns of usage labeled BE. For example: zero -s morpheme in sentences such as *He work all the time, Those scientist inventing many thing, My mother name Mary;* copula deletion as in *He a hippie* (also in the preceding example); multiple negation as *Can't nobody do nothin in his room;* and, of course, that famous and oft-quoted use of be as finite verb, as in *They be slow all the time.* And so on and so on. The point is that such a list contains only a very small ultimately unimportant set of *surface* grammatical features. One searches in vain for any discussion of surface vs. deep structure significance in the so-called "scholarly" literature on BI. I'm talkin bout deep structure in the Chomskian sense of the term. What, after all, is the underlying semantic differentiation between *He work all the time* and *He works all the time?* Or even between *My mother's name is Mary* and *My mother name Mary?* But this is logical. because if BI were really deep structurally different from WE, then there would be a situation of mutual unintelligibility. Oh, yeah, white folks understand BI speakers, it ain't a question of communication. Whites might not like what they hear, but they bees hearin and comprehendin every bit of it. Just as white speakers from one region of the country understand whites from another region. As a matter of fact, though I doubt if many white folks would admit it, they have far greater difficulty with British English than with BI. Yet British English commands great prestige in this country. (Outside thought: since America was once a British colony, this is what Frantz Fanon might call the "colonized mentality.")

10 This "much ado about nothing" is what led to the accusation by a Brother, at a recent Black professional meeting, that the research on BI was bogus scholarship, pseudo-intellectual attempts to create a field of knowledge or a discipline out of nothing. He was not misled, as, unfortunately, many English teachers are, by the overcomplexification, linguistic jargon, and statistical paraphernalia—i.e., scholarly trappings that make some of the articles on BI almost unreadable, and the linguists themselves nearly unintelligible. (Dig it, "zero -s morpheme" is just another way of saying that the kid left off an "s.") The dire consequence of this whole business to the English teaching profession can be illustrated by the case of a Black freshman at Wayne State, who submitted the following:

> [TEACHER'S, ASSIGNMENT: Take a position on the war in Viet Nam and present arguments to defend your position.]
>
> I think the war in Viet Nam bad. Because we don't have no business over there. My brother friend been in the war, and he say it's hard and mean. I do not like war because it's bad. And so I don't think we have no business there. The reason the war in China is bad is that American boys is dying over there.

The paper was returned to the student with only *one* comment: "Correct your grammar and resubmit." What sheer and utter nonsense!

Now, my advice to teachers is to overlook these matters of sheer mechanical "correctness" and get on with the educational business at hand. Don't let students get away with sloppy, irresponsible writing just because it happen to conform to a surface notion of correctness. Yeah, that's right, there is such a thang as sloppy "correct" writing—writing, for instance, where every statement is generalized comment without any specific, supporting details; or where the same modification structures or sentence patterns are used with tedious repetition; or where the student uses one simple kernel structure after another instead of combining and condensing. While *zero -s* and *-ed morphemes* may be easier "issues" for the already overworked English profs to deal with, I would warn such teachers not to abdicate their *real* responsibility: that of involving students in the totality and complexity of the communication process. And I would denounce as futile and time-wasting the attempts to move Black students from, for example, "He tired" to "He is tired" or from "They sold they house" to "They sold their house." Not only are such ventures misuses of important educational time, they are perhaps, albeit subtly, racist because such goals involve only lateral moves and Black folks need (upward) vertical moves. That what we mean when we sing with Curtis Mayfield "We movin on up," *Up,* not sideways.

None of this has been to assert that there is not a distinctive verbal style that characterizes contemporary Black American speech. But it is to reiterate a point I've made many times heretofore: it's *style, not language per se,* in which the uniqueness of Black expression lies. This style must be located in the situational context, in the Black Cultural Universe. And anybody who *knows* anythang about BI knows that that's where it's at. (Outside thought: emphasis on *knows,* cause like my daddy the preacher say, everybody talking bout Heaven ain't goin there.) I'm talking bout the Black Lexicon, and bout the rhetorical devices and unique patterns of communication found in what Richard Wright called the "Forms of Things Unknown." Such stylistic/language forms are an indigenous part of the Black historical past and are rooted in the Black Cultural sensibility. They achieve a dynamism of meaning which emanates from a shared sense of oppression, and they represent, perhaps, the continuity of our African sensibility in the New World. Although older Black writers used these forms only sporadically in they works (even Richard Wright himself), the new Black writers, the poets especially, are hip to the significance of these patterns from our Oral Tradition and have appropriated them with maximum power and poetic effect. I shall cite a few illuminating examples.

Don Lee effectively uses items from the Black Lexicon when he describes Malcolm X as being from "a long line of super-cools/doo-rag lovers/ revolutionary "pimps."[2] He employs Capping, Signification, and Black Rhythmic Pattern in his poem denouncing the self-styled Black revolutionary, who is all talk and no action—dig on the title alone: "But he was cool or: he even stopped for green lights."[3] Black prison poet Etheridge Knight does a poetic variation of the Toast in his poem about the Black prisoner Hard Rock, a super-bad dude, about whom there is a "jewel of a myth that Hard Rock had once bit/A screw on the thumb and poisoned him with syphilitic spit."[4] Maya Angelou plays the Dozens on both Blacks and whites in her companion poems "The Thirteens."[5] The ritualistic barbershop scene in John Oliver Killens' novel *Cotillion*[6] is shot through with a secular version of the Call-Response Pattern. And Richard Wright's own "Fire and Cloud,"[7] a short story about a militant Black minister, contains one of the most effective prose renditions of the sacred manifestation of this basic pattern.

Why is it that these substantive features of BI are never included in the descriptive monographs of "Black English"? Why is it that only the superfluous features of usage are extrapolated and dealt with in "language programs for the disadvantaged"? And isn't it interesting that these Superficial features of BI are easily translatable into WE? Whereas ain't no way in the world you can transform the "Forms of Things Unknown." Methinks there is some insidous design afoot to cut off Black students from they cultural roots, from, according to Frantz Fanon, "those they left behind," to create a new class of super-niggers, nouveau-white Blacks, who will rap in the oppressor's dialect, totally obliterating any knowledge or use of BI—a form of language firmly imbedded in the African-American past. Because, you see, the plain and simple fact is that language does not exist in a vacuum but in the socio-cultural reality. And with this broad view of BI, a view informed by cognizance of our historical past and political present, *even* those surface features take on a different meaning. As Baraka says:

> I heard an old Negro street singer last week. Reverend Pearly Brown, singing, "God don't never change!" This is a precise thing he is singing. He does not mean "God does not ever change!" He means "God don't never change!" The difference ... is in the final human reference ... the form of passage through the world. A man who is rich and famous who sings, "God don't never change," is confirming his hegemony and good fortune ... or merely calling the bank. A blind hopeless black American is saying something very different. ...

Being told to "speak proper," meaning that you become fluent with the jargon of power, is also a part of not "speaking proper." That is the culture which desperately understands that it does not "speak proper," or is not fluent with the terms of social strength, also understands somewhere that its desire to gain such fluency is done at a terrifying risk. The bourgeois Negro accepts such risk as profit. But does *close-ter* (in the context of "jes a close-ter, walk wi-thee") mean the same thing as *closer*"? Close-ter, in the term of its user is, believe me, exact. It means a quality of existence, of actual physical disposition perhaps in its manifestation as a *tone* and *rhythm* by which people live, most often in response to common modes of thought best enforced by some factor of environmental emotion that is exact and specific. Even the picture it summons is different, and certainly the "Thee" that is used to connect the implied "Me" with, is different. The God of the damned cannot know the God of the damner, that is, cannot know he is God. As no Blues person can really believe emotionally in Pascal's God, or Wittgenstein's question, "Can the concept of God exist in a perfectly logical language?" Answer: "God don't never change."[8]

Credit

Smitherman, Geneva. "'God Don't Never Change': Black English from a Black Perspective." *College English* 34.6. (1973): 828–833. Originally published 1973 by the National Council of Teachers of English.

Praisesong for a Mountain

BIANCA LYNNE SPRIGGS

O, mountain,
I am your daughter.

Once, before I knew you,
I mistook you
for a low-hanging thunderhead.

Or thought maybe
you were a blue whale
that had lost its way,
blinded by the sun.

O, mountain,
   linger—
be my whole horizon.

Let me never open
my eyes and see a thing
but your hoary grace.

You are the missing
rib of the Earth.

You are the climax
of a god's birth.

You are the mausoleum
of burnt-out stars.

O, mountain,
I wish one day
to be buried
in your third eye.

Lend me something
of yourself:
your posture,
your grip,
your innermost
jewel-toned seam,
so that I too, may endure.

Annoying Ways People Use Sources

KYLE D. STEDMAN

How Slow Driving Is Like Sloppy Writing

I hate slow drivers.* When I'm driving in the fast lane, maintaining the speed limit exactly, and I find myself behind someone who thinks the fast lane is for people who drive ten miles per hour *below* the speed limit, I get an annoyed feeling in my chest like hot water filling a heavy bucket. I wave my arms around and yell, "What ...? But, hey ... oh come *on!*" There are at least two explanations for why some slow drivers fail to move out of the way:

1. They don't know that the generally accepted practice of highway driving in the U.S. is to move to the right if an upcoming car wants to pass. Or,
2. They know the guidelines but don't care.

But here's the thing: writers can forget that their readers are sometimes just as annoyed at writing that fails to follow conventions as drivers are when stuck behind a car that fails to move over. In other words, there's something similar between these two people: the knowledgeable driver who thinks, "I thought all drivers *knew* that the left lane is for the fastest cars," and the reader who thinks, "I thought all writers *knew* that outside sources should be introduced, punctuated, and cited according to a set of standards."

One day, you may discover that something you've written has just been read by a reader who, unfortunately, was annoyed at some of the ways you integrated sources. She was reading along and then suddenly exclaimed, "What ...? But, hey ... oh come on!" If you're lucky, this reader will try to imagine why you typed things the way you did, giving you the benefit of the doubt. But sometimes you'll be slotted into positions that might not really be accurate. When this frustrated reader walks away from your work, trying to figure out, say, why you used so many quotations, or why you kept starting and ending paragraphs with them, she may come to the same conclusions I do about slow drivers:

1. You don't know the generally accepted practices of using sources (especially in academic writing) in the U.S. Or,
2. You know the guidelines but don't care.

And it will be a lot harder for readers to take you seriously if they think you're ignorant or rude.

This judgment, of course, will often be unfair. These readers might completely ignore the merits of your insightful, stylistically beautiful, or revolutionarily important language—just as my anger at another driver makes me fail to admire his custom paint job. But readers and writers don't always see eye to eye on the same text. In fact, some things I write about in this essay will only bother your pickiest readers (some teachers, some editors, some snobby friends), while many other readers might zoom past how you use sources without blinking. But in my experience, I find that teachers do a disservice when we fail to alert students to the kind of things that some readers might be annoyed at—however illogical these things sometimes seem. People are often unreasonably picky, and writers have to deal with that—which they do by trying to anticipate and preemptively fix whatever might annoy a broad range of readers. Plus, the more effectively you anticipate that pickiness, the more likely it is that readers will interpret your quotations and paraphrases in the way you want them to—critically or acceptingly, depending on your writing context.

It helps me to remember that the conventions of writing have a fundamentally *rhetorical* nature. That is, I follow different conventions depending on the purpose and audience of my writing, because I know that I'll come across differently to different people depending on how well I follow the conventions expected in any particular writing space. In a blog, I cite a source by hyperlinking; in an academic essay, I use a parenthetical citation that refers to a list of references at the end of the essay. One of the fundamental ideas of rhetoric is that speakers/writers/composers shape what they say/write/create based on what they want it to do, where they're publishing it, and what they know about their audience/readers. And those decisions include nitty-gritty things like introducing quotations and citing paraphrases clearly: not everyone in the entire world approaches these things the same way, but when I strategically learn the expectations of my U.S. academic audience, what

I really want to say comes across smoothly, without little annoying blips in my readers' experience. Notice that I'm not saying that there's a particular *right* or *wrong* way to use conventions in my writing—if the modern U.S. academic system had evolved from a primarily African or Asian or Latin American cultural consciousness instead of a European one, conventions for writing would probably be very different. That's why they're *conventions* and not *rules*.

The Annoyances

5 Because I'm not here to tell you *rules*, *decrees*, or *laws*, it makes sense to call my classifications *annoyances*. In the examples that follow, I wrote all of the annoying examples myself, but all the examples I use of good writing come from actual student papers in first year composition classes at my university; I have their permission to quote them.

Armadillo Roadkill

Armadillo Roadkill: dropping in a quotation without introducing it first

Everyone in the car hears it: buh-BUMP. The driver insists to the passengers, "But that armadillo—I didn't see it! It just came out of nowhere!"

Sadly, a poorly introduced quotation can lead readers to a similar exclamation: "It just came out of nowhere!" And though readers probably won't experience the same level of grief and regret when surprised by a quotation as opposed to an armadillo, I submit that there's a kinship between the experiences: both involve a normal, pleasant activity (driving; reading) stopped suddenly short by an unexpected barrier (a sudden armadillo; a sudden quotation).

Here's an example of what I'm talking about:

> We should all be prepared with a backup plan if a zombie invasion occurs. "Unlike its human counterparts, an army of zombies is completely independent of support" (Brooks 155). Preparations should be made in the following areas …

Did you notice how the quotation is dropped in without any kind of warning? (Buh-BUMP.)

The Fix: The easiest way to effectively massage in quotations is by purposefully returning to each one in your draft to see if you set the stage for your readers—often, by signaling that a quote is about to come, stating who the quote came from, and showing how your readers should interpret it. In the above example, that could be done by introducing the quotation with something like this (new text bolded):

> We should all be prepared with a backup plan if a zombie invasion occurs. **Max Brooks suggests a number of ways to prepare for zombies' particular traits, though he underestimates the ability of humans to survive in harsh environments. For example, he writes,** "Unlike its human counterparts, an army of zombies is completely independent of support" (155). **His shortsightedness could have a number of consequences …**

In this version, I know a quotation is coming ("For example"), I know it's going to be written by Max Brooks, and I know I'm being asked to read the quote rather skeptically ("he underestimates"). The sentence with the quotation itself also now begins with a "tag" that eases us into it ("he writes").

10 Here's an actual example from Alexsandra. Notice the way she builds up to the quotation and then explains it:

> In the first two paragraphs, the author takes a defensive position when explaining the perception that the public has about scientists by saying that "there is anxiety that scientists lack both wisdom and social responsibility and are so motivated by ambition …" and "scientists are repeatedly referred to as 'playing God'" (Wolpert 345). With this last sentence especially, his tone seems to demonstrate how he uses the ethos appeal to initially set a tone of someone that is tired of being misunderstood.

Alexsandra prepares us for the quotation, quotes, and then analyzes it. I love it. This isn't a hard and fast rule—I've seen it broken by the best of writers, I admit—but it's a wise standard to hold yourself to unless you have a reason not to.

Dating Spider-Man

Dating Spider-Man: starting or ending a paragraph with a quotation

An annoyance that's closely connected to Armadillo Roadkill is the tendency writers sometimes have of starting or ending paragraphs with quotations. This isn't technically *wrong*, and there are situations when the effect of surprise is what you're going for. But often, a paragraph-beginning or paragraph-closing quotation feels rushed, unexplained, disjointed.

It's like dating Spider-Man. You're walking along with him and he says something remarkably interesting—but then he tilts his head, hearing something far away, and suddenly shoots a web onto the nearest building and *zooms* away through the air. As if you had just read an interesting quotation dangling at the end of a paragraph, you wanted to hear more of his opinion, but it's too late—he's already moved on. Later, he suddenly jumps off a balcony and is by your side again, and he starts talking about something you don't understand. You're confused because he just dropped in and expected you to understand the context of what was on his mind at that moment, much like when readers step into a paragraph that begins with a quotation. Here's an example:

> *[End of a preceding paragraph:]* … Therefore, the evidence clearly suggests that we should be exceptionally careful about deciding when and where to rest.
>
> "When taking a nap, always rest your elbow on your desk and keep your arm perpendicular to your desktop" (Piven and Borgenicht 98). After all, consider the following scenario …

There's a perfectly good reason why this feels odd—which should feel familiar after reading about the Armadillo Roadkill annoyance above. When you got to the quotation in the second paragraph, you didn't know what you were supposed to think about it; there was no guidance.

The Fix is the same: in the majority of situations, readers appreciate being guided to and led away from a quotation by the writer doing the quoting. Readers get a sense of pleasure from the safe flow of hearing how to read an upcoming quotation, reading it, and then being told one way to interpret it. Prepare, quote, analyze.

I mentioned above that there can be situations where starting a paragraph with a quotation can have a strong effect. Personally, I usually enjoy this most at the beginning of essays or the beginning of sections—like in this example from the very beginning of Jennifer's essay:

> "Nothing is ever simple: Racism and nobility can exist in the same man, hate and love in the same woman, fear and loyalty, compromise and idealism, all the yin-yang dichotomies that make the human species so utterly confounding, yet so utterly fascinating" (Hunter). The hypocrisy and complexity that Stephen Hunter from the *Washington Post* describes is the basis of the movie *Crash* (2004).

Instantly, her quotation hooks me. It doesn't feel thoughtless, like it would feel if I continued to be whisked to quotations without preparation throughout the essay. But please don't overdo it; any quotation that opens an essay or section ought to be integrally related to your topic (as is Jennifer's), not just a cheap gimmick.

Uncle Barry and His Encyclopedia of Useless Information

Uncle Barry and his Encyclopedia of Useless Information: using too many quotations in a row

15 You probably know someone like this: a person (for me, my Uncle Barry) who constantly tries to impress me with how much he knows about just about everything. I might casually bring up something in the news ("Wow, these health care debates are getting really heated, aren't they?") and then find myself barraged by all of Uncle Barry's ideas on government-sponsored health care—which *then* drifts into a story about how his cousin Maxine died in an underfunded hospice center, which had a parking lot that he could have designed better, which reminds him of how good he is at fixing things, just like the garage door at my parents' house, which probably only needs a little ... You get the idea. I might even think to myself, "Wait, I want to know more about that topic, but you're zooming on before you contextualize your information at all."

This is something like reading an essay that relies too much on quotations. Readers get the feeling that they're moving from one quotation to the next without ever quite getting to hear the *real* point of what the author wants to say, never getting any time to form an opinion about the claims. In fact, this often makes it sound as if the author has almost no authority at all. You may have been annoyed by paragraphs like this before:

> Addressing this issue, David M. Potter comments, "Whether Seward meant this literally or not, it was in fact a singularly accurate forecast for territorial Kansas" (199). Of course, Potter's view is contested, even though he claims, "Soon, the Missourians began to perceive the advantages of operating without publicity" (200). Interestingly, "The election was bound to be irregular in any case" (201).

Wait—huh? This author feels like Uncle Barry to me: grabbing right and left for topics (or quotes) in an effort to sound authoritative.

The Fix is to return to each quotation and decide why it's there and then massage it in accordingly. If you just want to use a quote to cite a *fact*, then consider paraphrasing or summarizing the source material (which I find is usually harder than it sounds but is usually worth it for the smoothness my paragraph gains). But if you quoted because you want to draw attention to the source's particular phrasing, or if you want to respond to something you agree with or disagree with in the source, then consider taking the time to surround *each* quotation with guidance to your readers about what you want them to think about that quote.

In the following passage, I think Jessica demonstrates a balance between source and analysis well. Notice that she only uses a single quotation, even though she surely could have chosen more. But instead, Jessica relies on her instincts and remains the primary voice of authority in the passage:

> Robin Toner's article, "Feminist Pitch by a Democrat named Obama," was written a week after the video became public and is partially a response to it. She writes, "The Obama campaign is, in some ways, subtly marketing its candidate as a post-feminist man, a generation beyond the gender conflicts of the boomers." Subtly is the key word. Obama is a passive character throughout the video, never directly addressing the camera. Rather, he is shown indirectly through speeches, intimate conversations with supporters and candid interaction with family. This creates a sense of intimacy, which in turn creates a feeling of trust.

Toner's response to the Obama video is like a diving board that Jessica bounces off of before she gets to the really interesting stuff: the pool (her own observations). A bunch of diving boards lined up without a pool (tons of quotes with no analysis) wouldn't please anyone—except maybe Uncle Barry.

Am I in the Right Movie?

Am I in the Right Movie? failing to integrate a quotation into the grammar of the preceding sentence

When reading drafts of my writing, this is a common experience: I start to read a sentence that seems interesting and normal, with everything going just the way I expect it to. But then the unexpected happens: a quotation blurts itself into the sentence in a way that doesn't fit with the grammar that built up to quotation. It feels like sitting in a movie theater, everything going as expected, when suddenly the opening credits start for a movie I didn't plan to see. Here are two examples of what I'm talking about. Read them out loud, and you'll see how suddenly wrong they feel.

1. Therefore, the author warns that a zombie's vision "are no different than those of a normal human" (Brooks 6).
2. Sheila Anne Barry advises that "Have you ever wondered what it's like to walk on a tightrope—many feet up in the air?" (50)

In the first example, the quoter's build-up to the quotation uses a singular subject—*a zombie's vision*—which, when paired with the quotation, is annoyingly matched with the plural verb *are*. It would be much less jolting to write, "a zombie's vision *is*," which makes the subject and verb agree. In the second example, the quoter builds up to the quotation with a third-person, declarative independent clause: *Sheila Anne Barry advises*. But then the quotation switches into second person—*you*—and unexpectedly asks a question—completely different from the expectation that was built up by the first part of the sentence.

20 **The Fix** is usually easy: you read your essay out loud to someone else, and if you stumble as you enter a quotation, there's probably something you can adjust in your lead-in sentence to make the two fit together well. Maybe you'll need to choose a different subject to make it fit with the quote's verb (*reader* instead of *readers; each* instead of *all*), or maybe you'll have to scrap what you first wrote and start over. On occasion you'll even feel the need to transparently modify the quotation by adding an [s] to one of its verbs, always being certain to use square brackets to show that you adjusted something in the quotation. Maybe you'll even find a way to quote a shorter part of the quotation and squeeze it into the context of a sentence that is mostly your own, a trick that can have a positive effect on readers, who like smooth water slides more than they like bumpy slip-and-slides. Jennifer does this well in the following sentence, for example:

> In *Crash*, no character was allowed to "escape his own hypocrisy" (Muller), and the film itself emphasized that the reason there is so much racial tension among strangers is because of the personal issues one cannot deal with alone.

She saw a phrase that she liked in Muller's article, so she found a way to work it in smoothly, without the need for a major break in her thought. Let's put ourselves in Jennifer's shoes for a moment: it's possible that she started drafting this sentence using the plural subject *characters*, writing "In *Crash*, no characters were allowed …" But then, imagine she looked back at the quote from Muller and saw that it said "escape *his* own hypocrisy," which was a clue that she had to change the first part of her sentence to match the singular construction of the quote.

I Can't Find the Stupid Link

I Can't Find the Stupid Link: no connection between the first letter of a parenthetical citation and the first letter of a works cited entry

You've been in this situation: you're on a website that seems like it might be interesting and you want to learn more about it. But the home page doesn't tell you much, so you look for an "About Us" or "More Information" or "FAQ" link. But no matter where you search—Top of page? Bottom? Left menu?—you can't find the stupid link. This is usually the fault of web designers, who don't always take the time to test their sites as much as they should with actual users.

The communication failure here is simple: you're used to finding certain kinds of basic information in the places people usually put it. If it's not there, you're annoyed.

Similarly, a reader might see a citation and have a quick internal question about it: *What journal was this published in? When was it published? Is this an article I could find online to skim myself? This author has a sexy last name—I wonder what his first name is?* Just like when you look for a link to more information, this reader has a simple, quick question that he or she expects to answer easily. And the most basic way for readers to answer those questions (when they're reading a work written in APA or MLA style) is (1) to look at the information in the citation, and (2) skim the references or works cited section alphabetically, looking for the first letter in the citation. There's an assumption that the first letter of a citation will be the letter to look for in the list of works cited.

25 In short, the following may annoy readers who want to quickly learn more about the citation:

> *[Essay Text:]* A respected guide on the subject suggests, "If possible, always take the high ground and hold it" (*The Zombie Survival Guide* 135).
>
> [Works Cited Page:] Brooks, Max. *The Zombie Survival Guide: Complete Protection from the Living Dead*. New York: Three Rivers, 2003. Print.

The reader may wonder when *The Zombie Survival Guide* was published and flip back to the works cited page, but the parenthetical citation sends her straight to the *Z*'s in the works cited list (because initial *A*'s and *The*'s are ignored when alphabetizing). However, the complete works cited entry is actually with the *B*'s (where it belongs).

The Fix is to make sure that the first word of the works cited entry is the word you use in your in-text citation, every time. If the works cited entry starts with Brooks, use (Brooks) in the essay text.

Citations not including last names may seem to complicate this advice, but they all follow the same basic concept. For instance, you might have:

- **A citation that only lists a title**. For instance, your citation might read ("Gray Wolf General Information"). In this case, the assumption is that the citation can be found under the *G* section of the works cited page. Leah cites her paraphrase of a source with no author in the following way, indicating that I should head to the *G*'s if I want to learn more about her source:

  Alaska is the only refuge that is left for the wolves in the United States, and once that is gone, they will more than likely become extinct in this country ("Gray Wolf General Information").

- **A citation that only lists a page number.** Maybe the citation simply says (25). That implies that somewhere in the surrounding text, the essay writer must have made it stupendously clear what name or title to look up in the works cited list. This happens a lot, since it's common to introduce a quotation by naming the person it came from, in which case it would be repetitive to name that author again in the citation.

- **A quotation without a citation at all.** This happens when you cite a work that is both A) from a web page that doesn't number the pages or paragraphs and B) is named in the text surrounding the quotation. Readers will assume that the author is named nearby. Stephanie wisely leaves off any citation in the example below, where it's already clear that I should head to the O's on the works cited page to find information about this source, a web page written by Opotow:

  > To further this point, Opotow notes, "Don't imagine you'll be unscathed by the methods you use. The end may justify the means … But there's a price to pay, and the price does tend to be oneself."

I Swear I Did Some Research!

I Swear I Did Some Research: dropping in a citation without making it clear what information came from that source

Let's look in depth at this potentially annoying passage from a hypothetical student paper:

> It's possible that a multidisciplinary approach to understanding the universe will open new doors of understanding. If theories from sociology, communication, and philosophy joined with physics, the possibilities would be boundless. This would inspire new research, much like in the 1970s when scientists changed their focus from grand-scale theories of the universe to the small concerns of quantum physics (Hawking 51).

In at least two ways, this is stellar material. First, the author is actually voicing a point of view; she sounds knowledgeable, strong. Second, and more to the point of this chapter, the author includes a citation, showing that she knows that ethical citation standards ask authors to cite paraphrases and summaries—not just quotations.

30 But on the other hand, which of these three sentences, exactly, came from Hawking's book? Did *Hawking* claim that physics experts should join up with folks in other academic disciplines, or is that the student writer? In other words, at which point does the author's point of view meld into material taken specifically from Hawking?

I recognize that there often aren't clean answers to a question like that. What we read and what we know sometimes meld together so unnoticeably that we don't know which ideas and pieces of information are "ours" and which aren't. Discussing "patchwriting," a term used to describe writing that blends words and phrases from sources with words and phrases we came up with ourselves, scholar Rebecca Moore Howard writes, "When I believe I am not patchwriting,

I am simply doing it so expertly that the seams are no longer visible—or I am doing it so unwittingly that I cannot cite my sources" (91). In other words, *all* the moves we make when writing came from somewhere else at some point, whether we realize it or not. Yikes. But remember our main purpose here: to not look annoying when using sources. And most of your instructors aren't going to say, "I understand that I couldn't tell the difference between your ideas and your source's because we quite naturally patchwrite all the time. That's fine with me. Party on!" They're much more likely to imagine that you plopped in a few extra citations as a way of defensively saying, "I swear I did some research! See? Here's a citation right here! Doesn't that prove I worked really hard?"

The Fix: Write the sentences preceding the citation with specific words and phrases that will tell readers what information came from where. Like this (bolded words are new):

> It's possible that a multidisciplinary approach to understanding the universe will open new doors of understanding. **I believe that** if theories from sociology, communication, and philosophy joined with physics, the possibilities would be boundless. This would inspire new research, much like **the changes Stephen Hawking describes happening** in the 1970s when scientists changed their focus from grand-scale theories of the universe to the small concerns of quantum physics (51).

Perhaps these additions could still use some stylistic editing for wordiness and flow, but the source-related job is done: readers know exactly which claims the essay writer is making and which ones Hawking made in his book. The last sentence and only the last sentence summarizes the ideas Hawking describes on page 51 of his book.

One warning: you'll find that scholars in some disciplines (especially in the sciences and social sciences) use citations in the way I just warned you to avoid. You might see sentences like this one, from page 64 of Glenn Gordon Smith, Ana T. Torres-Ayala, and Allen J. Heindel's article in the *Journal of Distance Education*:

> Some researchers have suggested "curriculum" as a key element in the design of web-based courses (Berge, 1998; Driscoll, 1998; Meyen, Tangen, & Lian, 1999; Wiens & Gunter, 1998).

Whoa—that's a lot of citations. Remember how the writer of my earlier example cited Stephen Hawking because she summarized his ideas? Well, a number of essays describing the results of experiments, like this one, use citations with a different purpose, citing previous studies whose general conclusions support the study described in this new paper, like building blocks. It's like saying to your potentially skeptical readers, "Look, you might be wondering if I'm a quack. But I can prove I'm not! See, all these other people published in similar areas! Are you going to pick fights with all of *them* too?" You might have noticed as well that these citations are in APA format, reflecting the standards of the social sciences journal this passage was published in. Well, in this kind of context APA's requirement to cite the year of a study makes a lot of sense too—after all, the older a study, the less likely it is to still be relevant.

Conclusion: Use Your Turn Signals

35 You may have guessed the biggest weakness in an essay like this: what's annoying varies from person to person, with some readers happily skimming past awkward introductions to quotations without a blink, while others see a paragraph-opening quotation as something to complain about on Facebook. All I've given you here—all I *can* give you unless I actually get to know you and your various writing contexts—are the basics that will apply in a number of academic writing contexts. Think of these as signals to your readers about your intentions, much as wise drivers rely on their turn signals to communicate their intentions to other drivers. In some cases when driving, signaling is an almost artistic decision, relying on the gut reaction of the driver to interpret what is best in times when the law doesn't mandate use one way or the other. I hope your writing is full of similar signals. Now if I could only convince the guy driving in front of me to use *his* blinker ....

Works Cited

Barry, Sheila Anne. *Tricks & Pranks to Fool Your Friends*. New York: Sterling, 1984. Print.

Brooks, Max. *The Zombie Survival Guide: Complete Protection from the Living Dead*. New York: Three Rivers, 2003. Print.

"Gray Wolf General Information." *Environmental Conservation Online System*. U.S. Fish and Wildlife Service, 15 Oct. 2008. Web. 23 Oct. 2008.

Hawking, Stephen. *A Brief History of Time: From the Big Bang to Black Holes*. New York: Bantam, 1988. Print.

Howard, Rebecca Moore. "The New Abolitionism Comes to Plagiarism." *Perspectives on Plagiarism and Intellectual Property in a Postmodern World*. Ed. Lisa Buranen and Alice M. Roy. Albany: SUNY P, 1999. 87–95. Print.

Hunter, Stephen. "'Crash': The Collision Of Human Contradictions." *The Washington Post*. The Washington Post Company, 6 May 2005. Web. 21 Feb. 2008.

Muller, Bill. "Crash: LA Tale Confronts, Then Shatters, Stereotypes." *The Arizona Republic*. AZCentral.com, 6 May 2005. Web. 21 Feb. 2008.

Opotow, Susan. "Moral Exclusion and Torture: The Ticking Bomb Scenario and the Slippery Ethical Slope." *Peace and Conflict Studies* 13.4 (2007): 457–61. PsycINFO. Web. 27 Sept. 2008.

Piven, Joshua, and David Borgenicht. *The Worst-Case Scenario Survival Handbook: Work*. San Francisco: Chronicle, 2003. Print.

Potter, David M. *The Impending Crisis: 1848–1861*. Ed. Don E. Fehrenbacher. New York: Harper & Row, 1976. Print.

Smith, Glenn Gordon, Ana T. Torres-Ayala, and Allen J. Heindel. "Disciplinary Differences in E-learning Instructional Design: The Case of Mathematics." *Journal of Distance Education* 22.3 (2008): 63–88. Web. 10 Sept. 2009.

Toner, Robin. "Feminist Pitch by a Democrat Named Obama." *The New York Times*. The New York Times Company, 2 Dec. 2007. Web. 22 Oct. 2008.

Wolpert, Lewis. "Is Cell Science Dangerous?" *Journal of Medical Ethics* 33.6 (2007): 345–48. Academic Search Premier. Web. 28 Jan. 2009.

Credit

Stedman, Kyle D. "Annoying Ways People Use Sources" *Writing Spacess: Readings on Writing, Vol. 2. Eds. Charles Lowe and Pavel Zemiliansky. Anderson, SC: Parlor Press, 2011. 242–256.* Available online at http://writingspaces.org/sites/default/files/stedman--annoying-ways.pdf.

A Family Affair: Competing Sponsors of Literacy in Appalachian Students' Lives

SARA WEBB-SUNDERHAUS

> *My aunt teaches me how to do school.*
>
> —*Katie May*
>
> *He wants to blame me going back to school for his problems, which it is not.*
>
> —*Pamela, discussing her husband's drug addiction*
>
> *Sponsors [...] set the terms for access to literacy and wield powerful incentives for compliance and loyalty.*
>
> —*Deborah Brandt, Literacy in American Lives*

Growing up as an Urban Appalachian[1] in Cincinnati, Ohio, I became painfully aware of the stories that some people tell about Appalachians: stories of hillbillies, rednecks, and white trash; stories of incest and other deviant sexual practices; stories of laziness, ignorance, and hatred. When I entered graduate school, I became aware of other kinds of stories about Appalachians. While there were stories of illiteracy and relentless poverty, there were also stories that idealized Appalachian families and that venerated the "pure" Anglo-Saxon whiteness of the Appalachian people. But I didn't recognize the Appalachian people I knew and loved, or myself, in any of these stories. These stories demonized and romanticized Appalachians; as folklorist Patrick B. Mullen writes, "[T]he Anglo Appalachian is a complex construction containing both romantic and rational scientific elements; hidden beneath a romantic view is a pathological one" (129). The multifaceted stories I learned from my family about Appalachia and its people—the stories I learned down on the tobacco farms of Lewis County, Kentucky—usually were not being told in my fields of study. It was my awareness of these other stories of Appalachia that inspired my research, which examines the interplay of literacy and identity among Appalachians enrolled in college composition courses.

Deborah Brandt's *Literacy in American Lives* posits that literacy is not only an individual development, but also an economic one, since "literacy looms as one of the great engines of profit and competitive advantage in the twentieth century" (18). The individual and the economic are intertwined, Brandt argues, and she frames her analysis by examining what she calls "sponsors of literacy."

According to Brandt, sponsors are "any agents, local or distant, concrete or abstract, who enable, support, teach, and model, as well as recruit, regulate, suppress, or withhold, literacy—and gain advantage by it in some way" (19). These sponsors are conduits for the larger economic forces of literacy, as Brandt writes that they are "the means by which these forces present themselves to—and through—individual learners" (19). While interviewing the participants in the case studies that make up her book, Brandt found that sponsors were often individuals: "older relatives, teachers, religious leaders, supervisors, military officers, librarians, friends, editors, influential authors" (19). However, as Brandt notes, sponsors can include commercial entities, such as companies who award prizes in a jingle-writing contest and restaurants who offer gift certificates to children who read a designated number of books, as well as institutions, such as the African-American church.

I have found Brandt's concept of sponsorship useful in describing the literacy beliefs of students enrolled in an English Composition course at Riverton University and State University-Sciotoville, two open-admission universities in Central Appalachia.[2] When I began my project, I was particularly interested in the role of educational institutions in shaping literacy beliefs and the students' performance of identity, particularly their Appalachian identity. My research with these students led me to conclude that literacy beliefs and practices were part and parcel of the students' performance of identity, representing an important stage on which their Appalachian-ness—or non-Appalachian-ness, in some cases—was portrayed. Institutional beliefs about, and rewards for, certain types of literacy help foster or sponsor certain beliefs and performances from the students. Yet schools are not the only, or even necessarily the most influential, sponsors of literacy in American lives. Brandt writes that "sponsors of literacy are more prolific, diffused, and heterogeneous" (197) than in the past, when schools played a prominent role in literacy education; she later adds, "Schools are no longer the major disseminators of literacy" (198). Thus, the question that surfaced during my research was, if educational institutions are a key sponsor of these students' literacies, how do other sponsors impact the students' performance of identity, and more specifically Appalachian-ness, with regard to literacy? Who are the "prolific, diffused, and heterogeneous" sponsors in these students' lives?

This article will focus on one group of sponsors, namely immediate and extended family members, and the complexity of their sponsorship. Sponsorship is a messy process, one that cannot be neatly delineated. The same could be said of some Appalachian families as well. Appalachian Studies scholars often write of a romanticized Appalachian family that serves as a comforting fortress for its members; for example, Loyal Jones writes, "Mountain people usually feel an obligation to family members and are more truly themselves when within the family circle" (75). Other scholars write of conflicts between the culture of family and the culture of school, with family culture being more acceptable to Appalachians, according to Michael Maloney: "[T]here's a deep conflict between the values in school and the values at home [...] Appalachians expect relationships to be personal; they aren't comfortable with functional relationships" (34). Yet for the students in my study, the Appalachian family did not function only in the comforting, supportive ways typically described by scholars. While many individual family members were encouraging sponsors of their students' literacies, some of these same individuals also worked to inhibit the students' emerging literacy beliefs and practices. Seemingly contradictory messages about literacy could come from the same person, such that the same person could be both a sponsor and an inhibitor—or perhaps more accurately, a sponsor of a competing meaning of literacy—in a student's life. And it was through, and upon, these inhibitors of literacy that the larger social forces described by Brandt were often enacted. In other words, far from being a fortress from the outside world, the families of my participants created a space in which these social forces fostered particular kinds of sponsorship.

The Study

5 During the summer of 2004, I conducted an ethnographic case study of two English Composition classes and the students enrolled in them. The data I gathered came from multiple sources including participant-observations, transcripts of individual classes, a brief demographic survey, formal interviews, and, in the case of one class, an extended survey based on my interview script. I attended each class twice a week, making audio recordings of class sessions and taking notes so that I could paint a rich portrait full of "thick detail" for each course. I also made audio recordings of the five interviews I conducted with each of my case study participants, as well as the interviews with the instructors and other students. I asked each student to complete a brief demographic survey, and from those surveys I selected two to three students from each course to be my case study participants. My selections were based on students' willingness and availability to participate as well as their representativeness

of their respective classes. While two students from each course became case study participants who were interviewed weekly for the duration of each five-week course, many other students participated in my research, thanks to their contributions in class and their participation in short, occasional interviews inside and outside of class. Particular student voices you will hear in this article include those of Mike, Michelle, and Pamela, all of whom were students at Riverton University; and Katie May and Julie, students at State University-Sciotoville.

Tables 1 and 2 provide demographic information about the two classes and universities that were the focus of the project:

Table 1: Riverton

	Campus	**Class**
Enrollment	1,800 students	14 students
Male-Female Enrollment	40% M, 60% F	14% M, 86% F
Average Age of Students	33	23.8
Race of Students	93% white (all U.S. campuses)	86% white, 7% African-Amer., 7% Asian-Amer.
Commuting Students	All	All
First Generation College	"Most"	64%
Born and Raised in Local Area	"Most"	86%
Identify as Appalachian (All Students)	Unknown	64%
Identify as Appalachian (Students Raised in Region)	Unknown	64%

Table 2: Sciotoville

	Campus	Class
Enrollment	3,500 students	18 students
Male-Female Enrollment	40% M, 60% F	60% M, 40% F (50-50 in regular attendance)
Average Age of Students	25	26.8
Race of Students	86% white, 10% unknown, 4% students of color	94% white, 6% African-American
Commuting Students	90%	75%
First Generation College	"Most"	32%
Born and Raised in Local Area	"Most"	62%
Identify as Appalachian (All Students)	Unknown	28%
Identify as Appalachian (Students Raised in Region)	Unknown	45%

This demographic information confirms what I found in interviews: Riverton students were less likely to self-identify as Appalachian, even when they had been raised in the region, and had negative perceptions of Appalachian-ness; almost all of the Sciotoville students self-identified as Appalachian and performed Appalachian-ness in positive, even romanticized ways. These performances of identities would echo in interesting ways throughout the students' discussions of their literacy.

Multiple Sources of Sponsorship

Spiritual Influences

Interviews with all of my participants indicated several literacy sponsors at work in their lives. Michelle and Mike told of the influence of sports team and fraternity membership, respectively. Katie May, a 19-year-old pre-med student from State University-Sciotoville, shared intertwining stories of literacy and spirituality. Many Appalachian Studies scholars focus their attentions on the role of religion and the church in Appalachians' everyday lives. Jones represents this approach to Appalachians' religious lives when he writes, "Mountain people are religious. This does not mean that we always go to church regularly, but we are religious in the sense that most of our values and the meanings we find in life spring from the Bible. To understand mountaineers, one must understand our religion" (39). Thus, I was not surprised when the church appeared prominent in Katie May's discussions of her literacy.

Some of Katie May's sponsors include the church as an institution, as well as individuals (such as a youth pastor who encouraged her to take notes during church services) who were directly connected to the church and representative of the church's role in her literacy beliefs and practices. Katie May's descriptions of her brother's sponsorship of her spiritually-based literacy practices led me to focus on the role not only of religion, but also of family, in the development of her literacy life. While work by literacy scholars such as Shirley Brice Heath and Denny Taylor points to parents as significant forces in the development of literacy, my research points to multiple family members, including parents, as sponsors of literacy. This family sponsorship seems particularly important in the cultural context of Appalachia, since, as previously discussed, the work of many Appalachian Studies scholars emphasizes the value Appalachians place on family and extended kinship networks.

Immediate Family Members

10 Katie May's brother played an important role in the intertwining of literacy and religion in her life, since he recommended that she begin daily devotionals when she was in eighth grade.[3] He also offered specific suggestions of religious texts for her to read. Katie May recalled, "My brother encouraged me a lot with books that he had read. He'd say, 'Hey, try this one; it's good.'" Her brother was four years older than Katie May and, at the time he began to take on this sponsorship role in her life, he was preparing to attend Bible college. Given their age difference, Katie May's brother was more mature and knowledgeable about both spirituality and literacy, making him an appropriate sponsor in her life.

Katie May's brother demonstrated his sponsorship in other ways as well. Her brother offered her a ride to church until Katie May was old enough to drive herself, and as Katie May stated, he "encouraged" her spiritual development through various uses of literacy. Describing his influence, Katie May said his communication came "through notes. I'd find a note in my school notebooks. I'd turn the pages and there would be something he'd written me a couple nights before. Also with the books [the devotionals]. He recommended a lot of things to me." The notes usually had a theme of encouragement, drawing on stories from the Bible to make a point. Katie May said, "I think he was trying to encourage me. He'd write things like, 'I've been praying for you.' He'd mention things from the Bible, about people who had gone through the same thing. He'd talk about characters from the Bible that I could relate with." After Katie May's brother moved across the country to become a youth pastor, they began exchanging e-mails once or twice a week as a way to stay in touch and to continue this spiritual sponsorship. The spiritual sponsorship Katie May's brother offered was inextricably tied to literacy, as almost all instances of sponsorship that Katie May shared with me involved print such as recommendations of specific readings, writing notes, making Biblical analogies, and e-mailing.

Extended Family Members

While for some students immediate family members exerted the most influence in their literacy lives, extended family members, such as Michelle's grandparents and cousins and Katie May's aunt, acted as significant sponsors as well. Michelle, a 19-year-old, chemistry/pre-pharmacy student who had just completed her first year at Riverton University, lived in rural Massie County, a 30-minute drive from the campus. This distance made it difficult for her to return home for lunch or studying during the day. Her grandparents lived in town, however, and they invited their grandchildren to come to their house during the school day. Several of Michelle's cousins also attended Riverton University, and all of those cousins would gather at their grandparents' house for lunch and study breaks. In an interview, Michelle described these visits to her grandparents' home:

> Grandma will cook lunch for whoever's there, but we're all in and out at different times due to our class schedules, so we'll bring our own food to eat, too. But the main thing is that it's a quiet place to study. Grandma and Grandpa will ask how things are going and that sort of thing, but then they'll leave you alone so you can get your work done. And if they're not going to be home, they'll leave the door open so we can come in and do our work.

Michelle's grandparents did not sponsor her literacy through teaching her particular literacy practices, modeling textual interaction, and the like. Instead, Michelle's grandparents' sponsorship arose from their offer of material goods—namely food and study space—that would assist in the development of her academic literacy and education. Michelle's grandparents did not have the necessary academic literacy themselves to assist Michelle and her cousins with their homework; however, they could, and did, offer their approval of academic literacy by offering a warm meal and a quiet place to study. These acts, which on the surface may seem unconnected to literacy, were a powerful show of support for the educations of their grandchildren.

Michelle also commented on the role the cousins played in each other's educations, noting that since the cousins were at varying stages in their college careers and had different academic strengths, they could support each other:

> There is always somebody around who can help you with your homework. Or you can help them. It's really nice to be able to talk with them, if I'm stuck on something or have a question. Or sometimes we just give each other advice about what classes to register for, which professors are good, that sort of thing.

Through this support, Michelle and her cousins became sponsors of each other's academic literacy practices and education, broadly speaking.

Other students also discussed the importance of family members who helped them learn how to "do school." For Katie May, one of her aunts was a pivotal sponsor of literacy. Katie May stated in an interview that her aunt "teaches me how to do school," and we later talked further of the specific suggestions her aunt gave her for "doing school." Though Katie May was taking summer classes at State University-Sciotoville, she was actually a rising sophomore at Big State University, her state's flagship university. Katie May had a difficult time during her first two quarters at Big State. Always an A student in high school, she found herself struggling to make Cs in the chemistry and calculus courses required for pre-med majors—grades that put her in danger of losing her scholarships, which required a B average. Her aunt, a dentist who earned her undergraduate and professional degrees at Big State, sat Katie May down over a break and gave her a "talking-to," which Katie May discussed in an interview.

> **Katie May:** "I brought my grades up a lot last spring quarter, and she definitely influenced me in that area. I felt like I had what it took [to do well in school], but I didn't know how to channel that. And so she really guided me and showed me, this is the way you do it. It really was. At first I didn't believe her, because I'd never done study groups. But it really helped."
>
> **Sara:** "How did she, how did she show you, 'this is how you do it?' Was is just the study groups, or did she give you other kinds of advice?"
>
> **Katie May:** "She would talk to me, she talked to me at the end of fall quarter [Katie May's first term of college], and said, 'This is what you need to do and went down the list. And then …"
>
> **Sara [interrupting]:** "What was the list?"

> **Katie May:** "Do study groups. Talk to the professors. Do all the homework. She asked me how I studied, and I said I read the chapters but then I'm usually too tired to do the homework, so I just read the chapters. She was like, well maybe you should do the homework first and then go back and read the chapter. So she really helped me with that."

Katie May's responses indicate the pivotal acts of literacy sponsorship her aunt took on. Her aunt directed her as to which academic literacy practices were most important—doing the written homework as opposed to the reading homework—and directed her towards other, more local sponsors of literacy like her peers and professors. Here we see a sponsor whose importance came in part from her recommendations of other sponsors of literacy.

15 Katie May's aunt told her not only to seek out these other sponsors of literacy, but also how to approach them, and the aunt stayed in regular contact with Katie May so she could continue her sponsorship:

> **Sara:** "Did she give you strategies about how to talk to professors?"
>
> **Katie May:** "Yeah. She said, 'Go up to your Chemistry 122 professor and say, I got a C– in Chemistry 121, and I struggled for that, and I don't want to get another C– in this class. How can I improve?' [...] And then she'd talk to me once a week and ask me, so are you doing the things we talked about? Are you doing the study groups and talking to the professors? That sort of thing. [...] We have AIM instant messenger, so we talk at least once a week through that. At first it was probably two times a week, but then, as she saw I was doing what I needed to do, we went down to once a week."
>
> **Sara:** "How did she come to sit you down and give you the talking-to? Did you kind of come home and cry on her shoulder, or did your parents tell her something was up? Or did she just ask you about how you were doing in school?"
>
> **Katie May:** "My mom would call her and say, 'Katie May's crying! What should I do?!' That type of thing. And then I came home for break and we talked."

Here we see another sponsor of Katie May's literacy emerge: her mother, who first informed the aunt of Katie May's struggles in school. As I shall discuss in the next section, parents were important influences on the literacy practices and beliefs of many of the participants in my study.

Parents

In studies of family literacy, it is often parents who receive the most attention, and our culture's conventional wisdom places heavy emphasis on the role parents play in the development of their children's literacy practices. While part of my intent in this article has been to illustrate that many family members can become sponsors of literacy, I also recognize that for most individuals, their parents are among the earliest and most primary sponsors of literacy.

Parents' sponsorship can take different forms, however, as illustrated by the experiences of my case study participants. For some parents, such as Katie May's mother, sponsorship meant connecting their children with more knowledgeable sponsors. In the last transcribed section of the Katie May interview, Katie May stated that her mother had informed Katie May's aunt—her sister—of Katie May's problems with school and had asked for assistance: "Katie May's crying! What should I do?!." Katie May's mother did not attend college, whereas Katie May's aunt held undergraduate and professional degrees. Katie May's mother may not have had the knowledge of academic literacy practices to advise Katie May about difficulties in school, but she knew someone who did—her sister—and she asked her sister to work with Katie May. While this may have been an indirect form of sponsorship, it was incredibly important in helping Katie May acquire the literacy practices she needed during her first year of college.

Other parents engaged in indirect, as well as more direct, forms of sponsorship. Michelle's father earned two associate's degrees from Riverton University and worked at the local hospital as the supervisor of bio-medical engineering. He loomed large in Michelle's discussions of literacy. One of her earliest memories of books involved looking at her father's college textbooks when he was enrolled at Riverton while Michelle was a small child. After Michelle's father earned his last degree, he did not put away his books. Instead, he kept them displayed on the family bookshelf, and as she grew up, Michelle continued to read them:

> I loved looking at his books when I was little. Still do. I look at them now sometimes to see if they might explain something a little better, something I'm confused about. I know he's got a physics book up there that I should look at. [...] He never showed them to me. They were just always there. [...] As a kid I looked at them, not knowing what they were. But as I got older and thinking about college, it hit me, what they were, and I looked at them to see what college would be like.

In addition to the textbooks Michelle's father kept on hand, he also subscribed to and read several science magazines, partly to stay aware of new developments in his line of work, and partly for the pleasure of reading about science. Michelle frequently read these magazines and stated that she enjoyed doing so. While her father did not directly encourage her reading the magazines, his modeling of a certain type of behavior—an interest in continued learning and a love of science, combined with the easy availability of texts—led Michelle to develop an interest in science and read the books and magazines. Michelle directly credited her skill and interest in math and science to her father, an unsurprising development given the types of print materials her father brought into the house via his work and education. As Brandt notes:

> Though not always the focus of explicit instruction and not often school oriented, work-related reading and writing provided children real-world information about how literacy functions [... and] brought at least some children into contact with the material assets and social power of major literacy sponsors—corporations, industries, merchants, governments, and universities. (199)

While Michelle's mother worked at the hospital as well, she worked in the data entry department. She attended a business college for two years and did not earn a degree. Though Michelle did note in interviews that her mother always encouraged her to go to college, she made it clear that her father played a more active sponsorship role in her life through his sharing of texts and, as I will soon discuss, his specific guidance about her education. In Michelle's family, there was an unstated understanding that her father would be the one to develop Michelle's interest in science and to advise her about her education, since he had two associate's degrees and work experience in scientific fields.

Thus, it was Michelle's father who had the career path with more economic and cultural capital—one that a college-bound daughter would be more likely to emulate. Brandt writes that fathers are often overlooked in studies of family literacy, due to an emphasis on "the nurture of preschool children," a presumably "motherly" domain (200). But Michelle's case is representative of Brandt's notion that "[t]he historically privileged position that men have occupied in education and employment made fathers in many households the conduits of specialized skills and materials that could be of interest and use to other family members" (200). It was Michelle's repeated exposure to the world of scientific reading materials, via her father, that set her on the path of a chemistry/pre-pharmacy major.

20 Her father also played a direct role in her educational goals, advising her to take particular courses in high school:

> My sophomore year, I doubled up on math classes so I could go farther [take more advanced courses in high school]. I knew that I really wanted to go towards the medical field, and I knew, because my dad told me, that you had to have a lot of science, since obviously it's the big thing in the medical field. So you gotta get that in. So I doubled up in that.

The "doubling-up" in math and science courses paid off, as Michelle was quickly moving through her courses at Riverton and was looking into transferring to a joint B.S./PharmD program at a large state university a few hours from home. Given her father's educational background and work experience, he had the knowledge to tell Michelle what types of courses she needed to be taking and when—a critical factor in determining what careers would later be open to her and in enabling her success at Riverton. Michelle's father's ability to steer her towards particular courses—towards developing particular kinds of academic literacies, if you will—became a very important moment of sponsorship in her life.

Inhibitors of Literacy

While the students I interviewed told many positive and heart-warming stories of literacy sponsorship, as our interviews continued, other stories emerged as well. In these stories, a threatening side of literacy sponsorship emerged. Literacy, particularly academic literacy, became a dangerous force, one that could distance students from family members and loved ones. For a few students, their pursuit of academic literacy vis-à-vis a college degree put them at odds, in ways big and small, with some of the most important people in their lives. Some of these people sought to inhibit the students' development of this literacy through their sponsorship of competing meanings of literacy. These individuals did not inhibit the development of the students' literacy practices alone, however. Social forces, such as poor health care and stereotypical gender roles, played a significant part as well. Brandt writes, "Literacy spreads last and always less well to remote rural areas and newer, poorer industrial areas—a geographic and political legacy that, even today, in the United States, helps to exacerbate inequalities by race, region, and occupation" (88). The forces at work in these students' lives, sometimes presented in the form of individual inhibitors, reveal some of the inequalities still at work in parts of Appalachia.

Mike's Story

For Mike, attaining a college degree had been a long, drawn-out process. While he began college at the age of eighteen, at the time of our interview he was twenty-six and just entering his senior year. One reason why his college education had taken seven years to that point was repeated transfers between institutions, but his health was the factor that most slowed his progress to earning a degree. Mike developed a problem with his kidneys while he was enrolled in Riverton, a problem that required a minor surgery at the local hospital. The surgery involved inserting a stent into one of his kidneys to help improve its function and to reduce the pain he felt every day. While this was not a life-threatening operation, Mike had to withdraw from school for a quarter as he healed. As it turned out, however, Mike's surgery wasn't so simple: "I got an infection. It was pretty bad. They put me in the hospital for four or five days. I don't even remember being in the hospital, I was so sick. It was a staph infection. It was pretty bad."

After his hospital stay, Mike returned to his parents' home in a nearby town and continued to recover from the infection, which had left him weakened. During the course of his recovery, it was determined that the surgery had not corrected the problem with his kidneys. In fact, the condition had worsened. At this point, frustrated by the care their son was receiving and worried about his health, Mike's parents took him to the campus of Big State University so that he could be treated at the university's medical center:

> I was still in so much pain every day, which is what the first surgery was supposed to fix. And then I developed that staph infection, which you get from the [surgical] instruments not being sterile. So when that happened, we decided that I should change doctors, and I went up to Big State. They couldn't get me in for the surgery for a while, so I missed even more school. But at least they fixed my kidney.

All told, Mike lost a year of school as he went through the first surgery and recovery, the staph infection and recovery, and the second surgery and recovery. When I asked Mike if he ever wanted to give up during this time and quit school altogether, he responded, "Yes. But what kept me going was my parents. My parents were dead set on me getting through college."

Mike's story illustrates multiple forces at work in his literacy life. His first surgery, at a small country hospital, turned into a disaster, with the failure of the stent to treat the problem and the development of a staph infection. Mike attributed both of these problems to the health care he received, and, given the state of health care in Central Appalachia and Massie County, Riverton's home county, it is quite likely Mike received inadequate care. Massie County has been identified by the Appalachian Regional Commission as economically distressed, and, according to Richard P. Mulcahy, the "supply of doctors in the distressed counties is one primary-care physician for every 2,128 persons and one specialist for every 2,857 individuals" (1635). This is in comparison to one primary-care doctor for every 1,099 persons and specialist for every 588 in economically competitive Appalachian counties (1635). The lack of quality health care in the region caused serious hardship for Mike and very nearly derailed his college career.

25 But Mike's story also reveals the larger social forces that worked to help him return to college. His parents had the economic means to support him throughout his illness, to care for him in their home, to seek out second opinions, and to take him to Big State for further medical treatment. His parents also had the means to support him financially following the second surgery. Prior to these health problems, Mike had worked full time and gone to school. But Mike stated that after he recovered from his second surgery, "my parents told me they wanted me to focus on finishing school and staying healthy. They were afraid working would get me run-down and sick again. So they're paying for my school now and helping me with money to live on." The importance of this type of economic sponsorship, as well as his parents' insistence that he finish his degree, cannot be overrated. Simply put, without the sponsorship of his parents throughout this challenging time, it is highly debatable whether Mike would have returned to school or if his health would have permitted him to return.

Women's Stories

While Mike's story reveals some of the economic forces that sponsor or inhibit academic literacy, the stories of Pamela and Julie reveal how traditional gender roles can inhibit academic literacy—or, at the very least, sponsor competing notions of that literacy. I will first discuss Pamela, a thirty-three-year-old student at Riverton University.

Pamela

When I met Pamela during the first week of class, she was eager to participate in the case study, but she explained to me that she might have to drop the class due to problems at home. While she had just been accepted into the nursing program—a rigorous and competitive program at Riverton—she was considering withdrawing from it as well. Pamela was going through a divorce and was worried about its impact on her sons, who were nine and thirteen years old: "The kids, especially the little one, really need my support right now, and I'm worried he's not going to have that if I have my nose stuck in a book." There were also financial considerations. In order to accommodate the class schedule and homework the nursing major demanded, Pamela, who worked as a licensed practical nurse at the local hospital, would have to limit herself to sixteen hours of work a week. Given the pending divorce, she literally could not afford to make that change.

Pamela did in fact drop the course the following week; she also delayed her admission into the nursing program. Thus, what was to be our first interview became our only interview. During our short time together, Pamela explained why her plans for school were in a state of transition:

> I started here two years ago, full-time, but then last year I took a couple quarters off to deal with stuff at home. And now my status fluctuates. I can't predict what it will be. So much depends on my husband. Soon to be ex-husband. At first he was *very* supportive. And then his insecurities … [trailing off]. That's why we're getting a divorce. I'll just tell you: He's got a prescription drug abuse problem. He's buying them from the street.

Pamela's estranged husband suffered a back injury at work and, in the course of his treatment, was put on prescription painkillers, including OxyContin. During his disability leave from work and recovery, he eventually grew addicted to Oxy. His addiction is sadly representative of the problems facing many Central Appalachians. Oxy has become the drug of choice in the region, to such an extent that it is commonly referred to as "hillbilly heroin." And like heroin, Oxy can have a devastating effect. To give one example of the severity of the problem, the Appalachian Regional Commission states in "Substance Abuse in Appalachia" that "Appalachian Kentucky is experiencing drug related deaths at about four times the rate of the rest of the state"—deaths that, for the most part, are attributable to OxyContin. Though Pamela's estranged husband was alive, his addiction caused serious emotional and financial hardship for the family:

He had difficulty keeping a job, and he had emptied the joint bank accounts he had with Pamela in order to buy more Oxy. The consequences of his actions were mortgage and car payments so far behind that Pamela feared she might lose both her home and her car. Pamela continued to discuss her estranged husband and his addiction, directly relating his addiction to her pursuit of a college degree:

> And at first he was really supportive. In fact, before I went back to school, I actually wrote a paper about this for my first English class. It was something like, 'Why are you here?' And I had said, to my kids and my husband, I had said, 'Okay, here it is. I'm gonna go back to my school, you're going to have to help me pick up the slack with the house,' and everybody was in agreement. If one of them had said, 'No, I'm not willing to do that,' I probably wouldn't have come. But it was a family decision. And now his insecurities … [trailing off]. He thinks, he wants to blame me going to school for his problems, which it is not. It has nothing to do with me going back to school.

Indeed, even before we sat down for this interview after class, Pamela had related her estranged husband's attempts to attribute the cause of his addiction to her schooling. When she approached me after class, she told me that her husband had "problems" and stated, "He says it's my fault for going back to school. Because as the man, he should be the one to provide for the family, not me." Apparently, he was despondent over the loss of his income (due to his work injury) and threatened by Pamela's emergence as the breadwinner and most highly educated member of the family. In arguments with Pamela, her estranged husband connected these losses—both of money and of status—and perceived them as the cause of his subsequent addiction.

As this last anecdote suggests, gender roles can play a large part in circumscribing the opportunities available to men and women within the Central Appalachian region. More women go to college because they are deemed to "need" it, since it is hard for them to find a job that offers sustainable pay without a college degree. Men traditionally have not gone to college because jobs that could support a family were available to them without a degree. Yet given the exodus of jobs from this region, as well as changing life circumstances, gender roles are in flux. Whether it is due to a job being outsourced or being out of work due to workplace injury and subsequent addiction—as was the case in Pamela's marriage—many men are no longer the primary breadwinners for their families.

30 For couples steeped in the region's traditional gender roles (Bush and Lash 170), this break from tradition could have significant consequences. In her book *Whistlin' and Crowin' Women of Appalachia: Literacy Practices Since College,* Katherine Kelleher Sohn introduces us to Sarah, a former student of Sohn's and a woman whose marriage had been affected by her education, much like Pamela's. Sarah said of her husband, "He was a traditional man who wanted me to be more passive. He felt that he should be the breadwinner and felt that my being in college was a threat to his manhood in providing for his family" (131). Drawing on the old Appalachian maxim that "whistlin' and crowin' hens always come to no good ends," Sohn writes that in parts of Central Appalachia, "Women are not supposed to whistle or crow; those who objected [to women's changing roles] were threatened by these women's growth and change" (77). As we see from Sohn's study of Sarah and the example of Pamela in this study, some husbands may be intimidated by their wives' educations, given the confluence in the region of traditional gender roles, limited economic opportunities, and medical issues such as disability and addiction.

Julie

Like Pamela, Julie was also under a tremendous amount of pressure to live up to traditional gender roles and to abandon her pursuit of a college degree, though unlike Pamela, Julie's pressure came from multiple sources. Julie, a twenty-four-year-old mother of a kindergartner, first attended college as an eighteen-year-old fresh out of high school. Julie had been a good student throughout high school, and her mother and stepfather were generally supportive of her college plans. Thus, Julie enrolled at a community college in her hometown (while Julie is from Central Appalachia, she is not a native of Sciotoville or its home state). Soon after the fall semester started, however, Julie discovered she was pregnant, and her life quickly changed:

> I was under so much pressure. My mom and step-dad told me that I had to drop out of school, now that I was going to become a mother. I had to focus on my child and what was best for it. And he [the father of her child] and his mother said this, too. They all just wanted us to hurry up and get married. I really wanted to stay in school, but there was just no support for it at all. My ex-husband always went along with whatever his mother said, so there was no support there. And then I had terrible morning sickness and was constantly getting sick; I was so afraid of throwing up in class. Eventually, it seemed easier to stop fighting everybody and to quit, so I did.

For the first year of her son's life, Julie was a stay-at-home-mother, and while she enjoyed being home with her son, school was always in the back of her mind: "I knew I never should have dropped out." Then economic demands began taking a toll on the family. Julie described her ex-husband as young and irresponsible, and he lost several jobs. Julie found a job at a call center and went to work, eventually out-earning her husband—a fact that added stress to an already shaky marriage. When her son was four, Julie and her husband divorced. Shortly thereafter, Julie moved to Sciotoville and enrolled at the university. At the time of our interviews, she had just completed her first year.

Julie's family was aghast at these developments. Julie stated in interviews that numerous relatives told her she was "abandoning her child" by returning to school. Julie saw her return to school as a way to provide a better life for her son, but her relatives, especially her mother, did not agree:

> **Julie:** "Mom is always telling me that my place is in the home, that I should be taking care of him, that school is robbing him of me."
>
> **Sara:** "But you worked before you went back to school. So how is being away from him for work different from being away from him for school?"
>
> **Julie:** "That's just it. It's not. Well, I am working now, part-time, while I go to school, and they say it's too much, that I shouldn't be working and going to school. But I try to arrange my schedule so that I'm not away from him any more than I would be then if I worked full-time. Mom and my step-dad are always telling me that it's selfish for me to be in school, that I should just be working full-time and supporting my son. 'You made your bed, now you have to lie in it.' That's what they're always saying to me. It was one thing for me to go to school before I had him, but now it's something else."

Julie attributed her family's response to their strong religious beliefs, since "their church teaches a woman's place is in the home." But traditional gender roles were at work in complex and contradictory ways here. On one level, Julie's family recognized that her place was *not* in the home, since they felt she should be working full-time to support her son. Yet they also faulted her for not being home with him and told her she was "selfish"—an accusation typically hurled at working mothers. There was no way for Julie to win her family's approval, short of re-marrying and becoming a stay-at-home mother again.

Adding to her family's disapproval was the fact that Julie had come out as a lesbian. Shortly after moving to Sciotoville, Julie met Shelly, with whom she began a romantic relationship. They moved in together soon after they met. Her family's disapproval of homosexuality added to the already strained relationship and increased the tension in Julie's life. When I asked Julie in our first interview if Shelly had been a source of support for her during these trying times, she replied:

> **Julie:** "Oh, God, no. She's just as bad as they are about school. She tells me I have no business being in school. She says she was attracted to me because I was very femme, and she says school has changed that."
>
> **Sara:** "How?"
>
> **Julie:** "Well, she thinks it's my job to do all the stuff around the house, the cooking, the cleaning, and of course there's my son, who *is* my responsibility. She gets so mad when things aren't clean the way they should be and says that if I wasn't so busy with school I would take better care of the house."

Later in the same interview, Julie explained the other reasons why Shelly does not support her schooling:

> She says I don't have any time for her or our friends, that I'm always busy with homework. She says it can't be that hard, that it doesn't take that much time to do school work, that I just don't want to be with her. But how would she know? She came here a quarter when she was 18 and flunked out because all she did was party. So she never tried. (Sigh, then a short pause) She also says I think I'm better than everybody else now. She says I use big words and act all superior. And it's true, I do have a really good vocabulary, I've always been really verbal. But that's just the way I talk! It's not because I think I'm better than other people. I'm tired of fighting about it, though. So now I just don't talk about certain things, or say things in a certain way, just so I won't have to hear that.

Thus, Shelly emerged as an inhibitor of Julie's attempts to gain academic literacy, one who attributed academic literacy with other meanings. For Julie, her development of academic literacy was a way to gain a "better life" for her son. For Shelly, Julie's development of academic literacy was seen as an infringement on Julie's role in the home and their time together, as well as a force that distanced Julie from her, making her "uppity," to use another label Julie said had been applied to her by Shelly.

Shelly's disapproval of Julie's education had a noticeable impact on her schooling. As the summer term went on, Julie attended class less and less; she missed two classes to go on a camping trip that Shelly spontaneously announced, telling me, "I couldn't deal with telling her I couldn't go because of school." She also began a new job, one that required her to work more hours, because of pressure from Shelly that she wasn't contributing enough money to the relationship. The training for her new job overlapped with a couple of classes, and Julie missed class so she could attend those sessions. Before these absences, Julie was earning an A in the course. Between the penalty she earned due to the strict attendance policy and the self-admitted lack of time she put into doing assignments after she began her new job, Julie earned a B– for the course.

35 At the end of the summer, I met Julie for a follow-up visit, at which time she told me that she was taking fall quarter off: "I'm hoping it will make things better with Shelly," she said, sharing the details of their most recent argument about school. Throughout the summer, Julie had told me that she would not "give up" school for Shelly, noting, "If I have to choose between school or her, I'm choosing school." Yet, as fall approached, Julie's position had shifted: "I don't think it's worth it anymore. All the stress. All the fighting. I can't do it. Things are better now that I'm just working, and I want to keep it that way." I haven't been successful in contacting Julie since that day, and, as of the spring following that final conversation, her university e-mail account had been closed.

The Interplay of Literacy and Identity

The stories of literacy sponsorship presented here illustrate the complexities inherent in a discussion of literacy and identity. The sponsors profiled vary a great deal and at times exhibit contradictory or conflicting influences. The readily identifiable social problems discussed above affected my participants' literacy experiences in notable and dramatic ways. More pervasive, though harder to pinpoint, are the ways in which Appalachian identity—and the ways in which an individual performs that identity—affect his or her literacy beliefs and practices.

As noted in the introduction, familism is a value often constructed as part of a performance of Appalachian identity. Yet some of the most striking examples of those values in this article—Mike's relationship with his parents and Michelle's relationship with her grandparents—come from students who often sought to distance themselves from Appalachian identity in our interviews and in the classroom. What do the lives of these students suggest about Jones' construction of Appalachians?

Those students who most readily performed an Appalachian identity during my fieldwork evidenced ambivalence about their relationships with family members. While Katie May's mother was a sponsor of her literacy in important ways, Katie May also expressed a worry about being perceived by her mother as "rising above my raising"—similar to Julie's designation as "uppity" by her partner—when she talked about concepts she learned in school. Similarly, Julie appeared to embrace a romanticized performance of Appalachian identity more consciously and skillfully than any of the other students, yet in relation to her family and academic life, she stated, "All my life I've tried to do the absolute best I can do, and I never got the gratification from the people who love me. Most of the gratification I've got is from people who don't love me, my teachers and the students around me." This statement stands in stark contrast to Jones' description of Appalachians as "more truly themselves" when among family, a conceptualization that essentializes Appalachian-ness and assumes there is a stable, authentic Appalachian identity. Julie's comment undercuts this notion and reveals that the metaphor of the Appalachian family as a fortress is also a performance, much like the facets of Julie's romanticized Appalachian identity. But what might this "undercutting" reveal about overlapping and contesting performances of identity? How much of Julie's conflict, for example, is rooted in her performance of gender—a performance that clashes with the expectations for gender performance by Appalachian women? These are the questions that remain with me as I conclude.

Works Cited

Abramson, Rudy, and Jean Haskell, eds. *Encyclopedia of Appalachia.* Knoxville: The University of Tennessee P, 2006.

Borman, Kathryn, and Phillip J. Obermiller, eds. *From Mountain to Metropolis: Appalachian Migrants in the American City.* New York: Greenwood, 1993.

Brandt, Deborah. *Literacy in American Lives.* New York: Cambridge University P, 2001.

Bush, Kevin Ray, and Sheryl Beaty Lash. "Family Relationships and Gender Roles." *Encyclopedia of Appalachia.* 2006 ed.

Jones, Loyal. *Appalachian Values.* Ashland, KY: The Jesse Stuart Foundation, 1994.

Mulcahy, Richard P. "Health." *Encyclopedia of Appalachia.* 2006 ed.

Mullen, Patrick B. "Belief and the American Folk." *Journal of American Folklore* 113: 119–143.

Sohn, Katherine Kelleher. *Whistlin' and Crowin' Women of Appalachia: Literacy Practices since College.* Carbondale: Southern Illinois University P, 2006.

United States. Appalachian Regional Commission. *Substance Abuse in Appalachia.* 28 May 2006. Web.

Credit

Webb-Sunderhaus, Sara. "A Family Affair: Competing Sponsors of Literacy in Appalachian Students' Lives." *Community Literacy Journal 2.1* (2007): 5–24. Reprinted with the author's permission.

Mother Tongue

AMY TAN

I am not a scholar of English or literature. I cannot give you much more than personal opinions on the English language and its variations in this country or others.

I am a writer. And by that definition, I am someone who has always loved language. I am fascinated by language in daily life. I spend a great deal of my time thinking about the power of language—the way it can evoke an emotion, a visual image, a complex idea, or a simple truth. Language is the tool of my trade. And I use them all—all the Englishes I grew up with.

Recently, I was made keenly aware of the different Englishes I do use. I was giving a talk to a large group of people, the same talk I had already given to half a dozen other groups. The nature of the talk was about my writing, my life, and my book, *The Joy Luck Club*. The talk was going along well enough, until I remembered one major difference that made the whole talk sound wrong. My mother was in the room. And it was perhaps the first time she had heard me give a lengthy speech, using the kind of English I have never used with her. I was saying things like, "The intersection of memory upon imagination" and "There is an aspect of my fiction that relates to thus-and-thus'—a speech filled with carefully wrought grammatical phrases, burdened, it suddenly seemed to me, with nominalized forms, past perfect tenses, conditional phrases, all the forms of standard English that I had learned in school and through books, the forms of English I did not use at home with my mother.

Just last week, I was walking down the street with my mother, and I again found myself conscious of the English I was using, the English I do use with her. We were talking about the price of new and used furniture and I heard myself saying this: "Not waste money that way." My husband was with us as well, and he didn't notice any switch in my English. And then I realized why. It's because over the twenty years we've been together I've often used that same kind of English with him, and sometimes he even uses it with me. It has become our language of intimacy, a different sort of English that relates to family talk, the language I grew up with.

5 So you'll have some idea of what this family talk I heard sounds like, I'll quote what my mother said during a recent conversation which I videotaped and then transcribed. During this conversation, my mother was talking about a political gangster in Shanghai who had the same last name as her family's, Du, and how the gangster in his early years wanted to be adopted by her family, which was rich by comparison. Later, the gangster became more powerful, far richer than my mother's family, and one day showed up at my mother's wedding to pay his respects. Here's what she said in part:

> Du Yusong having business like fruit stand. Like off the street kind. He is Du like Du Zong—but not Tsung-ming Island people. The local people call putong, the river east side, he belong to that side local people. That man want to ask Du Zong father take him in like become own family. Du Zong father wasn't look down on him, but didn't take seriously, until that man big like become a mafia. Now important person, very hard to inviting him. Chinese way, came only to show respect, don't stay for dinner. Respect for making big celebration, he shows up. Mean gives lots of respect. Chinese custom. Chinese social life that way. If too important won't have to stay too long. He come to my wedding. I didn't see, I heard it. I gone to boy's side, they have YMCA dinner. Chinese age I was nineteen.

You should know that my mother's expressive command of English belies how much she actually understands. She reads the *Forbes* report, listens to *Wall Street Week,* converses daily with her stockbroker, reads all of Shirley MacLaine's books with ease—all kinds of things I can't begin to understand. Yet some of my friends tell me they understand 50 percent of what my mother says. Some say they understand 80 to 90 percent. Some say they understand none of it, as if she were speaking pure Chinese. But to me, my mother's English is perfectly clear, perfectly natural. It's my mother tongue. Her language, as I hear it, is vivid, direct, full of observation and imagery. That was the language that helped shape the way I saw things, expressed things, made sense of the world.

Lately, I've been giving more thought to the kind of English my mother speaks. Like others, I have described it to people as 'broken" or "fractured" English. But I wince when I say that. It has always bothered me that I can think of no way to describe it other than "broken," as if it were damaged and needed to be fixed, as if it lacked a certain wholeness and soundness. I've heard other terms used, "limited English," for example. But they seem just as bad, as if everything is limited, including people's perceptions of the limited English speaker.

I know this for a fact, because when I was growing up, my mother's "limited" English limited *my* perception of her. I was ashamed of her English. I believed that her English reflected the quality of what she had to say That is, because she expressed them imperfectly her thoughts were imperfect. And I had plenty of empirical evidence to support me: the fact that people in department stores, at banks, and at restaurants did not take her seriously, did not give her good service, pretended not to understand her, or even acted as if they did not hear her.

10 My mother has long realized the limitations of her English as well. When I was fifteen, she used to have me call people on the phone to pretend I was she. In this guise, I was forced to ask for information or even to complain and yell at people who had been rude to her. One time it was a call to her stockbroker in New York. She had cashed out her small portfolio and it just so happened we were going to go to New York the next week, our very first trip outside California. I had to get on the phone and say in an adolescent voice that was not very convincing, "This is Mrs. Tan."

And my mother was standing in the back whispering loudly, "Why he don't send me check, already two weeks late. So mad he lie to me, losing me money.

And then I said in perfect English, "Yes, I'm getting rather concerned. You had agreed to send the check two weeks ago, but it hasn't arrived."

Then she began to talk more loudly. "What he want, I come to New York tell him front of his boss, you cheating me?" And I was trying to calm her down, make her be quiet, while telling the stockbroker, "I can't tolerate any more excuses. If I don't receive the check immediately, I am going to have to speak to your manager when I'm in New York next week." And sure enough, the following week there we were in front of this astonished stockbroker, and I was sitting there red-faced and quiet, and my mother, the real Mrs. Tan, was shouting at his boss in her impeccable broken English.

We used a similar routine just five days ago, for a situation that was far less humorous. My mother had gone to the hospital for an appointment, to find out about a benign brain tumor a CAT scan had revealed a month ago. She said she had spoken very good English, her best English, no mistakes. Still, she said, the hospital did not apologize when they said they had lost the CAT scan and she had come for nothing. She said they did not seem to have any sympathy when she told them she was anxious to know the exact diagnosis, since her husband and son had both died of brain tumors. She said they would not give her any more information until the next time and she would have to make another appointment for that. So she said she would not leave until the doctor called her daughter. She wouldn't budge. And when the doctor finally called her daughter, me, who spoke in perfect English—lo and behold—we had assurances the CAT scan would be found, promises that a conference call on Monday would be held, and apologies for any suffering my mother had gone through for a most regrettable mistake.

15 I think my mother's English almost had an effect on limiting my possibilities in life as well. Sociologists and linguists probably will tell you that a person's developing language skills are more influenced by peers. But I do think that the language spoken in the family, especially in immigrant families which are more insular, plays a large role in shaping the language of the child. And I believe that it affected my results on achievement tests, I.Q. tests, and the SAT. While my English skills were never judged as poor, compared to math, English could not be considered my strong suit. In grade school I did moderately well, getting perhaps B's, sometimes B-pluses, in English and scoring perhaps in the sixtieth or seventieth percentile on achievement tests. But those scores were not good enough to override the opinion that my true abilities lay in math and science, because in those areas I achieved A's and scored in the ninetieth percentile or higher.

This was understandable. Math is precise; there is only one correct answer. Whereas, for me at least, the answers on English tests were always a judgment call, a matter of opinion and personal experience. Those tests were constructed around items like fill-in-the-blank sentence completion, such as, "Even though Tom was ______, Mary thought he was ______." And the correct answer always seemed to be the most bland combinations of thoughts, for example, "Even though Tom was shy, Mary thought he was charming:' with the grammatical structure "even though" limiting the correct answer to some sort of semantic opposites, so you wouldn't get answers like, "Even though Tom was foolish,

Mary thought he was ridiculous:' Well, according to my mother, there were very few limitations as to what Tom could have been and what Mary might have thought of him. So I never did well on tests like that.

The same was true with word analogies, pairs of words in which you were supposed to find some sort of logical, semantic relationship—for example, "*Sunset* is to *nightfall* as ______ is to ______." And here you would be presented with a list of four possible pairs, one of which showed the same kind of relationship: *red* is to *stoplight, bus* is to *arrival, chills* is to *fever, yawn* is to *boring*. Well, I could never think that way. I knew what the tests were asking, but I could not block out of my mind the images already created by the first pair, "*sunset* is to *nightfall*"—and I would see a burst of colors against a darkening sky, the moon rising, the lowering of a curtain of stars. And all the other pairs of words—red, bus, stoplight, boring—just threw up a mass of confusing images, making it impossible for me to sort out something as logical as saying: "A sunset precedes nightfall" is the same as "a chill precedes a fever." The only way I would have gotten that answer right would have been to imagine an associative situation, for example, my being disobedient and staying out past sunset, catching a chill at night, which turns into feverish pneumonia as punishment, which indeed did happen to me.

I have been thinking about all this lately, about my mother's English, about achievement tests. Because lately I've been asked, as a writer, why there are not more Asian Americans represented in American literature. Why are there few Asian Americans enrolled in creative writing programs? Why do so many Chinese students go into engineering! Well, these are broad sociological questions I can't begin to answer. But I have noticed in surveys—in fact, just last week—that Asian students, as a whole, always do significantly better on math achievement tests than in English. And this makes me think that there are other Asian-American students whose English spoken in the home might also be described as "broken" or "limited." And perhaps they also have teachers who are steering them away from writing and into math and science, which is what happened to me.

Fortunately, I happen to be rebellious in nature and enjoy the challenge of disproving assumptions made about me. I became an English major my first year in college, after being enrolled as pre-med. I started writing nonfiction as a freelancer the week after I was told by my former boss that writing was my worst skill and I should hone my talents toward account management.

20 But it wasn't until 1985 that I finally began to write fiction. And at first I wrote using what I thought to be wittily crafted sentences, sentences that would finally prove I had mastery over the English language. Here's an example from the first draft of a story that later made its way into *The Joy Luck Club,* but without this line: "That was my mental quandary in its nascent state." A terrible line, which I can barely pronounce.

Fortunately, for reasons I won't get into today, I later decided I should envision a reader for the stories I would write. And the reader I decided upon was my mother, because these were stories about mothers. So with this reader in mind—and in fact she did read my early drafts—I began to write stories using all the Englishes I grew up with: the English I spoke to my mother, which for lack of a better term might be described as "simple"; the English she used with me, which for lack of a better term might be described as "broken"; my translation of her Chinese, which could certainly be described as "watered down"; and what I imagined to be her translation of her Chinese if she could speak in perfect English, her internal language, and for that I sought to preserve the essence, but neither an English nor a Chinese structure. I wanted to capture what language ability tests can never reveal: her intent, her passion, her imagery, the rhythms of her speech and the nature of her thoughts.

Apart from what any critic had to say about my writing, I knew I had succeeded where it counted when my mother finished reading my book and gave me her verdict: "So easy to read."

Full Frontal Feminism: A Young Woman's Guide to Why Feminism Matters—Boys Do Cry Excerpt

JESSICA VALENTI

Be a man. Boys don't cry. Boys will be boys.

Men are affected by sexism too, but it's not often talked about—especially among men themselves. That's where feminism should step in.

The same social mores that tell young women that they should be good little girls are telling guys to be tough, to quash their feelings, and even to be violent. Their problems are our problems, ladies. Men aren't born to rape and commit violence. Men aren't naturally "tougher" emotionally. These gendered expectations hurt men like they hurt us.

I mean, really, can you imagine what it must be like to know that one of the only ways to demonstrate your "masculinity" is to do violence to someone else? To never let your guard down? Seems pretty goddamn awful to me.

5 Feminism can help men too, but only if they're open to it. We can't have a fully successful feminism if we're missing half the population. The thing is, how can we relay the superfabulous stuff feminism is made of to the men in our lives?

I am by no means an expert on masculinity. There are great people doing amazing work on how sexism hurts men—like academic and masculinity expert Michael Kimmel and organizations like Men Can Stop Rape. I'd highly recommend checking these folks out if you're looking for in-depth information on masculinity.

My thoughts on men and feminism are really just starting to be formed, but it's too important a topic to not get into it. Especially now, in a world where what it means to be "a man" has the potential to damage both men and women. Whether it's a consequence of the way that masculinity is used during wartime, or the way it's presented in pop culture—something just isn't right.

Without dissecting how masculinity standards affect men, we'll never be able to comprehensively address sexism and how it affects women. They're linked like a motherfucker. Besides, imagine how much easier it will be to develop male allies in feminism when they realize that they have something to gain from the movement as well.

Men Should Act Like Men

A commercial for Milwaukee's Best beer shows three guys digging a ditch in a back yard (can you smell the testosterone?). When a bee buzzes too close to one of the men, he frantically tries to wave it away while giving off a little high-pitched (you know, girlie) scream. His friends look on in horror. A huge can of Milwaukee's Best falls from the sky and crushes the offending man—who clearly is too femmey to live. The voice-over says, "Men should act like men." The same thing happens to another man who dares to soak up his pizza grease with a napkin. The moral of the story? Act like "a girl" and be killed by giant beer cans. Lovely.

Read this book: Manhood in America: A Cultural History, *by Michael S. Kimmel*

10 What I find truly interesting about this commercial—and this limited view of what it means to be a man in general—is that masculinity is defined as whatever *isn't* womanly. So long as you're not acting like a girl (or a gay!), you're all good.

It's kind of along the same lines as that "what's the worst thing you can call a girl/guy?" exercise. The idea being that there is nothing worse than being a girl, and that being a man is simply the polar opposite of whatever "woman" is. So really, masculinity as it's defined in our society is ridiculously tied up in sexism. How sad is that?

So back to "men should act like men." I think the Milwaukee's Best commercial is so telling—it really does represent the current state of masculinity in a lot of ways. Not only does it define what it means to be a man by pitting it directly against girlishness, but it also implies that what's really important is that you "act" like a man. In a way, the commercial recognizes masculinity as a performance. So even if you are freaked out by bugs or don't want nasty grease on your pizza—suck it up and act like men "are supposed" to. Creepy, right?

But of course, expecting guys to "act" like men isn't limited to beer commercials—it's everywhere. How many times have you heard "Boys don't cry," or "Be a man"? Or even my personal favorite, especially when it was said to me as a kid, "Don't be a girl."

The new trend, however, seems to be deviating from manhood altogether, and instead fetishizing boyhood.

Men Should Act Like Boys

15 Something kind of new in American masculinity—at least in terms of pop culture—is the resurgence of boyhood as the cool standard. Like, back in the day, being a man meant taking care of your family and having a good job and all that. Now, at least if you look at commercials and television shows and the like, it seems that the ultimate way to be a man is to stay a boy.

You know what I mean—the new cool is this "bros over hos" mentality that seems to be inundating our culture. Just think of all the commercials in which perpetual boyhood is the ultimate—where playing cards, watching football, drinking beer, and picking up chicks is the norm (even for "older" guys), and girlfriends and wives are annoying, nagging, distractions from fun.

In a March 2006 article entitled "Men Growing Up to Be Boys," Lakshmi Chaudhry says that an "infantilized" version of manhood is making its way to the mainstream:

> These grown men act like boys—and are richly rewarded for it. ... Where traditional masculinity embraced marriage, children, and work as rites of passage into manhood, the twenty-first-century version shuns them as emasculating, with the wife cast in the role of the castrating mother. The result resembles a childlike fantasy of manhood that is endowed with the perks of adulthood—money, sex, freedom—but none of its responsibilities.[1]

Some say that this goes beyond pop culture silliness where *Maxim* magazine is king. In 2005, Rebecca Traister wrote about "listless lads," men who "are commitmentphobic not just about love, but about life. They drink and take drugs, but even their hedonism lacks focus or joy.... They exhibit no energy for anyone, any activity, profession, or ideology."[2] Traister theorizes that maybe this is a crisis in masculinity—where men don't want to be men.

But what does that mean, anyway?

Snips and Snails?

20 It seems unclear what "being a man" actually is. Is it simply *not* being a woman? Or is it something more?

According to Michael Kimmel, there are "rules of manhood":

> No sissy stuff, that's the first rule. You can never do anything that even remotely hints of femininity. The second rule is to be a big wheel. You know, we measure masculinity by the size of your paycheck, wealth, power, status, things like that. The third rule is to be a sturdy oak. You show that you're a man by never showing your emotions. And the fourth rule is give 'em hell. Always go forward, exude an aura of daring and aggression in everything that you do. And this model of masculinity has been around for an awfully long time.[3]

Kimmel describes it as "relentless pressure on men." I would imagine so. I can't imagine it's easy living that way. But unfortunately, this limited view of what it means to be a man truly fucks up the way men treat women.

Kimmel says that feminist-hating can be tied to masculinity as well. Because for men who are holding on for dear life to the traditional idea of what it means to be a man, feminism is a real threat—because it asks people to question traditional gender roles. He also believes that "manliness" can be tied to violence against women: "Men tend to be violent against women when they feel that their power is eroding when it's slipping."[4] Ugh.

But this seems par for the course in terms of feminist backlash. Feminism changed things around in a lot of ways, and that is scary as hell to a lot of men—because they benefit from sexism. Sexism means that they're the ones with the power, with the rights, and with their dinner made every night. It's no wonder feminism scares the shit out of them.

Feminist Phobia

25 My first real taste of feminist phobia came when I taught Intro to Feminisms at SUNY Albany in upstate New York. I taught the class as part of a teaching collective program in which undergraduates could teach other undergraduates. So I was pretty psyched, but not so much with all of my students.

One guy, who was my age, took the class just to be disruptive. I knew it wasn't going to go well when, on the first day of class, we asked everyone to write their names on a piece of paper and hang it from their desks so we could all talk roundtable-style, and the guy wrote WOMAN HATER.

The semester was pretty miserable, with him trying to make me feel like shit at every turn. He wrote "Jessica is a bitch" on every test he handed in. He showed up at the antirape rally Take Back the Night to tell me that he had had sex with a girl when she said no (but that she liked it). He even had occasion to wander past my apartment drunk one night, just to yell out not-so-nice things. At the time, I just thought he hated me because he was a fucked-up person. Looking back, I realize that this guy was terrified of what he was being confronted with in class. It was going against everything he had ever learned, and his immediate reaction was to lash out. Plus, he was just a dick. He was acting out and felt he could without consequence because I was a woman his age—not an authority figure.

Since I've started Feministing, I've seen similar reactions online. We've gotten our fair share of hateful comments on the site, but none have compared to the vitriol spewed our way from a group of guys on the Internet who call themselves "men's rights activists."

Basically, their deal is that they blame feminism for everything from not being able to get dates to increasing crime rates. Weird stuff. Some of them hated what we were doing so much that they created a parody site modeled after Feministing! They stole our logo (though they made it look like she was fingering herself—classy), our name, and put this tagline on it: "Because women are never sexist. So there." Uh huh.

A great organization, Men Can Stop Rape, created this awesome website: Masculinities in Media: http://mencanstoprape.org.

30 They posted articles every day and even talked to each other in comments using female pseudonyms and language they thought feminists would use: "You go grrrl!" Yeah, I know. It was amazing to me that anyone would spend so much time creating and keeping up a site that no one really looked at or read besides their small group of online buddies. Besides, why weren't they out being active on behalf of men?

Again, it's the fear of feminism. They are terrified by the idea that women could actually be autonomous people with opinions. Interestingly, they blame feminism for ruining American women; on one of their websites (which has the lovely header "Ameriskanks suck"), they often discuss how Asian women are "real women" because they adhere to traditional gender roles. I won't even get into how dumb and racist that is, but the idea is that the perfect woman is one who doesn't, you know, talk back or have opinions.

This kind of misogyny (and yes, I do think a hatred of feminists is based in an overwhelming hatred of women) is unfortunately fairly widespread. There is just something about feminism that really pisses some guys off. Us gals from Feministing have actually received death threats, threats to cuts off our breasts (seriously), and threats of rape. Which is insane. But it's because feminism is powerful. If these same men who hate feminism so much weren't threatened by it and its power, they wouldn't waste their time creating sites, causing disturbances, and emailing threatening letters.

In a way, this fear of feminism is a testament to its strength.

When I had that kid in my Intro to Feminisms class, I used to think that if only he would really try to understand feminism, it could really help him. Because it was clear that he was looking for something. And at times I felt that way about our online "admirers." The truth is, some guys will never be open to feminism because misogyny is just too ingrained in them. Which is sad. But that doesn't mean that there aren't amazing men out there who support the cause.

Boys Will Be Feminists

35 Can men be feminists? Hell yeah; I've been lucky in my life to be surrounded by feminist men (hi, Dad!) and I see the difference it makes, so I'm all for men joining in on the fun, and I believe we need male allies. But not everyone agrees. Some feminists think that the movement needs to be womancentered, and I can understand this hesitancy to include men.

There is a fear that they wouldn't be willing to learn, and that they would try to take shit over, because they're used to leading. I even have friends who take issue with men calling themselves feminists. They think that women need a word all their own, and that only someone who experiences life as a woman can truly understand feminism.

Check out the organization Dads and Daughters, whose tagline reads "making the world safe and fair for our daughters": www.dadsanddaughters. Aww.

So, some guys call themselves "pro-feminist" as a way to stand in solidarity with feminists without co-opting the word/movement. As far as I'm concerned, they can call themselves whatever they want, so long as they're down to do the feminist work.

Self-identified pro-feminist blogger and academic Hugo Schwyzer says it's imperative that men mentor other men in order to spread a nonsexist message.

> We owe it to them to make it clear that we have grown up with the same pernicious cultural influences that have taught us to objectify women. They need to know what tools we ourselves have used to change our behavior, and they need to know—in detail—how we live out egalitarian principles in our relationships with women. We can't preach gender justice; we have to live it out in our actions and we have to be willing to do so publicly, as role models.[5]

Unfortunately, it's not just men like Hugo who are trying to reach out to younger men.

Traditional Gender Roles on Crack

40 The same conservative messes that are telling young women that they have to be chaste, married, and popping out babies are telling young men that they have to be strong, be "soldiers."

James Dobson, daddy of the terrifying conservative religious group Focus on the Family, wrote a book called *Bringing up Boys* in which he tells parents how to raise their male children. A lot of it is concerned with nurturing boys' "natural" masculinity and making sure they don't turn out to be homos. Seriously. The Focus on the Family website (which promotes Dobson's book at every turn) says much the same thing:

> God designed boys to be more aggressive, excitable, and wild in their behavior. Despite the claims made a generation ago, boys are different … To help a boy develop a healthy gender identity, make sure he receives appropriate affection, attention, and approval from his father (or, in the father's absence, a trustworthy male role model).[6]

There's even a section on "Countering Radical Feminism's Agenda"![7] The idea is that boys need their "masculine" side praised and their "feminine" side quashed.

Is the Military the Ultimate in Masculinity?

I couldn't write about men and masculinity without at the very least mentioning militarization and war. They're all too tied up with each other not to talk about it. Something superfucked up that will give you a good idea of why I'd feel remiss if I didn't write about militarization: During the Gulf War (and who knows how many other wars), Air Force pilots watched porn movies before they went off on bombing missions in an attempt to "psyche [sic] themselves up."[8] Ugh. But that's par for the course for an institution that relies on the feminization of the enemy as a way to dehumanize them.

Feminists who study men and the military are quick to point out that the military itself is built on sexist ideals. Cynthia Enloe, a professor and an expert on feminism, militarization, and globalization, writes frequently about how militarization is dependent on women in "supporting" roles—whether as military wives or prostitutes on military bases.[9] Interesting stuff (though disturbing).

45 Even Amnesty International reports that women are disproportionately affected by war:

> [T]here is still a widespread perception that women play only a secondary or peripheral role in situations of conflict … The use of rape as a weapon of war is perhaps the most notorious and brutal way in which conflict impacts on women. As rape and sexual violence are so pervasive within situations of conflict the "rape victim" has become an emblematic image of women's experience of war.
>
> [W]omen and girls are targeted for violence, or otherwise affected by war, in disproportionate or different ways from men.[10]

Clearly, this is a huge issue, one that requires a lot more conversation than I can fit in this book. So this is just something to get you thinking.

Men Moving Forward

I think it's clear that everything—from social norms to pop culture—presents an insanely limited definition of masculinity, one that not only does damage to men, but harms women as well. So what to do now?

Robert Jensen, a journalism professor at the University of Texas, argues that the whole concept of masculinity as we know it has to go, because it creates a life for men that is marked by "endless competition and threat" and a quest for control and domination:

> No one man created this system, and perhaps none of us, if given a choice, would choose it. But we live our lives in that system, and it deforms men, narrowing our emotional range and depth. It keeps us from the rich connections with others—not just with women and children, but other men—that make life meaningful but require vulnerability.[11]

50 Men's lives are being damaged by sexism—we can't separate it out from how sexism affects women. Because every time someone calls a guy a "pussy" or a "mangina," every time someone tells a little boy not to "throw like a girl," the not-so-subtle message is that there is something inherently wrong with being a woman. And that's a message I think we could all live without.

Credit

Islamophobia in Classrooms, Media, and Politics

MAYIDA ZAAL

It was the second week of school in a sleepy town on the eastern coast of the U.S. Middle school students (mostly White, Christian, and middle class) were becoming familiar with one another, their routines, and their teachers.

Their history teacher had a special activity planned to commemorate the 10th anniversary of the attacks that occurred on September 11, 2001. First, students were to describe in writing how they felt about the building of a mosque near the World Trade Center site in New York City. Second, they were given the following vocabulary words and asked to construct a paragraph: *Al Qaeda, terrorist, Islam, Muslim, hijacker, and Islamist.*

The teacher did not provide any context (historical, political, or social) for the assignment, and several students were uncomfortable with it. A few students asked one another in disbelief, "Why is he saying that all Muslims are terrorists?" Becky (all names are pseudonyms) worried how her friend Aysha, a Muslim American, felt about the activity. Although they complied with the assignment, Becky and others did not agree with their teacher's implications.

Becky told Aysha after class, "I don't believe that all Muslims are terrorists and I'm sorry you had to hear that." After being alerted by Becky's parents about the U.S. History lesson, Aysha's parents knew they needed to address the issue.

5 At a meeting with the principal and the teacher, Aysha's parents described their concerns. They wished the teacher had taken a different approach, one that did not equate Islam with terrorism. The teacher was apologetic, but did not understand that pathologizing Islam could have a direct effect on his students. The principal exclaimed that he would have never taught a lesson on that topic, even though it was a significant event discussed in the news media.

Critical Pedagogy

Becky and Aysha's story was brought to my attention when Aysha's parents sought guidance regarding this incident. This classroom example and others like it point to the necessity for a critical pedagogical stance that addresses the manifestation of Islamophobia in the classroom.

The example raises many difficult questions and ethical considerations. What are the consequences (whether intended) of such a lesson taught in isolation? How could a lesson on the events of September 11th have been taught differently? How can educators use literacy as a way to engage with most pressing social contexts instead of oversimplifying or barring them? How do young Muslims across the U.S. experience growing anti-Muslim sentiment? What are our responsibilities as educators to create safer spaces for Muslim students and for all of our students?

Currents of Islamophobia

According to the Council on American Islamic Relations (2009), civil rights violations targeting Muslims in the workplace, at religious institutions, and in schools have escalated. For instance, in 2007 there were 118 reported cases of discrimination in schools, and in 2008 there were 153 reported cases.

Moreover, the Pew Research Center's (2010) survey in the wake of public debate on the proposed construction of an Islamic cultural center and mosque near the site of the former World Trade Center reveals that since 2005, Americans are tending towards less favorable views of Islam. In 2005, 41% of those surveyed held a favorable view of Islam, while 36% held an unfavorable view. In 2010, only 32% held a favorable view, while 38% looked at Islam unfavorably.

10 Remarkably, the Center for American Progress reports that over the last decade $43 million dollars in funding was contributed to support anti-Muslim thinkers in the U.S. (Hing, 2011). These are the same thinkers who are credited with influencing the Norwegian mass murderer, Anders Breivik, whose intent was to wage war against Muslims in Europe.

What fuels these acts of hatred? What influences the general public's perceptions of Muslims as a group? There are many inputs from mass media, both historical and current, that have served to facilitate people's perceptions of Muslims as a threat.

The effects of Islamophobia, defined as a generalized fear of Islam and Muslims (Shryock, 2010; Zine, 2004), are felt by Muslims and non-Muslims alike. For instance, Arabs, Sikhs, and South Asians are some of the groups that are often targets of anti-Muslim discrimination (American-Arab Anti-Discrimination Committee Research Institute [ADC], 2010).

Politics of Representation

Muslim Americans are not a monolithic group, nor can they be described in terms of one common experience. Nonetheless, it is a term that millions of Muslims living in the U.S. use to identify themselves (Bakalian & Bozorgmehr, 2009; Pew Research Center, 2011). Muslims in the U.S. originate from at least 77 countries and include native-born African Americans and other converts to Islam (Pew Research Center, 2011).

Therefore, it is imperative not to homogenize or essentialize the experiences of Muslims across the country. I employ the category of "Muslim Americans" to situate a growing Islamophobic trend within its historical, social, and political context and to generate discussion and interrupt the pedagogical practices that contribute to further oppression of Muslim students.

15 Muslims in the U.S., and Arabs specifically, have been vilified in images, cartoons, film, and television for many decades (and long before the attacks of September 11th took place). Social scientist Jack Shaheen (2001) has extensively documented the hundreds of images that portray Arabs as violent and barbaric. (Many Arabs, usually represented as Muslims, are Christians, Jews, and even Quakers [ADC, 2008]).

These demonized and dehumanizing images (often depicted in seemingly harmless ways, as in the Disney film *Aladdin*) have served to desensitize the U.S. populace and to legitimize fear and hatred against Muslims and Islam. Moreover, the persistent discourse in the media and in politics (e.g., Peter King's Congressional hearings on Muslim Americans and radicalization) that equates Muslims with terrorism and violence (Nisbet & Garrett, 2010) perpetuates Islamophobia.

How do these popular, discriminatory discourses manifest themselves in schools and in classrooms? They inform literacy practices like the ones illustrated in the opening vignette. These mainstream images, texts, and narratives form the basis of how students and teachers make sense of the world and reinforce the official curriculum in textbooks and state standards.

Common Concerns

In previously conducted research, the Muslim youth who shared their stories with me in the U.S. (Zaal, Salah, & Fine, 2007) and in the Netherlands (Zaal, 2009) had many concerns in common. They spoke of experiencing Islamophobia in blatant and insidious ways—being called names, being told they were oppressed by their backward religion, and told to return to where they came from. They reported feeling targeted at school, on the playground, and on the bus. They did not want to be burdened with educating others about their faith or to defend their religion or ethnicity. They described feeling alienated when adults and peers promoted stereotypes about Islam.

The young women who participated in my research based in New York City resisted having their identities defined in polarizing dichotomies—devout or progressive, Muslim or American, good citizen or feared neighbor. They wanted to claim all their identities—student, sister, national origin, friend, daughter, law-abiding citizen, Muslim—without compromise.

20 We have a responsibility as educators to expand our students' understanding of the world by engaging them critically in analyzing the social, political, and historical contexts in which they live. This responsibility can and should include difficult conversations about conflicts, war, discrimination, and oppression.

Unlike the principal in the vignette, I do not agree that the teacher should not have conducted a lesson about the events of September 11, 2001. But teachers must be prepared with pedagogical tools and age-appropriate curricula (see Table 1). When approaching socially sensitive issues, it is critical to deconstruct stereotypes and create anti-oppressive classrooms that allow for difficult dialogue in a responsible way.

Table 1: Resources for Educators

Organization	Websites
Colorlines	www.colorlines.com/911-anniv/
Rethinking Schools	www.rethinkingschools.org/war/readings/index.shtml www.rethinkingschools.org/static/special_reports/sept11/pdf/911insrt.pdf
Teaching Tolerance	www.tolerance.org/activity/debunking-muslim-myths
American-Arab Anti-Discrimination Committee	www.adc.org/education/educational-resources/

Classrooms are not simply spaces reserved for fiction, mock debates, and role-plays. They are microcosms where global–political, social, and historical tensions are enacted and reinforced in every action and interaction. Young people must negotiate torrents of information, and as educators we need to provide counternarratives and create learning environments in which students can engage as critical readers of their world.

Works Cited

American-Arab Anti-Discrimination Committee Research Institute. (2008). *2003–2007 Report on hate crimes and discrimination against Arab Americans.* Washington, DC: American-Arab Anti-Discrimination Committee. Retrieved August 15, 2011, from www.adc.org/PDF/hcr07.pdf

Bakalian, A., & Bozorgmehr, M. (2009). *Backlash 9/11: Middle Eastern and Muslim Americans respond.* Berkeley: University of California Press.

Council on American–Islamic Relations. (2009). *The status of Muslim civil rights in the United States 2009: Seeking full inclusion.* Washington, DC: Council on American-Islamic Relations.

Hing, J. (2011, September 11). The $43 million Islamophobia machine. *Colorlines*. Retrieved January 15, 2011, from colorlines .com/archives/2011/09/the_43_million_islamophobia_machine.html

Nisbet, E., & Garrett, K. (2010). *FOX News contributes to spread of rumors about proposed NYC Mosque: CNN and NPR promote more accurate beliefs*. Retrieved November 11, 2010, from www.comm.ohio-state.edu/kgarrett/MediaMosqueRumors.pdf

Pew Research Center. (2010). *NYC mosque opposed, Muslims' right to build mosques favored: Public remains conflicted over Islam*. Retrieved June 11, 2011, from pewforum.org/Muslim/ Public-Remains-Conflicted-Over-Islam.aspx

Pew Research Center. (2011). *Muslim Americans: No signs of growth in alienation or support for extremism mainstream and moderate attitudes*. Retrieved November 5, 2010, from people-press.org/files/legacy-pdf/Muslim-American-Report.pdf

Shaheen, J.G. (2001). *Reel bad Arabs: How Hollywood vilifies a people*. New York: Olive Branch.

Shryock, A. (2010). *Islamophobia/Islamophilia: Beyond the politics of enemy and friend*. Bloomington: Indiana University Press.

Zaal, M. (2009). *Neglected in their transitions: Second generation Muslim youth search for support in a context of Islamophobia*. Unpublished dissertation. Graduate Center, New York.

Zaal, M., Salah, T., & Fine, M. (2007). The weight of the hyphen: Freedom, fusion and responsibility embodied by young Muslim-American women during a time of surveillance. *Applied Developmental Science, 11*(3), 164–177. doi:10.1080/10888690701454674

Zine, J. (2004). Anti-Islamophobia education as transformative pedagogy: reflections from the educational front lines. *The American Journal of Islamic Social Sciences, 21*(3), 110–119.

Credit

Zaal, Mayida. "Islamophobia in Classrooms, Media, and Politics." *Journal of Adolescent and Adult Literacy 55.6* (2012): 555–558. Republished with permission of John Wiley and Sons Inc.

Collected Notes from Essays

How to Tame a Wild Tongue by Gloria Anzaldúa

[1] Ray Gwyn Smith, *Moorland is Cold Country,* unpublished book.

[2] Irena Klepfisz, "*Di rayze aheym*/The Journev Home," in *The Tribe of Dina: A Jewish Women's Anthology,* Melanie Kaye/Kantrowitz and Irena Klepfisz, eds. (Montpelier, VT: Sinister Wisdom Books, 1986), 49.

[3] R. C. Ortega, *Dialectologia Del Barrio,* trans. Hortencia S. Alwan (Los Angeles, CA: R. C. Ortega Publisher & Bookseller, 1977), 132.

[4] Eduardo Hernandéz-Chávez, Andrew D. Cohen, and Anthony F. Beltramo, *El Lenguaje de los Chicanos: Regional and Social Characteristics of Language Used by Mexican Americans* (Arlington, VA: Center for Applied Linguistics, 1975), 39.

[5] Hernandéz-Chávez., xvii.

[6] Irena Klepfisz, "Secular Jewish Identity: Yidishkayt in America," in *The Tribe of Dina,* Kaye/Kantrowitz and Klepfisz, eds., 43.

[7] Melanie Kaye/Kantrowitz, "Sign," in *We Speak in Code: Poems and Other Writings* (Pittsburgh, PA: Motheroot Publications, Inc., 1980), 85.

[8] Rodolfo Gonzales, *I Am Joaquín/Yo Soy Joaquín* (New York, NY: Bantam Books, 1972). It was first published in 1967.

[9] Gershen Kaufman, *Shame: The Power of Caring* (Cambridge, MA: Schenkman Books, Inc., 1980), 68.

[10] John R. Chávez, *The Lost Land: The Chicago Images of the Southwest* (Albuquerque, NM: University of New Mexico Press, 1984), 88–90.

[11] "Hispanic" is derived from *Hispanis* (*España,* a name given to the Iberian Peninsula in ancient times when it was a part or the Roman Empire) and is a term designated by the U.S. government to make it easier to handle us on paper.

[12] The Treaty of Guadalupe Hidalgo created the Mexican-American in 1848.

[13] Anglos, in order to alleviate their guilt for dispossessing the Chicano, stressed the Spanish part of us and perpetrated the myth of the Spanish Southwest. We have accepted the fiction that we are Hispanic, that is Spanish, in order to accommodate ourselves to the dominant culture and its abhorrence of Indians. Chávez, 88–91.

Trans Media Moments: Tumblr, 2011–2013 by Marty Fink and Quinn Miller

[1] Georgia Tech, Atlanta, GA, USA

[2] University of Oregon, Eugene, USA

Is He Boyfriend Material?: Representation of Males in Teenage Girls' Magazines by Kirsten B. Firminger

1 Percentage of male-focused pages was taken out of total editorial pages, not including advertising pages. Confessional/embarrassing stories did not count toward the total number of pages because of inconsistencies in unit of analysis, with the confessional stories having a variable number of male-focused stories. I analyzed those separately. Feature articles (unique, nonregular) counted if the article focused on or if males significantly contributed to the narrative in the article (for instance, "Out of bounds: A cheerleader tells the story of how the coach she trusted attacked her"). If the feature was equally balanced with focused sections on both boys and girls (for example, if the article is sectioned into different topics or interviews), only pages that focused on males were counted.

Because of the limited nature of the study, I chose to focus purely on the content that was decided upon by the editorial/writing (called "editorial content" within this article) staff of the magazines, since they establish the mission and tone of the content across all of the issues of the magazine. While I acknowledge the influential presence of advertising, I did no analysis of the content of the advertising pages or photographs. The analysis consists only of the written content of the magazines.

2 The magazines report that the question-and-answer columns and embarrassing/confessional tales are "submitted by readers." However, they do not report how they choose the questions and stories that are published, or whether the magazine staff edits this content.

3 *ELLEgirl* did not contain embarrassing or confessional stories.

4 The unit of analysis was the smallest number of sentences that contained a complete thought, experience, or response, ranging from one sentence to a paragraph. For example, "The fact is you can't change other people. He has to change himself—but perhaps your concern will convince him to make some changes." I took this approach so that the meaning and context of a statement was not lost in the coding. Whole paragraphs could not always be used because they sometimes contained contrasting or multiple themes.

5 The other articles that were not included in the coding focused predominantly on a specific boy or a celebrity male and his interests/activities, or on stories including a boy, or activities to do with a boy, rather than making broad statements about how all boys act (for example, "When he was in kindergarten, his mom enrolled Elijah [Wood] in a local modeling and talent school." or "One time, my boyfriend dared me to sneak out of the house in the middle of the night while my parents were sleeping and meet him at a park.").

Learning to Read by Malcolm X

1 Charles H. Parkhurst (1842–1933); American clergyman, reformer, and president of the Society for the Prevention of Crime.

2 A native Egyptian Christian church that retains elements of its African origins.

3 Evil plots or schemes. Faust was a fictional character who sold his soul to the devil for knowledge and power.

4 The "Opium War" of 1839–1842 was between Britain and China and ended when Hong Kong was handed over to Britain.

5 The Boxer Rebellion of 1898–1900. An uprising by members of a secret Chinese society who opposed foreign influence in Chinese affairs.

Reading Games: Strategies for Reading Scholarly Sources by Karen Rosenberg

1 In this discussion I draw on Norgaard's excellent discussion of reading as joining a conversation (1–28). By letting you, the reader, know this in a footnote, I am not only citing my source (I'd be plagiarizing if I didn't mention this somewhere), but I'm also showing how I enter this conversation and give you a trail to follow if you want to learn more about the metaphor of the conversation. Following standard academic convention, I put the full reference to Norgaard's text at the end of this article, in the references.

2 I draw on—and recommend—Rounsaville et al.'s discussion of rhetorical sensitivity, critical reading and rhetorical reading (1–35).

Queer Characters in Comic Strips by Edward H. Sewell, Jr.

1 Terminology is always something of a problem. Throughout this chapter, the term "queer" is used rather than cumbersome combinations of gay, gay men, lesbian, bisexual, and transgender. It is used in two different ways. First, it is used to identify a sexual orientation different from heterosexual or straight. Second, it is used as a collective term for all the combinations of gay, gay men, gays, lesbians, bisexuals, homosexuals, and transgendered. In instances of direct quotations or paraphrases, the term used by the quoted or paraphrased source is retained. For a recent discussion of this debate, see Rotello (2000).

2 The role of the Internet in the queer community cannot be overemphasized. It provides a type of "community forum" where people can meet, talk, and have no fear of being "outed" or harassed.

3 The Doonesbury website (http://www.doonesbury.com) has an excellent search engine that locates all dates when a specific topic or character appeared in the strip.

4 Robert Triptow (l989) provides an excellent collection of early queer comics art that is not readily available from any other source. A brief overview of the beginnings of queer comic books and strips is also found in Sabin (1996, p. 124), but without any visual examples.

5 *Kyle's Bed & Breakfast* can be found on-line at URL members.aol.com/KylesB&B

"God Don't Never Change": Black English from a Black Perspective by Geneva Smitherman

[1] For examples of such programs, see *Non-Standard Dialect,* Board of Education of the City of New York (National Council of Teachers of English, 1968); San-Su C. Lin, *Pattern Practices in the Teaching of Standard English to Students with a Non-Standard English Dialect* (USOE Project 1339, 1965); Arno Jewett, Joseph Mersand, Doris Gunderson, *Improving English Skills of Culturally Different Youth in Large Cities* (U.S. Department of Health, Education and Welfare, 1964); *Language Programs for the Disadvantaged* (NCTE, 1965).

[2] Don L. Lee. "Malcolm Spoke/Who Listened?" *Don't Cry, Scream.* Detroit: Broadside Press, 1969. 33.

[3] Don L. Lee, "But He was Cool or: he even stopped for green lights,: ibid., pp. 24–25.

[4] Etheridge Knight, "Hard Rock Return to Prison from the Hospital for the Criminal Insane," *Poems from* Prison (Detroit: Broadside Press, 1968), p. 12.

[5] Maya Angelou, *Just Give me a Cool Drink of Water 'fore I Diiie* (New York: Random House, 1971), pp. 46–47.

[6] John Oliver Killens, *The Cotillion or One Good Bull is Half the Herd* New York: Trident Press, 1971), pp. 29–42.

[7] Richard Wright, "Fire and Cloud," *Uncle Tom's Children* New York: Harper and Row, 1936), pp. 137–39.

[8] Imamu Amiri Baraka (LeRoi Jones), "Expressive Language," *Home* (New York: William Morrow & Co., 1996), pp. 171–72.

A Family Affair: Competing Sponsors of Literacy in Appalachian Students' Lives by Sara Webb-Sunderhaus

[1] Urban Appalachian is a term that refers to a subgroup of Appalachians who migrated out of the Appalachian region and relocated to urban centers; the term also includes the children of these migrants. See Borman and Obermiller's *From Mountain to Metropolis: Appalachian Migrants in the American City* for further discussion.

[2] Pseudonyms have been substituted for the names of all locations and individuals in order to protect participant anonymity.

[3] Devotionals are short books designed to reinforce daily prayer and reading of the Bible. They direct readers to read a particular Bible passage and to use the devotional as supplementary material that encourages further reflection. Finally, the readers are to conclude the reading with prayer. Some devotionals even include suggested prayers for the day, though not all do, thus blending silent reading of the devotional with the reading aloud of prayers.